Devices of Curiosity

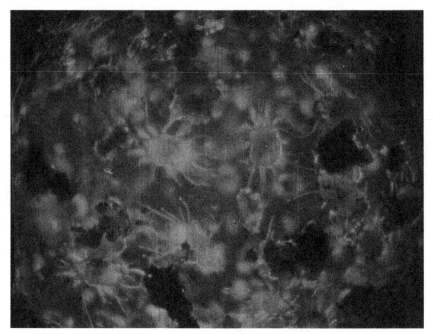

A frame enlargement from the second shot of *Cheese Mites* (1903). BFI.

Devices of Curiosity

EARLY CINEMA AND POPULAR SCIENCE

Oliver Gaycken

OXFORD

UNIVERSITY PRESS

OXFORD
UNIVERSITY PRESS

Oxford University Press is a department of the University of Oxford.
It furthers the University's objective of excellence in research, scholarship,
and education by publishing worldwide.

Oxford   New York
Auckland   Cape Town   Dar es Salaam   Hong Kong   Karachi
Kuala Lumpur   Madrid   Melbourne   Mexico City   Nairobi
New Delhi   Shanghai   Taipei   Toronto

With offices in
Argentina   Austria   Brazil   Chile   Czech Republic   France   Greece
Guatemala   Hungary   Italy   Japan   Poland   Portugal   Singapore
South Korea   Switzerland   Thailand   Turkey   Ukraine   Vietnam

Oxford is a registered trade mark of Oxford University Press
in the UK and certain other countries.

Published in the United States of America by
Oxford University Press
198 Madison Avenue, New York, NY 10016

© Oxford University Press 2015

Library of Congress Cataloging-in-Publication Data
Gaycken, Oliver.
Devices of curiosity : early cinema and popular science / Oliver Gaycken.
p.   cm.
Includes index.
ISBN 978-0-19-986068-5 (cloth) — ISBN 978-0-19-986070-8 (pbk.) —
ISBN 978-0-19-986069-2 (ebook) — ISBN 978-0-19-023598-7 (online version)
1. Science in motion pictures. 2. Science films—History and criticism.
3. Motion pictures in science. I. Title.
PN1995.9.S265G39 2015
791.43'66—dc23

2014031218

1   3   5   7   9   8   6   4   2

Printed in the United States of America on acid-free paper

What is the meaning of the Artifact? And why did the people of Atlantis go to such lengths in making it? Hope seems to be waning that the riddle will be solved. The answer rests, finally, upon the decipherment of two words, both hopelessly ambiguous, that appear on nearly every page of the Codex. Barring the chance discovery of a Rosetta Stone, we may never understand them, since they defy contextual analysis.

The first of these is "science." And the second is "art."[1]

{ CONTENTS }

{ ACKNOWLEDGMENTS }

On a train in December 2008, I am returning from a workshop at the National Library of Medicine, reading Adolf Nichtenhauser's unpublished manuscript "History of Motion Pictures in Medicine." Written over the course of more than twenty years (1933-1955), Nichtenhauser's opening remarks (written in the third person) contain a number of striking parallels to my own experiences in writing this book: "Without being quite aware of what was happening, he found himself surrounded by volumes on the prehistory of motion pictures; by the original works of those men whose desire to understand the physiology of movement had stimulated the invention of the motion picture; and by written reports of the physicians who first attempted to utilize the new invention in their teaching and research." After submitting an initial draft of his research, Nichtenhauser concluded his reflections by noting, "As may happen in similar situations, the writer became more and more a prisoner of his subject." I experienced a jolt of recognition upon reading this passage, not only because of the shared area of interest—motion pictures in the service of science—but also in the sense that I, too, have become, without being quite aware of what was happening, a prisoner of my subject. The incarceration has not been unpleasant, though. And even though this book has taken longer to complete than I care to recall (if I count my initial interest in this general field of cinema and science, which dates to 1993, then I, too, have been pursuing this subject for more than twenty years), and while there are many things I would have done differently, there are many more things I would never want to change, and the people and institutions that have supported me in the course of this work deserve acknowledgment and thanks.

Looking back on the process of writing this book brings to mind geological time. To invoke geological time here is perhaps misleading; the earth, to say nothing of the cosmos, will have no concern for the few extra years it took for this book to appear. But the image seems apt because this book's genesis and development contain distinct strata. The earliest stratum dates to the final years of my undergraduate studies, when Tom Levin, Thomas Keenan, and Eduardo Cadava were influential in my intellectual development as I unwittingly laid this book's groundwork. The book's formative period occurred during my time in graduate school. Tom Gunning was an unfailingly generous and inspiring teacher and dissertation advisor, from the first meeting where we discussed the dissertation that would become this book (and where he provided its title) to the final stages of that project to his willingness to be the officiant at my wedding. The other members of my dissertation committee, Jim Lastra, Yuri Tsivian, and Scott Curtis, also provided valuable feedback. Scott, in particular, has been an invaluable source of criticism, good cheer, and cocktail recipes. I look forward to toasting the appearance of our books soon. I was fortunate to have had the opportunity to present early versions of this material at the Mass Culture workshop. Thanks so much to my friends from those days— Noel Jackson, Michael Antenbring, Jennifer Peterson, Paul Young, Paula Amad, Jean Ma, Doron Galili, Michelle Puetz, Josh Yumibe Charles Tepperman, Josh Malitsky, and Dan Morgan—graduate school was a better place with you around. Julia Gibbs was a wonderful boss and fun to hang out with, too. Bob von Hallberg and Jessica Burstein at *Modernism/modernity* taught me an awful lot about how to write. I learned a great deal about cinema at Doc Films, especially in programming committee meetings, where Seth Johnson was a notable presence, whom I miss. Thanks as well to fellow Chicago lovers of the image James Bond, Alan Lesage, and Will Schmenner. Dr. Jeffrey Stern provided patient and loyal support. Finally, I'd like to thank Miriam Hansen, who was not able to have the kind of sustained engagement with this project that we initially envisioned, and who will not be able to read these words, but whose influence was and remains significant.

A project based primarily on archival research incurs tremendous debts to the keepers of primary sources. Madeleine Matz served as a guide to my earliest archival excursion at the Library of Congress, and Nico de Klerk aided me in accessing the collections of the Nederlands Filmmuseum in Amsterdam. I watched many early popular-science films in the British Film Institute National Archive in London, where Bryony Dixon was especially helpful. I also am grateful for the assistance of the staffs of the Science Museum, where Charles Urban's papers were originally housed, and the National Media Museum in Bradford, UK, where they currently reside. My trips to London allowed me to have conversations with Tim Boon and Luke McKernan, both of whom provided meaningful insights, especially into the careers of Charles Urban, F. Martin Duncan, and Percy Smith.

An American National Can Fellowship and a Society for French American Cultural Services and Educational Aid (FACSEA) Scholarship for French Cinema Studies allowed me to spend the academic year 2001-2002 in Paris. During my stay, I conducted archival research at the Cinémathèque de la Ville de Paris, where I received excellent support and guidance from Béatrice de Pastre, and at the Archives du Film at the Centre National de la Cinématographie, Bois d'Arcy. My time in Paris was especially enriched by my interactions with Thierry Lefebvre, who was a marvelous mentor.

I spent a year as a Visiting Assistant Professor at York University in Toronto, where Mike Zryd, Janine Marchessault, Tess Takahashi, Barbara Evans, and Philip Hoffman helped make my stay pleasant and productive. My first job was in the English Department at Temple University. I am especially thankful for Sue Wells's and Peter Logan's unwavering support, as well as for the friendship of colleagues—James Salazar, Sue-Im Lee, Jenna Osman, Gabe Wettach, Chris Cagle, Kevin Arceneaux, Megan Mullin—and for the work of able research assistants Bayard Miller, Gabe Cutrufello, and Kellen Graham. Thanks are due to other Philadelphia-area friends and colleagues: Karen Beckman, Peter Decherney, Emily Steiner, Tim Corrigan, John Tresch, Homay King, Bob Rehak, Jay Schwartz of Secret Cinema, Thad Squire, Meredith Rainey, Susan Glassman and Lynne Dorwaldt at the Wagner Free Institute of Science, and Babak Ashrafi and the Philadelphia Area Center on History of Science.

I had several opportunities to spend time at the Max Planck Institute for the History of Science, first as a participant in the summer seminar "Science on Screen" in 2004; and later as a visiting fellow in Lorraine Daston's department II in 2009 and 2013. The Institute's intellectual atmosphere was a spur to my research, and I had particularly productive exchanges with Tania Munz, Jeff Schwegman, Andreas Meyer, Henning Schmidgen, and Charlotte Bigg. While in Berlin, I also benefitted from conversations with Barbara Wurm, Anja Laukötter, and Vinzenz Hediger. My interest in the history of science has allowed me to strike up conversations with valuable interlocutors—Hannah Landecker, Hanna Rose Shell, David Kirby, Jimena Canales—who should not be held accountable for what I am sure is my imperfect assimilation of their discipline's insights. David Cantor and Mike Sappol at the National Library of Medicine kindly invited me to present a portion of the book at their works-in-progress seminar, which led to helpful revisions. James Cahill and Kirsten Ostherr, also primarily cinema historians, share my commitment to the cross-disciplinary conversation with historians of science, and their insights, encouragement, and friendship have meant a great deal to me.

I have not been at University of Maryland for a long time, but I already have a long list of people who have supported me and my scholarship. My friends and colleagues in the film program—Jonathan Auerbach, Luka Arsenjuk, Peter Beicken, Caroline Eades, Saverio Giovacchini, Reggie Harrison, Jason Kuo, Valérie Orlando, Elizabeth Papazian, Eric Zakim—and departmental friends and colleagues—Christina Walter, Orrin Wang, Matt Kirschenbaum, Randy Ontiveros, Sheila Jelen, Bill Cohen—are responsible in equal measure for making UMD such a welcoming and rewarding place to work. Thanks as well to my research assistants Peter Garafolo and Brian Davis.

Penultimately, thanks to the editorial group at Oxford University Press— Shannon McLaughlin, Brendan O'Neill, Stephen Bradley, and Gogulanathan Bactavatchalane—for your expert management of the final stages of the process. I am especially grateful to the manuscript's anonymous readers, whose suggestions prompted valuable changes.

The most extraordinary debts accrue to family. To the McGraths—Gary, Melinda, and Sean—I look forward to seeing a copy of this book on the shelves of your bookstore, where I imagine it will be well looked after for a good long while. To my parents Hans-Jürgen and Hanne Gaycken, my brother Karsten and my sister Bettina, I cannot thank you enough for your patient love and support. And finally, to my own, most immediate family—Caitlin, Iris, and Oscar—I owe the most of all. In your love I see my best self, the me I try to be every day. This book is for you.

Part of the introduction (on *L'Âge d'or*) appeared as "Das Privatleben des Scorpion Languedocien: Ethologie und *L'Âge d'or* (1930)," *Montage A/V: Zeitschrift für Theorie und Geschichte audiovisueller Kommunikation* 14 (November 2005): 44–51.

Early versions of sections of Chapter 1 appeared as "The Sources of the Secrets of Nature: The Science Film at Urban, 1903–1911," in Scene-Stealing: Sources for British Cinema before 1930, ed. Alan Burton and Laraine Porter (Trowbridge, Wilts: Flicks Books, 2003), 36–42; and in "'The Living Picture': On the Circulation of Microscope-Slide Knowledge in 1903," *History and Philosophy of the Life Sciences* 35, no. 3 (2013): 319–39.

An early version of Chapter 3 appeared as "'A Drama Unites Them in a Fight to the Death': Some Remarks on the Flourishing of a Cinema of Scientific Vernacularization in France, 1909–1914," *Historical Journal of Film, Radio, and Television* 22, no. 3 (2002): 353–374.

Portions of Chapter 4 (on *The Fly Pest*) appeared in "The Cinema of the Future: Visions of the Medium as Modern Educator," in *Learning with the Lights Off: Educational Film in the United States*, ed. Dan Streible, Marsha Orgeron, and Devin Orgeron (New York: Oxford University Press, 2011), 67–89.

A German translation of an early version of Chapter 5 appeared as "'Stetige Verwandlung und eine beunruhigende Allgegenwärtigkeit': Der Superverbrecher als 'Mad Scientist' im französischen Kriminalmelodrama, 1911–1919," in *Verrückt, prophetisch, unheimlich: Ansichten wissenschaftlicher Charaktere*, ed. Doerthe Ohloff and Torsten Junge (Aschaffenburg: Alibri Verlag, 2004), 149–170.

Devices of Curiosity

Introduction

Prologue: Where Did These Scorpions Come from?

L'Âge d'or (1930) begins with footage of scorpions (Fig. 1). Initially, Luis Buñuel wanted to start the film with the scene of a scorpion encircled by a ring of fire stinging itself to death, an opening sequence that would measure up to the eyeball-slicing scene with which his previous film, *Un Chien Andalou* (1929), began.[1] *Chien*'s radical gesture of blinding was to be followed by an example of suicide from the animal kingdom.

That scene was never shot, however, because scorpions do not, in fact, become suicidal when surrounded by flames. After fruitless attempts to capture the mythical behavior, Buñuel sent his assistant director Jacques-Bernard Brunius to Paris to search for other forms of scorpion footage. Brunius returned with a print of *Le Scorpion Languedocien*, a film made by the Éclair company in 1913 as a part of its "Scientia" series. Buñuel cut the six-minute *Scorpion* down to a two-minute sequence, condensing the film's account of the arthropod's anatomy and behavior by selecting evocative images and intertitles. Although a compromise of sorts, the embedded story of the reedited footage from *Le Scorpion Languedocien* makes the prologue arguably a more interesting sequence than anything Buñuel could have shot himself, exemplifying the Surrealist interest in mass-cultural detritus and collage.[2]

The use of parts of a popular-science film in a famous Surrealist provocation serves as an emblem of this book's dual concerns. First, *Le Scorpion Languedocien* was part of the history of popular-science filmmaking prior to Buñuel's repurposing of it, and much of this book is dedicated to tracing this kind of filmmaking, both its sources and how it developed in its earliest period, between 1903 and 1913. A central aim of this book is to recover the outlines and key examples of popular-science filmmaking by describing its historical and stylistic parameters as well as the contexts in which it appeared.

FIG. 1   Borrowed scorpions (video still from *L'Âge d'or*).

Second, however, as the fact of *Le Scorpion Languedocien*'s appropriation attests, popular-science films circulated beyond their original contexts, a tendency
that is not an epiphenomenon but rather a defining feature. A history of the early
popular-science film thus requires not only a description of core features, key
filmmakers, important institutions and producers, and so forth, but also an account of how the films exemplified what historian of science James Secord has
termed "knowledge in transit."[3] Attention to the dynamic, communicative aspect
of this kind of filmmaking entails, on the one hand, an appreciation of how
popular-science films relied on a variety of media predecessors, which is to say the
inheritance as well as transformation of preexisting discourses that can be designated with the term "intertextuality." On the other hand, the circulatory model
also leads to the consideration of how popular-science films display affinities with
other types of filmmaking (e.g., trick films, serials, and the film experiments of
the avant-garde). The detective genre provides a primary example of this type of
circulation, constituting a particularly rich area of overlap that demonstrates how
the techniques of popular-scientific filmmaking resonated with the style and
thematic preoccupations of a fictional genre. And while this book concentrates
on the early silent era of cinema history, as I elaborate in the conclusion, the circulatory tendencies of popular-science films have remained prominent, from the
sustained interest in the avant-garde in the scientific moving image, to the

institutionalization of educational cinema from the 1920s onward, to the continued transit between the imaging cultures of scientific visualization and entertainment cinema. Indeed, the earliest era of popular-science filmmaking prefigures a wide range of contemporary uses of the moving image, such as the continuing importance of moving images in education to the circulation of popular-science sequences in Hollywood specialeffects and television dramas like *CSI*.

From Cinema, a Curiosity, to a Cinema of Curiosity

The first public screening of the Lumière cinematograph took place on December 28, 1895, at the Salon Indien, in the basement of the Grand Café on the Boulevard des Capucines in Paris. After this screening Georges Méliès was said to have approached Antoine Lumière, father to Auguste and Louis and the evening's impresario, to ask whether he could purchase a cinematograph. Antoine replied, "Young man, my invention is not for sale.... For you it would be ruinous. It may be exploited for a while as a scientific curiosity; beyond that it has no commercial future."[4] The obvious irony here is that Lumière *père* was mistaken; the cinema, after all, had an extraordinarily robust commercial future. As interesting as this lack of appreciation for the cinema's potential as an entertainment device, however, is the description of it as a "scientific curiosity," a designation that invokes a lineage of optical toys, such *jouets philosophiques* as the thaumatrope, the phenakistascope, and the zoetrope, which also included the deployment of chronophotography in physiology.

Cinema's initial debt to this imaging tradition has received substantial attention.[5] One influential account describes scientific cinema as "a mode geared to the temporal and spatial decomposition and reconfiguration of bodies as dynamic fields of action in need of regulation and control," thus emphasizing the scientific film's place among techniques for social regulation.[6] The question of how scientific modes of visualization have figured in cinema history beyond the experimental achievements of the medium's pioneers has been largely ignored, however. The cinema's indisputable involvement with a disciplining gaze is only part of the story of the interaction of cinema and science. A different type of gaze emerges by considering the fluid boundaries between science and entertainment in the culture of modernity and modernization, which I designate with the strategically multivalent keyword "curiosity."

Curiosity is a capacious concept. There are sexual and scientific curiosities as well as a generalized form that inheres in all narrative—the question "what happens next" that propels stories forward. In an evolutionary sense, curiosity can be seen a core human characteristic.[7] Curiosity is also a capricious concept. Historically, the term has transformed from a sin to a virtue, a spectrum of meaning that is retained in common

usages that are antithetical, such as "morbid curiosity" versus "intellectual curiosity."[8] My own use of the term is indebted to Hans Blumenberg's
argument that curiosity is a signal characteristic of modernity.[9] Blumenberg's periodization of modernity goes back well beyond the nineteenth
century; in his account, curiosity distinguishes the modern from the medieval.[10] Curiosity thus functions as a shifter, designating the novelty of
the popular-science film's emergence from the knowledge cultures of the
late nineteenth century while also recognizing links to traditions that
extend much farther back, such as the cabinet of curiosities, helping to
account for how early popular-science films are simultaneously modern
and venerable.

Curiosity also deemphasizes objectivity as a preeminent principle for understanding popular-science films. While Lorraine Daston and Peter Galison trace how objectivity came to be installed as a "ubiquitous and irresistible"
epistemic virtue around 1850, they also acknowledge that objectivity's en-
thronement was far from a monolithic occurrence, consisting instead of "innovation and proliferation rather than monarchic succession. . . . This is not
some neat Hegelian arithmetic of thesis plus antithesis equals synthesis, but
a far messier situation in which all the elements continue in play and in interaction with one another."[11] Thus, this argument expands on Daston's and
Galison's observation that the rise of objectivity did not eradicate other epistemic forms. So while many practitioners of science were turning away from
the kinds of thinking and expression that characterized popularization and
the fluidity of the cultures of art and science prior to the mid-nineteenth
century, a prominent site for the cultivation of curiosity in modernity was
the domain of popular science. Instead of objectivity's restraint, nineteenth-
century popular science retained ties to previous traditions of display and
their engagement with the senses and the affective states of curiosity and
wonder.

The "devices" of curiosity in the book's title, then, refer on the one hand
to material contrivances—the machines, films, and the exhibition spaces
that constitute the range of physical artifacts related to popular-science
films. Devices encompass less tangible manifestations as well, however,
such as the cinema's ability to visualize the invisible and provide a form of
enriched vision. In this sense, the devices refer to the various techniques for
producing novelty and revelation that include slow motion, magnification,
or time lapse (which are certainly entwined with physical artifacts). Finally,
devices also can be thought of as akin to literary devices. In this sense, to
call these films "devices of curiosity" is to suggest that they function as
contrivances of the concept of curiosity itself, that they are curious experiences that invigorate the senses and activate the sense of wonder. The devices of curiosity in this sense are stimuli for knowledge, products of and
for epistemophilia.[12]

Late in his life, Michel Foucault expressed a desire for a different relationship to vision/knowledge that turned on the concept of curiosity:

> Curiosity is a vice that has been stigmatized in turn by Christianity, by philosophy, and even by a certain conception of science. Curiosity, futility. The word, however, pleases me. To me it suggests something altogether different: it evokes "concern"; it evokes the care one takes for what exists and could exist; a readiness to find strange and singular what surrounds us; a certain relentlessness to break up our familiarities and to regard otherwise the same things; a fervor to grasp what is happening and what passes; a casualness in regard to the traditional hierarchies of the important and the essential.[13]

Acknowledging the modern skepticism about curiosity, a kind of attention both stigmatized and "futile" from certain modern perspectives, Foucault's description highlights characteristics that are crucial for understanding popular-science films. To be sure, early popular-science films do not always live up to Foucault's ambitions for curiosity. Many of these films were part of traditional and even conservative approaches to knowledge that did not break up familiarities and instead domesticated the strange and singular.

To view popular-science films as agents of stultification is ungenerous, however. Many of these films do exhibit a concern for what exists and could exist, rendering the familiar strange and singular, often by virtue of cinematic mediation. Indeed, this aspect of popular-science films has served as a vital resource for the avant-garde as well as scientists and scholars. "To regard otherwise" encapsulates what, at their best, these films can do, and the reclamation of early popular-science films promises a multiplication of the paths of cinema history and the history of science. The keyword "curiosity" opens up a pathway to early popular-science films so that they appear not as short-lived novelties leading nowhere but rather as coming out of a long tradition of science's visual culture that they both inherit and transform.

Into the Drop of Water: Locating Popular-Science Films in Documentary History

In a familiar popular-science image, a device—a story, a microscope, a film—reveals teeming life within some small thing, thus transforming a drop of pond water or blood or a piece of cheese into a vibrant world.[14] This image provides, on the one hand, an apt encapsulation of the process of writing this book; what initially seemed an inconsequential blank spot in cinema history has expanded to become a complex area with manifold ramifications. This image, on the other hand, is particularly opportune because it involves the aforementioned dynamic of inheritance and transformation of previous traditions. The methodological consequence of this dynamic is that these films need to be approached not only from the perspective of cinema studies but also from the history of science. Indeed, the obscurity in which popular-science films lie is due in no small part to their location in an area of interdisciplinary overlap, belonging to the histories of both cinema and popular science but generally understood and appreciated by neither discipline.

For much of the twentieth century, cinema historians tended to ignore films made between the medium's emergence around 1895 until 1913, at which point the narrative, feature-length film began to predominate. Films from this era often were described as "primitive" cinema, an epithet based on a characterization of them as embryonic forms of a cinema that would emerge fully fledged only later. At the end of the 1970s, however, this era of cinema history underwent a reevaluation that revealed not an underdeveloped media form but rather an alternative cinematic mode, which has come to be known as "early cinema" and whose particularity is signaled by the phrase "the cinema of attractions."[15]

Initially, fiction films received the lion's share of scholarly attention, even though nonfiction films were known to have played a critical, and even for a time predominant, role in early cinema culture. The lack of attention to early nonfiction films in discussions of documentary cinema is due largely to John Grierson's influential redefinition of documentary in the 1930s. For Grierson, the term "documentary" designated the reinvention of prior modes of nonfiction filmmaking practice.[16] His pithy and frequently quoted formula—documentary is "the creative treatment of actuality"—distinguished the new documentary from prior forms, about which he wrote, "they describe, and even expose, but in any aesthetic sense, only rarely reveal."[17] The hierarchy in Grierson's redefinition led to a slippage, from an understanding of early nonfiction as descriptive filmmaking to a conception of it as an unreflective practice, a cinema of "uninterpreted fact," as a program note for an early program of Griersonian documentaries at the Museum of Modern Art would have it.[18]

The result of Grierson's appropriation of the term "documentary" was to create what Tom Gunning has called a "polemical periodization."[19] The unfortunate, and lasting, effect of Grierson's intervention was to deny the films that preceded "the documentary" of both their argumentative structures and their status as films worthy of attention. Nonfiction films from the 1900s and 1910s consistently have been excluded from histories of documentary cinema; for example, Lewis Jacobs's *The Documentary Tradition* (1971) began in the early 1920s with *Nanook of the North* (Robert Flaherty, 1922), consigning "precursors" to a brief preface.[20] More recent scholars of documentary, while nuancing this line of demarcation by, for instance, expanding the purview of documentary studies to include the modernist avant-garde, have continued to exclude early cinema from the documentary tradition.[21]

The title of one of the first essay collections on early nonfiction films tellingly referred to *Uncharted Territory*, but fortunately the neglect of nonfiction filmmaking vis-à-vis the early fiction film shows signs of abating. In the two decades since the publication of *Uncharted Territory*, scholars have begun to fill in the map of this terrain.[22] Charles Acland, Paula Amad, Jennifer Bean, Scott Curtis, Lee Grieveson, Vinzenz Hediger, Luke McKernan, Kirsten Ostherr, Jennifer Peterson, Matthew Solomon, Dan Streible, Nana Verhoeff, Valérie Vignaux, Haidee Wasson, and Kristin Whissel have all contributed to recovering early nonfiction cinema history, developing the insights of a prior generation of cinema scholars who also showed an interest in early nonfiction—Stephen Bottomore, Lisa Cartwright, Alison Griffiths, Tom Gunning, Frank Kessler, Thierry Lefebvre, Charles Musser, and Greg Waller.[23] This book builds on the historiography of early nonfiction cinema while adding early popular-science films, which have received the least attention of early nonfiction's major genres, to the map.

Simply adding popular-science films to the history of early cinema would do these films a disservice, however, since without insights from the history of science, crucial aspects of these films remain opaque.[24] Perhaps the most important of these contexts is the attention historians of science have bestowed upon the notion of "popularization" itself, which I will discuss in more detail below. The work historians of science have done to excavate and theorize popular science as a cultural practice has provided an essential resource for my engagement with popular-science films, which often rely on and incorporate themes and techniques of nineteenth-century popular-scientific media.

Early popular-science *films* have received almost no attention from historians of science, however. This lack of attention is not unfamiliar from the way the history of science has treated film more generally. Whereas the investigation of science's visual dimension has been a lively area in the last thirty years, an engagement with the moving image has not been pursued with nearly the same thoroughness as the static image.[25] And approaches to cinema from within the history of science often are limited to a relatively impoverished conceptualization of films as transparent representations to be mined for content. One familiar and limited optic asks the question whether a particular fiction film, usually from the genre of science fiction, has gotten a scientific concept "right."[26] Another approach has been to produce catalogues of films according to the logic of a particular scientific discipline—psychology, anthropology, and so forth—"at the movies," or to look at single films as a way to illuminate particular scientific issues.[27]

Beyond these limited cross-border forays into the land of the moving image, some historians of science have taken up the question of cinema's role in the history of science in more sustained and sophisticated ways, including Hannah Landecker, Jimena Canales, Tania Munz, David Kirby, and

Hanna Rose Shell.[28] Scholars in the history of medicine also have investigated the impact film had on the medical profession.[29] Finally, accounts of "natural history" filmmaking overlap most strongly with the central concerns of this book, occasionally even discussing some of the same films.[30] Unlike previous approaches, however, this book considers how early popular-science films constituted a tradition of their own.

The choice of the term "popular science" to describe the films discussed in this book requires justification, since the notion of popular science itself is neither straightforward nor uncontroversial. The status of popular science within the history of science has been through several stages. A seminal article by Roger Cooter and Stephen Pumfrey problematized an earlier "diffusionist" model in which popular science was understood as a secondary and often debased version of knowledge generated by professional scientists.[31] The rejection of the diffusionist model has become, as Jonathan Topham notes, "de rigeur," but problems related to the conceptualization of popular science as an area of inquiry persist, and as Topham writes, "the historiography of the field has become increasingly uncertain."[32] A sign of this uncertainty is that James Secord has called for the abandonment of "popular science" as a "neutral descriptive term," calling instead for an understanding of scientific knowledge that "eradicat[es] the distinction between the making and the communicating of knowledge."[33] So while popularization has moved from a marginal position to occupy a more central category in the history of science, the affirmation of its importance is intertwined with a countertendency that seeks to dissolve the category altogether.

One way to address this issue would be to choose a term that avoids the problematic qualities of "popular," which, after all, can mean both science produced for the people and science produced by the people. One alternative that has been employed by both historians of science and cinema historians is "vernacular."[34] The reasons for the choice of "vernacular" vary, but Miriam Hansen's justification for choosing it over "popular," to which I am particularly partial and indebted, places an emphasis on how "the term vernacular combines the dimension of the quotidian, of everyday usage, with connotations of discourse, idiom, and dialect, with circulation, promiscuity, and translatability."[35] Many of the reasons Hansen enumerates accord with Secord's notion of "knowledge in transit," especially the vernacular's emphasis on circulation.

To designate these films as "vernacular science," however, creates more problems than it solves (not the least of which is the inkhorney inelegance of the phrase "cinema of scientific vernacularization"). "Vernacular science," with its suggestion of knowledge created by laypeople, distorts the social position of these filmmakers, who were largely aligned with the scientific establishment.[36] Of the three filmmakers to whom I devote the most detailed discussion—F. Martin Duncan, Percy Smith, and Jean Comandon—only

Smith could be considered a producer of vernacular knowledge, and only somewhat, since he became increasingly drawn into the ambit of professional science over the course of his career. My choice of "popular science" as a general descriptor thus follows Topham's and Bernard Lightman's arguments for retaining the term. As Topham notes, "While [popular science] may fail us as a fixed and supposedly neutral descriptive vocabulary to be applied retrospectively to past events, the lexicon of 'popular science,' and the work that it has done for historical actors, is itself richly deserving of historical study."[37] Ultimately, "popular science" is a useful term because it constitutes what historians of science call an "actor's category"—which is to say, it is a term that was in use at the time as opposed to a later term imposed onto the past.

Of course, "popular science" was not the only label for these films; indeed, a wide variety of terms designated this kind of filmmaking: "natural history," "educational," "interest," "factual," *"films de vulgarisation," "scènes instructive,"* and hundreds of other terms of varying degrees of specificity, from apiculture to zoology. Popular science can function as an umbrella term, however, gathering these films together into a more or less coherent genre. As Ralph O'Connor has noted, "When it comes to pointing up the wider significance of our research, connecting it to large-scale narratives, the umbrella-category comes into its own. For many people, the most exciting and challenging feature of this research is its revelation that popular and elite scientific practices turn out to be so much more interdependent than was previously assumed."[38] The gesture of gathering together that popular science performs is particularly appropriate insofar as an aim of this book is to provide an overview of this kind of filmmaking, putting it onto the map, so to speak, by outlining its historical developments and major practitioners and taking care to emphasize its circulation across the boundary between nonfiction and fiction.

O'Connor's second point about how research into popular science reveals the interdependence of the popular and elite scientific spheres applies to popular-science filmmakers as well. As Lightman has noted, "Perhaps the most important changes to the old map indicated by this study of popularizers have to do with the status of 'professional' science in this period."[39] So while the first half of the nineteenth century saw the formation of a modern scientific identity, with the creation of both the word "scientist" and a particular kind of persona associated with that term, and while it was the period during which scientific disciplines became established together with the related institutional infrastructure, the rise of popularization was entwined with the developing identities and procedures of professional science.[40] In other words, the professionalization of science formed a dyad with popular science; "if it was the age of the (would-be) professional scientists, it was also the age of the popularizer of science."[41]

Historians of science have elaborated the conditions of popular science's emergence over the course of the nineteenth century, how it was an outgrowth of certain attitudes toward knowledge and transformations in mass-cultural technologies, in particular the popular-science press. Secord has labeled the two-part industrial revolution in the book market (the first from 1830 to 1855 and the second from 1875 to 1914) the "greatest transformation in human communication since the Renaissance."[42] This transformation constitutes a precondition for popular-science films, which are themselves extensions of this transformation in the production and circulation of knowledge.

One particularly pronounced aspect of nineteenth-century popularization was its appeal to vision. As Lightman notes, "Popularizers responded to the pictorial turn in Victorian culture by increasing the use of illustrations and vivid literary images in their books, and, in the case of those who were active speakers, by incorporating spectacles into their lectures."[43] Early popular-science films were exemplary of this visual turn in mass culture that took place during the second half of the nineteenth century. Popular-science films often drew visual strategies from the public display of science at the great exhibitions, or in the popular press, lectures, popular shows, and textbooks. This intertextuality requires attention to other histories, such as how popular-science films relate to the histories of education or popular literature.

Finally, it bears emphasizing that these films are "popular" not just in terms of the traditions of display that they inherit but also because they are commercial products.[44] Knowledge in transit often involves the flow of commodities, and these films circulated primarily in the context of a market economy. Relatedly, as Topham emphasizes, popular science requires a consideration of transnational dynamics, which my account takes as fundamental by tracing the genre's development from its genesis and growth in England to its elaboration in France to its attempted institutionalization in the United States before finally returning to France for an example of the circulation of popular-science moments in fiction films.[45]

While the focus in this book is on the period from 1903 to 1918, as the invocation of the scorpion footage at the beginning of L'Age d'or indicates, it has a wider historical radius. The avant-garde's fascination with popular science indicates the importance of a documentary aesthetic prior to and different from the Griersonian mode, and it serves as an initial example of how early popular-science films had notable afterlives. Additionally, the popular-science films of the pre-World War I era constituted the precursors of educational cinema, which came into its own around the turn of the 1920s. And finally, the circulation of the visual knowledge that underpins popular-science films also included fiction films, as my discussion of French serials will demonstrate.

As lectures on magnified drops of water occasionally pointed out, the tiny creatures seen through the microscope could have profound effects on much larger organisms. Similarly, the role of popular-science films in the media ecology of the long twentieth century, while generally beneath the notice of historians, constitutes a vital, continuous tradition. Taking notice of these films reshapes both the histories of cinema and science.

* * *

The first three chapters of this book chart the emergence of popular-science films, tracking their appropriation of previous presentational forms (e.g., the magic-lantern lecture) as well as the creation of new forms of popular-scientific imaging specific to cinema (e.g., time-lapse cinematography). The Charles Urban Trading Company was the first company to create a significant catalogue of popular-science films. Chapters One and Two describe the work of Urban's two key collaborators, F. Martin Duncan and Percy Smith. Chapter One, "'Revealing Nature's Closest Secrets': F. Martin Duncan's Popular-Science Films at the Charles Urban Trading Company," describes the earliest popular-science films at Urban that were made by Duncan and how the lantern-slide lecture served as a primary model for the films' format. During the period that Smith, Duncan's successor at Urban, worked for Urban, a more self-contained type of film emerged. Chapter Two, "Juggling Flies and Gravid Plants: Percy Smith's Early Popular-Science Films," investigates the beginning of Smith's filmmaking career, which saw the former civil servant introduce numerous innovations in the field of popular-science cinema, from time-lapse color cinematography of blooming flowers to some of the first animated maps that were used in World War I propaganda films. This chapter includes a discussion of Smith's amateur detective stories, introducing an argument about the affinities between popular-science films and the scientific detective tradition, which reappears in Chapter Five.

These chapters highlight the importance of the aesthetics of wonder, demonstrating how from their beginnings popular-science films presented an experience of science as affective and spectacular. One way this experience was particularly evident was the perceived proximity of popular-science films to the trick film, a similarity that arose in contemporary reactions to Duncan's microcinematography, Smith's *The Birth of a Flower*, and his juggling fly films. These chapters detail how such signal moments of popular-science cinema involve a return to the first film screenings and their particular constellation of affects, particularly the fascination with the apparatus itself and its perceptual capabilities. In this foregrounding of the cinema's novel effects, these films incite a curiosity similar to that of the first cinema audiences, demonstrating a peculiarly modern fascination with seeing how things work, what Neil Harris has dubbed the "operational aesthetic."

At the turn of the 1910s, French companies produced a large number of popular-science films. The third chapter, "'A Drama Unites Them in a Fight to the Death': The Flourishing of Popular-Science Films in France, 1909–1914," provides a comparative analysis of popular-science films produced by Pathé, Gaumont, and Éclair. It begins with an account of the early work of Jean Comandon, whose films for Pathé inaugurated the popular-science cycle in France. The chapter then moves to a detailed analysis of a number of films, especially *Le Scorpion Languedocien* (Éclair, 1913), whose borrowings, particularly from Jean-Henri Fabre's ethological writings, are a further indication of the persistence of intertextuality in popular-science filmmaking. In addition to detailing the stylistic parameters of individual nonfiction films in France before World War I, the chapter investigates the importance of the films' reception contexts, from the calculated jumble of genres at a typical neighborhood cinema to scholastic screenings that were part of attempts to incorporate the cinema into visual education curricula. The chapter concludes with a consideration of how the exhibition context, specifically the films' incorporation into the program format, suggests a stronger continuity between nonfiction and fiction genres than has previously been assumed, a point further elaborated in Chapter Five.

The first half of the book sketches the contours of how popular-science films developed over their first decade, from 1903 to 1913. Each of the chapters takes as its focal point a single filmmaker, and taken together these three figures—Duncan, Smith, and Comandon—represent a spectrum of approaches to popular-science filmmaking. Duncan was most indebted to nineteenth-century cultures of popularization, and his filmmaking career represented only a brief interlude in his lifelong work as a researcher and popularizer. Alternately, Smith and Comandon were the first examples of a new figure, the popular-science filmmaker. And while both Smith and Comandon devoted themselves fully to cinema, they came from different backgrounds, with Smith emerging from the milieu of amateur naturalism while Comandon was trained as a laboratory scientist. Smith worked almost exclusively for commercial film companies (Charles Urban, British Instructional Films, Gaumont-British Instructional), while Comandon spent his life working both for commercial enterprises (Pathé) and in private research institutions (Albert Kahn's *Archives de la planète* project, and finally the Institut Pasteur).

In the final two chapters, the question of how these films circulated becomes a central concern. Here the story shifts from one of how early popular-science films were produced to how they moved through the world. In 1910 George Kleine published an ambitious catalogue of "educational motion picture films" that consisted of titles he had collected from a number of European companies, notably Pathé, Gaumont, and Urban. The fourth chapter, "A Modern Cabinet of Curiosities: George Kleine's Collection of Popular-Science

Films," argues that Kleine's catalogue demonstrates an ambivalence that can be traced back to the concept of curiosity itself. On the one hand, his project was aligned with modern pedagogical research that argued for education via visual means as the most efficient form of instruction. In this sense, visual curiosity offered a powerful way to arouse interest, and the cinema's unique visual qualities made it the most modern mode of instruction. Simultaneously, however, Kleine's film catalogue recalled the collections of natural artifacts that were called "cabinets of curiosities" in the seventeenth and eighteenth centuries.

So while the Kleine collection was described generally as part of a modern plan for the rational deployment of the cinema, the description and content of individual films frequently displayed powerful contiguities with the wonders and marvels associated with an earlier era, where rationality and enchantment had not yet become antithetical. In this mixed appeal, the catalogue embodied a number of the contradictions often associated with visual education, such as the ineradicable presence of the image's sensual and sensational dimensions. The catalogue's most successful and best-documented film, *The Fly Pest*, exemplifies this dynamic, oscillating between a hygienic argument that construes the fly as a disease vector and an appreciation of the magnified fly images that participates in the aesthetics of wonder.

The final chapter considers the ramifications of popular-science filmmaking for fictional genres, in particular the crime melodrama. Parallel to the popularity of the one-reel popular-science film, the serial film was emerging as an important new genre of the early 1910s. The final chapter, "Popular Science and Crime Melodrama: Louis Feuillade and the Serial," argues that the serial film as pioneered by Feuillade contained significant similarities to popular-science films. These similarities are both stylistic, as manifested in the tendency to use more close-ups than was typical for fiction films of the time, and thematic, i.e., the preoccupation with registering the impact of science and technology on modern life.

This link between popular-science films and the serial helps to modify an enduring aspect of the reception of the crime melodrama, the invocation of the term "fantastic realism" to characterize its aesthetic distinctiveness. An artifact of the Surrealist appreciation of the serial, "fantastic realism" usually describes how the films are filled with moments of the bizarre and the unexplainable, such as the detective Juve's suit of spikes to counteract Fantômas's "silent executioner," a giant python. In my analysis, elements such as Juve's spikes are revealed less as mysteries than as effects from the domain of popular science. What is fantastic, in other words, is usually the latest technological device adapted to the struggle between criminal and police (and, indeed, Juve's spikes refer to a celebrated news story involving an anarchist's battle with the police). In these moments, the crime melodrama shares the popular-science film's ability to arouse and satisfy curiosity, taking as its source the ubiquity of the inexplicable in modernity. In my reading, then, the crime melodrama becomes a form of popular-science film, providing its audience with examples of the pleasures and the pitfalls of scientific advances.

Of the more than three hundred films viewed in the course of my research, only a handful receive careful attention in this book, and those that do are some of the best-known examples of early popular-science films. In other words, this account is an introductory rather than an exhaustive study, surveying the tip of an iceberg. One aim of this study, then, beyond an engagement with exemplary films, is to gesture to the large amount of material that awaits future research. F. Martin Duncan once ended the introduction to one of his books by writing that if it should "awaken and stimulate an interest in the wonders and beauties of animal life, then my labours have not been in vain."[46] I harbor a similar hope, namely that this book will lead to greater interest in both the particular popular-science films I discuss and the category of popular-science films more generally. May this book serve as an invitation to watch these films, to reconsider their place in history, and to multiply the means of appreciating them.

{ Chapter 1 }

"Revealing Nature's Closest Secrets": F. Martin Duncan's Popular-Science Films at the Charles Urban Trading Company

> To-day animated photography stands upon the threshold
> of a new epoch of its existence.
>
> —F. MARTIN DUNCAN, "THE APPLICATION OF ANIMATED
> PHOTOGRAPHY TO SCIENCE AND EDUCATION," *BRITISH JOURNAL OF
> PHOTOGRAPHY*, JULY 10, 1903, 549.

In the earliest film shows, the display of cinema technology itself was of as much interest as the images on the screen, which is emblematized by the projector's location in the middle of the audience in early Lumière shows. By 1903, however, cinema had been around for almost a decade, and the device that had appeared as a technological curiosity was developing into a fledgling global industry. 1903 represents a landmark year in cinema history, marking a turn toward longer story films, epitomized by *The Great Train Robbery* (Edison/Porter), as well as other advances in narrative form that emerged in 1903, including the use of intertitles, as in *Uncle Tom's Cabin* (Edison/Porter).[1] The "new epoch" signaled by F. Martin Duncan in the epigraph did not refer to this elaboration of narrative form in the cinema, however. 1903 may have marked the beginning of fictional narrative as the predominant form of cinema, but it also witnessed the emergence of another cinematic genre, the popular-science film.

The first examples of this new form of cinema came from the combined efforts of F. Martin Duncan and Charles Urban. Urban, the son of German immigrants, began his business career with a variety of sales jobs, and he soon began to concentrate his efforts in a particular branch of book salesmanship that presaged his interests in film production. Urban specialized in big, expensive compendia of information and collections of cultural icons. The first book that he sold was Rand McNally's *Railway Guide and World's Atlas*. Thereafter, he peddled fine-art images called "The World's Masterpieces," which consisted of twenty-five $1 photogravures, delivered weekly.

A bound version of the images also was available in a deluxe edition for $125, partly in color and printed on India and parchment paper. Finally, Urban sold *The Stage and Its Stars*, a set of images of American and British theater stars, which also was available in a standard and deluxe version.[2] This first stage of Urban's sales career contained an attitude toward cultural commodities that later would characterize his popular-science filmmaking as well. As Luke McKernan has noted, "[Urban] used his super-salesman image of superiority and quality to shape a cinema based on information, science, education, and wonder at what was natural."[3]

Following his days as a traveling salesman, Urban bought a stationery store in Detroit, which brought him into contact with the world of business machines. He began to trade in typewriters and phonographs, and in 1895 his phonograph parlor merged with the local Edison kinetoscope concession. After a trip to New York City, where he saw the Lumière cinematograph and the Edison Vitascope shows, Urban began to pursue motion-picture projection technology, and, together with the engineer Walter Isaacs, he developed a motion-picture projector that he dubbed the Bioscope. Soon thereafter, the firm Maguire and Baucus hired Urban to run their London office, which he renamed the Warwick Trading Company. The company thrived under Urban's management and became one of the leading British film companies of the period, distributing films by James Williamson, G. A. Smith, and Georges Méliès. It specialized, however, in producing actuality films, an area of expertise that indicated Urban's conception of the cinema as primarily a nonfictional medium.

The Unseen World

On July 20, 1903, Urban established the Charles Urban Trading Company (CUTC), which produced the first series of popular-science films in the history of cinema. For his company's first major independent production, Urban hired Francis Martin Duncan, a microphotographer and naturalist, to produce films on various natural history subjects[4] (Fig. 1.1). Duncan was the son of Dr. P. Martin Duncan, the multifaceted scientist and popularizer who edited *Cassell's Natural History* (1883), a six-volume, profusely illustrated reference work.[5] F. Martin, as his name tends to be written, made photographs for *Cassell's* and soon established himself in the field of popular-science publishing in his own right with such titles as *Some Birds of the London Zoo* (1900) and *Some Curious Plants* (1900). His *First Steps in Photo-Micrography: A Hand-Book for Novices* (1902) provided information about how to obtain images of the "beauties" of zoology and botany through the microscope for the interested amateur, who could be a medical student, a practicing doctor, or a curious hobbyist, which corresponded with the kind of genteel audience

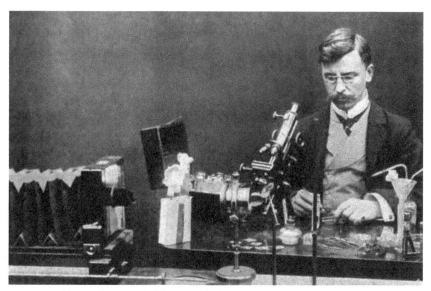

FIG. 1.1 Publicity photograph of F. Martin Duncan reproduced in Urban's catalogues. Courtesy of Stephen Herbert.

Urban sought to engage.[6] This book also exemplifies Duncan's involvement with what Tim Boon, referring to Duncan's films for Urban, terms "the visual and participatory culture of science."[7] Duncan's background as a popularizer formed the critical cultural background for his involvement with early cinema.

Urban began press preview screenings of his new film program in early July 1903 at his offices at 48 Rupert Street. The first published review appeared in *The Daily Mail* on July 10 under the title "New Camera Wonders: Living Pictures of Nature's Closest Secrets," and other newspapers such as the *Daily Express, Le Figaro,* the *Morning Post, The Amateur Photographer,* and *Focus* soon followed with articles on the innovative motion-picture program.[8] The first lines of the *Daily Mail* article positioned Urban's films as signaling a change in the status of moving pictures: "Although the kinematograph in its various forms has so far been a toy, or has served as a music-hall 'turn,' it has been realised from the first that as its processes improved it would open out enormous new possibilities of scientific application. How great these possibilities are will be realised in a few weeks when Mr. Charles Urban, the proprietor of the 'Bioscope' gives to the scientific world the results of a series of experiments he has made in the combination of the bioscope and the microscope."[9] The appeal to the "scientific world" was of course a familiar feature of popular-scientific gestures toward cultural legitimation, and it continued to figure prominently in the rhetoric surrounding Urban's science productions. Urban repeatedly stressed the "high-class" appeal of his films, but the writer of these sentences erred in assuming that the films were made for exhibition to "the scientific world." If the scientific world took notice of Urban's films, as was occasionally the case, Urban gladly included these reactions in his publicity materials, but the first screenings of his films were aimed at a music-hall audience. The article in *The Amateur Photographer* gave a better sense of Urban's public when it stated that "[Urban] has succeeded in making a number of cinematographic records of microscopic observations, so that it is now possible to watch upon the screen the actual processes of protoplasmic life, and show a large audience what has hitherto only been observable by the scientist."[10]

The showman's tendency toward overstatement also appeared in another, more oblique fashion. As the *Focus* remarked, "We have often been promised startling wonders by scientists, but when the time came for making them public, it has turned out that the report was premature. It remains to be seen whether this will be so in the present instance."[11] Although Urban's public premiere of these films met with enthusiasm, he did promise more than he delivered. The *Daily Mail* review mentioned that "[Urban] has designed an automatic camera which can be set to take a series of photographs at any interval that may be desired. The week's growth of a plant might be recorded in this way by a series of snapshot photographs taken at intervals of, say, one minute. Those photographs may then be projected upon the screen with ordinary kinematograph rapidity, so that processes of growth of the entire period might be made visible in a minute." Other reviews allude to this apparatus as well, and the *Daily Mail* reviewer wrote, "Mr. Urban has succeeded in taking a photograph through a red screen in one-seventieth of a second, an achievement which brings instantaneous color photography within sight."[12] These announced innovations—time-lapse and color—took some time to develop; the first commercially released popular-science films that featured time-lapse and color did not appear until 1910, and they were made with the help of Duncan's successor, F. Percy Smith.[13]

These reviews established what Yuri Tsivian has referred to as "tropes of reception."[14] The reviews and Urban's publicity frequently returned to the extreme manipulation of space involved in the microcinematographic films; the claims for magnification ranged from 2,200,000 to 76,000,000 times when the films were viewed on a 20- to 25-foot screen. This almost unfathomable play of scale presented spectators with a visual experience that was difficult to understand on its own terms. The *Daily Express* reviewer, for instance, had recourse to a pastoral image: "More remarkable still are the pictures of the veins in the web of a frog's foot and in the point of a leaf. You see blood rushing through the frog's artery like water down a mill-stream."[15] The *Daily Mail* review likewise scaled up the microscopic doings to human scale: "Mr. Urban's greatest achievement, however, is the series of films which reproduce on the screen as clearly as a bioscope picture shows the movement of a crowd the actual processes of protoplasmic life in a bit of common water-weed."[16] This reviewer recognized the cinema's celebrated ability to show complex movements in photorealistic detail at a macroscopic level—leaves blown by the wind, dust, smoke, or crowds—in Urban's scenes from the world as revealed by the microscope.

The *Daily Express* review continued its reaction to the preview screening by spinning out a remarkable extended metaphor that first envisioned the films as political allegories and then speculated about the possible ramifications of the play of scale that the films raised:

These very bodies of ours support and nurture as crowded a life as throngs the outer surface of the globe. Through our veins wander tribes of Bedouin bacteria, possessed, we doubt not, of recognized forms of communal existence. The pain which we call colic may conceivably be due to a South African war of bacilli, and a twinge of toothache to some upheaval in microbe politics equivalent to a change in our fiscal policy. The suggestion sounds ludicrous, but so little do we know of the lesser life that it is well within the range of possibility. If man's entity indeed began as an amoeba in the primeval slime, there is no law of evolution which forbids the possibility of his nurturing in his veins to-day a microbe that millions of years hence shall attain to an infinitely higher degree of civilisation than he will ever reach.[17]

Here the microcinematography has prompted the reviewer to imagine the body as a planet, where microbial processes resemble contemporary geopolitical struggles (the Boer War). In addition, the manipulation of space leads to speculation about manipulating the scale of time, hence the vision of a time "millions of years hence" when a microbe may evolve into humanity's better.[18]

Other reactions speculated about the films' function. "As the principal purpose in life of most of these tiny organisms seems to be to devour those belonging to a different species, Mr. Urban's photographs should show plenty of excitement, and we may expect such advertisements as 'Great Battle of Microbes now on—'Orrible Slaughter.' We only fear less [sic] the Society for the Prevention of Cruelty to Animals will step in and stop these exhibitions."[19] The tendency to read the films as scenes of spectacular action qualifies Urban's high-class rhetoric, and, indeed, early popular-science films often had recourse to scenes of remarkable violence. As the dropped "h" from the hypothetical advertisement indicates, this reviewer took Urban's pronouncements about the elevating intentions of his films with a grain of salt, and this reaction provides an example of the multivalent possibilities that these films provided.

Having used the press preview screenings to build publicity for his new entertainment, the time had come for the public premiere. After Charles Morton at the Palace Theatre declined to book the show, Urban found an interested impresario in Douglas Cox, the manager of the Alhambra Theatre, who agreed to a screening of Urban's films during the relatively low-risk summer season.[20] The show was billed as "'The Unseen World' A Series of Microscopic Studies, Photographed by Means of The Urban-Duncan Micro-Bioscope," and was exhibited publicly for the first time at the Alhambra on August 17, 1903. One account of the opening performance recalled, "Scientists were present in great number, journalists in force, a crowded house. Enthusiasm was the order of the night, and the great London press was unanimous in praise the next morning. . . . The program was presented every night to delighted audiences for a period of nine months, and proved one of the principal attractions at the Alhambra."[21] Although the number of scientists in attendance may be exaggerated, the press reaction was, indeed, considerable, and Urban's skills at self-promotion and archival instincts led him to reprint pages of press reviews in his catalogues.

An Alhambra program of the screening does not seem to survive, but a comparison of the reviews to the descriptions of the film in Urban's first catalogue, which appeared in late 1903, allows the certain identification of the following titles: *Cheese Mites* (50ft), *Circulation of Blood in the Frog's Foot* (75ft), *The Pugilistic Toads and the Tortoise Referee* (60ft), *The Fresh-Water Hydra* (75ft), *Chameleons Feeding* (100ft), *The Circulation of Protoplasm in the Waterweed* (75ft), and *Typhoid Bacteria* (50ft). *The Meal of the American Toad* (75ft) and *The Boa Constrictor* (200ft) are likely titles, although the scenes described in the reviews could also refer to *The Toad's Luncheon* (75ft) or *The Greedy Toad* (75ft) and *The Boa Constrictor Crushing and Swallowing a Rat* (100ft) or *A Snake in the Grass* (60ft). *The Busy Bee* (450ft), "a series of 15 pictures showing every phase of Bee Culture," formed the "second part" of the program.[22] The total footage of these films was at least 1,000ft, which would have meant that the program lasted roughly twenty minutes.

Many reviews noted the show's novelty. *The Standard* declared, "most shows may be described as novel, but none are more entitled to the adjective than that presented for the first time last night at the Alhambra." *The Era* remarked, "it is as beautiful as it is novel and curious," and the *Daily Telegraph* observed, "Science has just added a new marvel to the marvelous powers of the Bioscope."[23] As McKernan has noted, with *The Unseen World*, "Urban had taken the cinema back to its roots. The sense of astonished marvel in this review [the *Daily Telegraph*'s] echoes accounts of the first film shows."[24] Some eight years after cinema first had received widespread attention, the appeals of its emergence had been reinvigorated and made to seem novel once again.

Duncan's images returned spectators to the sense of wonder that the first projections had inspired by seeing a photographic image in unprecedented motion. This fascination is registered in some of the catalogue descriptions of the films, as when a description of *The Boa Constrictor* states, "An animated head of a young boa showing the play of the tongue is next seen."[25] An image of a boa constrictor's head was not particularly novel, and microscope shows or aquarium slides had offered images of animals and microbes in motion on a screen for decades, but the locution "an animated head" and the mention of the "play of the tongue" point to the dimension of the image that the reviewer found noteworthy. As the *Daily Express* wrote, "The chief impression [the films] leave behind is an extraordinary sense of movement. Rest, repose, stillness, seem absolutely opposed to all principles of Nature. At the very moment of death new life in some form or other is born."[26] This emphasis on movement both recalls the reactions to the earliest cinematic projections and extends those reactions into new optical realms.

The sense of the familiar mingled with the novel evoked echoes of older entertainments as well. While stressing the show's originality, the reviewer for the *Free Lance* also connected it to a mid-nineteenth-century popular-science venue: "All last week the house was crowded nightly and this I should think is largely due to the novelty. What a sensation it would have been for the Polytechnic in the old days if it could have had something of this kind."[27] Another review referred to the Polytechnic as well:

> I wonder who remembers that the original Alhambra was a competitor of the old Polytechnic, called the Panopticon, opened with prayer, operated under a Royal charter, and filled with scientific toys? It does not matter much; but the thought occurred to me when I inspected Mr. Douglas Cox's collection of scientific toys in the shape of animated photographs the other evening. Science, to be sure, has progressed a little since 1854. The microscopic and bioscopic studies of blood in circulation, vegetation in growth, cheese in animation, and so forth, that nightly enthrall the Alhambra audience are weird and fascinating.[28]

While both reviews implied that the Alhambra show outdid what the Polytechnic offered, the comparison attests to enduring similarities. The Polytechnic, which was founded in 1838 and received a royal charter in 1839, initially devoted itself to popular lectures and demonstrations of scientific devices. Its commitment to public education, however, contained a strain of indulgence in what Richard Altick has described as the "popular appetite for the light, sweet tarts of amusement rather than the nutritious loaf of instruction."[29] "The Unseen World" thus evoked a familiar mode of entertainment, in terms of its images that resembled both the public lantern lecture and the microscope show as well as in terms of its mixture of the perceived sweetness of amusement with the more substantial fare of education.

A further element that *The Unseen World* inherited from its nineteenth-century forebears was precisely the dimension that Altick signals with his gustatory metaphor, which recurred in various guises in reviews of *The Unseen World*. The reviewer for *The Referee* wrote, "By means of these pictures the management has contrived to 'combine instruction with amusement' for the grown-up Sandfords and Mertons who have patronized the

Alhambra, and to administer, as it were, several sugar-coated science pills."[30] And the reviewer for *The People* remarked, "The way in which the Alhambra audiences watch the screen during the presentation of the pictures of insect life is significant. Here there is something new to so many that if the educational pill is gilded, as it is at the Alhambra, that is so much gained from the entertainment point of view."[31] These pharmaceutical figures for *The Unseen World* contain a crucial dynamic for popular-science films: To provide its educational medicine, an antidote for the entertainments of the music hall, some accommodation to popular taste was required. This concept of "sugar-coated science," which Percy Smith would echo, encapsulates how popular-science films appealed to both the sensuous and the intellectual faculties.

One reaction to this dual appeal was discernment, an attempt to parse the cultural elements that *The Unseen World* fused. *Nature*, for instance, was of the opinion that "Those interested in science need not spend the evening there [at the Alhambra]; they could go to see just what concerned them."[32] Instead of being seen as a compromise, however, the show's mixed appeals also could be appreciated as having a peculiar power, as the reviewer for the *Morning Post* recognized:

> As a music hall turn, last night's production was an unqualified success. People like to be interested, and they don't in the least mind being interested by something worth knowing, if only someone will provide it for them. And surely the performance must also show that the usefulness of animated pictures is not limited to amusement, but that developed on considered lines it must be of value to science, not only as an automatic and unerring record of experiments, but as a potent aid in the dissemination of knowledge.[33]

This view of the cinema signaled an increase of its purview, from a role as the so-called retina of the scientist to an educative force.

The strategy of elevating the status of the motion picture also met with a more jaundiced reception, however. The review in the *Court Circular* revealed an understanding of Urban's attempt to create a "high-class" motion-picture show that emphasized its financial calculation:

> The yearning for instruction of a popular order which characterises the British race is extraordinary. By playing delicately on this peculiarity, astute speculators have disposed of hundreds of sets of curiously-antiquated encyclopaedias, and increased by thousands the circulations of unspeakably dull weekly papers of the cheaper kinds. Instruction blended with entertainment and administered in homoeopathic doses will draw money from the major class of Englishman. Mr. Douglas Cox, the experienced general manager of the Alhambra, understands his public, and he is filling that hall nightly by an appeal to this national trait.[34]

The encyclopedias mentioned here recall Duncan's work for his father's editions of *Cassell's Natural History* as well as Urban's encyclopedia peddling, and Urban's vision of the cinema as educator was indeed indebted to the proliferation of what this reviewer saw as "unspeakably dull weekly papers." As noble as Urban's aims may have been, they also were inseparable from a commercial interest that relied on the widespread appeal of popular-scientific products. In this sense, the Alhambra shows could be seen as another instance of an onslaught of entertainments that catered to an interest in scientific innovation. As *The Morning Advertiser* put it, "'The Unseen World' is a scientific novelty, calculated to create a sensation for many weeks."[35] This emphasis on the show's transitory nature adds a shade of meaning to the celebrations of its novelty. While *The Unseen World* made gestures toward its noncommercial value, it remained subject to the law of obsolescence that ruled over other popular entertainments.

FIG. 1.2 *Unseen World* poster. Courtesy of Stephen Herbert.

The Intertextuality of *The Unseen World*

As with most films from this period, *The Unseen World* drew from other media practices, although its intertextuality is less indebted to the frequent sources for fiction films (comic strips, theater, newspaper illustrations, etc.). The partially drawn curtain in a promotional lantern slide provided an introductory image for the program, concretizing the concept of revelation promised by the program's title (Fig. 1.2). The curtain also evoked a theatrical stage, and the empty circle recalled both a spotlight and the circular frame typical of lantern slides, an iconography that provided an initial indication of the importance of the lantern-lecture tradition for *The Unseen World*. The lantern lecture was a widespread way popular science reached audiences from the mid-nineteenth to early twentieth centuries, and *The Unseen World* could be described as an animated photography lecture. There are several similarities between the two forms of entertainment, beginning with the fact that the shows consisted of a series of photographic images projected onto a screen. Beyond this fundamental resemblance, there was the more specific context of lantern lectures that included photomicrographs; lantern lectures such as *The Inhabitants of a Drop of Water under the Microscope* or Arthur J. Doherty's *Bacteria; and an Hour with the Microscope* consisted almost entirely of views taken through a microscope. A lecture on human physiology could contain a photomicrograph of a fly's eye, included as an illustration of the various possible types of eye structures.[36]

The presence of the lecturer provided another link to the exhibition strategies of the lantern-lecture format. Duncan lectured with *The Unseen World*, and certain reviews preserve impressions of his lecturing style. These references make a distinction between Duncan's performance and a typical popular-science lantern lecture. "'The popular lecture,' with its accompanying slides, would be regarded as intolerable. At the Alhambra the living picture of animal life, with its brief description given in a resonant voice, is quite another story."[37] *The Court Circular* mentioned the lecturer in its reviews of the show, commenting, "The subjects . . . are described in a concise and cheery manner that is quite to the taste of spectators."[38] The second review stated, "the orator, who discourses on the pictures as they are thrown upon the screen, is brief in his remarks and to the point."[39] Based on these comments, Duncan's comments were notably brief and, as the word "cheery" suggests, humorous. *The Unseen World* thus seems to have represented a departure from some lantern lectures, appealing to an audience that demanded diversion and amusement in addition to edification.

Lantern culture also informed *The Unseen World* because lantern slides were a prominent component of Urban's products. In catalogues from 1903 to 1905, a separate section was dedicated to the company's inventory of lantern slides, which increased from 258 slides in 1903 to 596 slides in 1905[40] (Fig. 1.3).

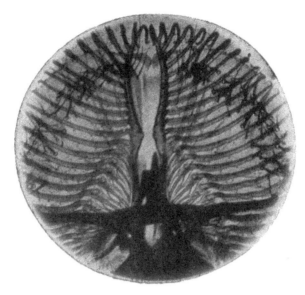

Tongue of Fly. . .

FIG. 1.3 Lantern slide of a fly's tongue from Urban's *1905 catalogue.* Courtesy of
Stephen Herbert.

Urban and Duncan saw lantern slides and films as functioning together, as this
introductory text to the lantern slide section of the 1905 catalogue indicates:

> We beg to draw the attention of Principals of Colleges, Schools, and Educa-
> tional Institutions; the Secretaries and Committees of Natural History, Sci-
> entific, Literary and Photographic Societies, and all who are engaged in
> Lecturing, Teaching, etc., to the remarkable and unique series of Films and
> Lantern Slides listed in this Catalogue.
>
> These Films and Slides have been specially prepared to meet the require-
> ments of Educational and Scientific Establishments, Lecturers, etc., and are
> throughout of the highest standard of perfection. We were the first to apply
> Animated Photography to the recording of living Microscopic organisms,
> to Zöology, Botany, Physics, Electricity, Entomology, Anthropology, etc.,
> and the **URBAN-DUNCAN MICRO-BIOSCOPE FILMS** are in demand
> all over the world. Modern educational methods all prove the importance
> of teaching through the agency of the eye as well as the ear. A lecture or
> lesson demonstrated by a graphic series of pictures remains vividly im-
> pressed on the mind. –F. Martin-Duncan, F.R.H.S., Director Scientific and
> Educational Department.[41]

Lantern slides figured not as something for motion pictures to overcome but
as a companion medium in the effort to promote "modern educational
methods."

The Unseen World fit in quite well with modern theories of education, as is evident from its relation to the nature-study movement. A little more than a month after its public debut, the program was screened at the Home Counties Nature-Study Exhibition in Burlington Gardens:

> Tickets at special rates for teachers and pupils. The programme includes conferences for teachers on practical methods of nature-study in elementary and secondary schools. The latest scientific developments of the Urban-Duncan microbioscope will be shown on the evenings of Friday and Saturday, and well-known lecturers on natural history subjects, such as Mr. Douglas English, Mr. Richard Kearton, Mr. R. B. Lodge, and Mr. Oliver Pike will give addresses from time to time, and exhibit their slides during the exhibition.[42]

Kearton and Pike both became noteworthy nature filmmakers, and their exhibition of slides at this event is a further indication of the fluidity between lantern and cinema culture in this period. A report on the exhibition noted, "Mr. Martin Duncan proved the great possibilities of the Urban Duncan micro-bioscope for recording natural history observations in the ordinary way and under the microscope."[43]

A specific film from the program furnishes a final example of *The Unseen World*'s intertextuality. In the aforementioned promotional lantern slide, five of the six smaller images illustrate microscopic scenes. Four images, all in circular frames, are taken from films shot using light-field microscopy; one image, in a rectangular frame, is from a film shot using the dark-field technique. The remaining image, of a toad atop a skull next to which a viper lies coiled, comes from *The Toads' Frolic* (Fig. 1.4):

> This is a subject full of most laughable, grotesque, and sensational effects. The toads ride along on a tortoise, thoroughly enjoying themselves. Then a chameleon mounts on to the flagstaff carried on the back of the tortoise, and shouts his orders as he rides along to the toad escorting him. Once again the toad, riding along on the trusty steed, and having gone far enough, dismounts. The scene changes, and we see the toad resting after his frolic on top of a skull; while a viper coils its body in and out of the jaws and round the base of the skull. Length 100ft.[44]

The final image of the toad atop the human skull with the viper on the side served as the introductory image for the entire natural-history section of the 1903 catalogue, making it an emblem of Urban's natural-history filmmaking. An iconographically rich image, it recalls the tradition of vanitas painting as well as images of the grotesque, and thus participates in a form of art-historical intertextuality.[45]

In the 1905 catalogue, this shot became part of a series entitled *Amongst the Reptiles*, where it received the title "A Deadly Combination." The catalogue

FIG. 1.4 Catalogue illustration for *The Toad's Frolic*. Charles Urban Papers, National Media Museum, Science & Society Picture Library.

blurb indicated ambivalence about how to read the image: "A giant toad seated upon a human skull, from the base of which glides a snake is indeed to the ignorant mind a deadly and fearsome combination; yet the toad is a most harmless and useful creature, while the snake helps the farmer by swallowing the field-mice which would devour his grain."[46] The description both evokes and attempts to contain the image's associations; it is an image of a deadly and fearsome combination, but only for an ignorant mind. The toad and snake are presented in a fashion that emphasizes their associations with things frightening and deadly, and yet they are harmless and even helpful. In this instance, an internal form of intertextuality is operative as well, in which Duncan's footage was recycled and recirculated, which often involved a modification in meaning.

Together these factors demonstrate how *The Unseen World* was located at the confluence of several contexts. The show was modeled on the lantern lecture, resembling a natural-history lantern show. It was recognized as relevant to the nature-study movement, and some of its films attested to Duncan's involvement in scientific networks of early-twentieth-century microscopy.

Situated between older traditions of scientific display and a new mass-cultural technology, *The Unseen World* was at once novel while also relying on established display traditions.

"A Fine Attack of the Jim-Jams"

A characteristic response to *The Unseen World* was horrified fascination. One reviewer noted, "To say that it is a wonderful advance is to put it very weakly, and I look to this class of living pictures to provide a popular form of scientific education. 'Arriet, for instance will no longer speak of the bee as a 'pretty fly with 'ot feet,' for the Micro-bioscope reveals the working life of the busy bee. We are shown animals ranging in size from the cheese mite to the boa-constrictor, and the sight of an ugly toad contentedly consuming a worm made some of us shudder."[47] Alongside the familiar praise for how *The Life of the Bee* and *The Boa Constrictor* could educate and amaze, this review reveals a different type of response to *The Meal of the American Toad*—a shudder. Another reviewer had a similar reaction to *The Meal of the American Toad* and *The Pugilistic Toads and the Tortoise Referee*: "Some of these views were to the amateur in natural history rather horrible, notably one of a toad eating worms and another of two toads fighting and grabbing at each other's eye."[48] These reactions signaled that the show's effect on audiences was not solely uplifting and edifying; the gluttonous and disputatious toads indicated a strain of the grotesque that ran counter to the current of uplift and gentility that *The Unseen World* promoted.

The microcinematographic films proved even more disturbing than the films about animals visible to the naked eye. The review in the *Sunday Special* provided a typical reaction:

> A visit to the Alhambra last Monday evening resulted in a firm resolve never to eat cheese or drink water again. A microscopic examination of the former, magnified to the size of a Bioscope screen, revealed one of the most blood-curdling pictures imaginable with mites of various shapes and sizes, but all equally hideous, prowling around in the most businesslike manner. As regards the fresh water hydra, he was a horror built on more graceful lines; but to see the tentacles shooting out for food was sufficient to shake the confidence of the most rabid teetotaler.[49]

Instead of providing views of grotesque but recognizable creatures from the visible universe, *Cheese Mites* and *The Fresh-Water Hydra* revealed an invisible world that was both fascinating and threatening (Fig. 1.5). The extension of the boundaries of the visible resulted in a defamiliarization of everyday objects, like cheese and water, which Bernard Lightman and Melanie Keene have shown was a widespread component of nineteenth-century popular

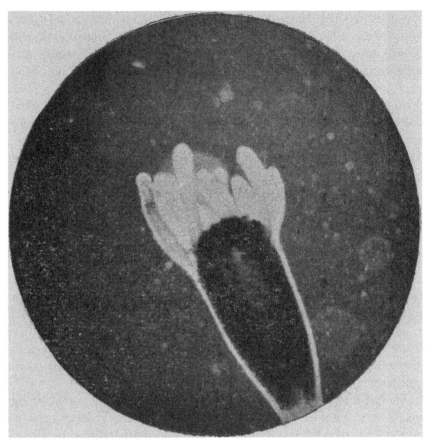

FIG. 1.5　Catalogue illustration for *The Fresh-Water Hydra*. Charles Urban Papers, National Media Museum, Science & Society Picture Library.

science.[50] Another reviewer wrote, "No micro-bioscopes and no Alhambra in Cornaro's days; else Cornaro might not have been a centenarian. I think it would have prostrated, if not killed, the dear old gentleman to see those many-armed, angry, spiteful little mites waging war against one another in cheese and water. Heavens, what combatants, what warriors! Many an abstainer has gone shuddering out of the Alhambra, and many a cheesemonger foresees failure."[51] The Micro-Bioscope revealed something seemingly inanimate as in fact teeming with life, calling forth, verily, a gut reaction. The writer for the *Topical Times* provided the most colorful language about his bodily reaction to the microscopic films, "Anyone in want of a fine attack of the jim-jams cannot do better than hurry up to the Alhambra, but if you feel a bit 'jumpy' I should advise you to leave these latest exhibits of the Charles Urban Trading Company severely alone. There is also a screen full of cheesemites magnified to the size of turtles. Ugh!"[52]

Suggestions that cheesemongers might have reservations about *Cheese Mites* appeared: "Purveyors and consumers of cheese will probably not relish the exposure of life in that article of diet, and some of the other displays are a trifle uncanny."[53] An article in the *Daily Express* entitled "Microbic Monsters" contained the following imagined dialogue: "'Well, this is the last time that I ever eat cheese!' said the man in the stalls. 'If you want to be logical,' said his friend, 'it would be the last time that you ever drank water.'"[54] Unsurprisingly, given these reactions of disgust, a story arose about how *Cheese Mites* was censored at the behest of the cheese industry, although no evidence of such repression exists.[55] The persistence of this anecdote, however, attests to *Cheese Mites'* long-term notoriety; it remains the best-known film from *The Unseen World.*[56]

What made *Cheese Mites* more memorable than *The Fresh-Water Hydra* or *Typhoid Bacteria*? Visually, the hydra and the bacteria simply may not have generated as much displeasure as the mites, since the appearance of the mites tapped into the perennial power of arachnophobia. Additionally, the cheese mite has a long history in the field of microscopy, having been used as a test object in the beginning of the nineteenth century. This interest in the cheese mite was marked by an appreciation of its perceptual novelty. As Jutta Schickore recounts, "The cheese mite could serve as a test because it offered surprising, unexpected views" that were capable of exciting "great curiosity," and the mite's delicate double teeth and jaws were described as "exquisite microscopic objects."[57]

Another reason for the film's appeal, however, relates to the particular cinematic treatment it received. Quite soon after the initial screenings, a review mentioned a second shot in its description of *Cheese Mites*: "Now the Alhambra has got one of the most fascinating turns I have seen in the shape of a series of bioscoped microphotographs showing all sorts of things that we have seen under a microscope. For example, a picture of a man eating cheese is thrown on the screen and then a second picture of the cheese showing the mites actually moving."[58] By including an introductory shot that depicted a man eating a piece of cheese, Urban and Duncan visualized the experience of consuming living, microscopic creatures (Fig. 1.6). The initial description of the two-shot version of *Cheese Mites* describes the response being modeled.

2501 Special . . . CHEESE MITES

A gentleman reading the paper and seated at lunch, suddenly detects something the matter with his cheese. He examines it with his magnifying glass, starts up and flings the cheese away, frightened at the sight of the creeping mites which his magnifying glass reveals. A ripe piece of Stilton, the size of a shilling, will contain several hundred cheese mites. In this remarkable film, the mites are seen crawling and creeping about in all directions, looking like great uncanny crabs, bristling with long spiny hairs and legs.

Magnified 30 diameters on film.   Length 150ft.[59]

FIG. 1.6 Stills from *Cheese Mites*. British Film Institute.

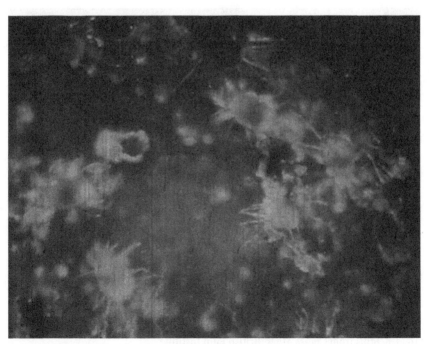

FIG. 1.6 Continued.

The "frightened" reaction of the man with the magnifying glass suggests a depiction of the gentleman as a rube, similar to the country bumpkin attending his first cinema experience in *Uncle Josh at the Moving Picture Show* (Edison, 1902).

The recent rediscovery of a more complete print of this film allows for a different understanding of the gentleman's performance, however.[60] The first additional insight is that Duncan himself plays the role of the "gentleman." Duncan's decision to play the role of the discoverer, which contains a hint of self-mockery, accords with other indications of his personality, both his "amiable" lecturing style and the presence of humor in such films as *A Toad's Frolic*. The more complete version of *Cheese Mites*, in other words, reveals that the film's tone is closer to comedy than horror.

Another noteworthy detail of the first shot is its unusual framing. Not only is the gentleman shot from the side, which is a rare angle for an era of cinema history dominated by frontality, but it also is framed at a surprisingly close distance, constituting a medium shot. The motivation for this framing seems to be the necessity of showing the details of Duncan's performance, which consists of a number of relatively restrained gestures. Duncan goes through a progression of expressions when registering his reactions to the food items he regards with the magnifying glass, from amusement when examining the bread to a double take when he looks at the cheese. His surprise, expressed through an open mouth and widened eyes, escalates to astonishment, which is indicated by the gesture of his right hand being spread.

The catalogue's description of the man's reaction to the sight of the mites through the magnifying glass as "frightened" is thus misleading. Of course, the rediscovered print of *Cheese Mites* is missing certain details mentioned in catalogue descriptions, both how the gentleman "flings . . . away" the cheese and how he leaves the table "in disgust."[61] One explanation for this discrepancy is that yet another, missing, version of the film does contain this action, perhaps as a brief, final shot.[62] So perhaps the original, complete film did involve a less ambiguous performance of fear. Nevertheless, the emotion that Duncan expresses in the first shot is not simply fear; his reactions are better described as wonder and astonishment. In fact, this reaction to an unfamiliar sight seems akin to a familiar form of knowing parody, a recapitulation of what Stephen Bottomore has termed the "train effect," that oft-repeated story about the first cinema audiences fleeing from the image of an oncoming train.[63] Duncan's response to the magnified view, in other words, is a self-conscious performance of experiencing perceptual novelty.

Relatedly, the catalogue's description of the mites as "uncanny" seems grounded in details linked partially to magnification; the mites look like crabs, but distorted and made "great," which is to say giant.[64] This sense of the uncanny, however, also is related to the peculiarities of the mites' movement. The reaction to cinematic motion that sees it as uncanny is a minor but

significant reaction to cinema in general.[65] There are also specific qualities to
the movement in the film that amplify its uncanniness. The animal activity
in *Cheese Mites*, as in many popular-science films, contains multiple interruptive splices, which add to the impression of hectic, erratic movement, and
several reframing camera movements contribute to the sense of profilmic
activity, adding to the impression of the mites "creeping and crawling about
in all directions."

Indeed, their movement could even seem mechanical, an impression that
was taken up in a fascinating parody of *Cheese Mites*, Cecil Hepworth's *The
Unclean World: The Sururban-Bunkum Microbe-Guyoscope* (Percy Stow,
1903).[66] A catalogue description explains the film as follows:

> For the first time in the history of the Cinematograph, that instrument has
> been used to burlesque a popular application of itself. As everyone knows,
> the Microscope has recently been wedded to the Bioscope, and the result is
> an interesting and valuable series of scientific films. In this parody one of
> these films is ridiculed in a good humoured, but wonderfully funny
> manner. A quasi-scientific gentleman sits eating a plebeian lunch of bread
> and cheese. The ancient taste and predatory habits of the latter engage his
> disgusted attention and he places a crumb under the microscope. The un-
> earthly looking swarming creatures are most grotesque and realistic, and
> the audience is completely taken in until at the end the game is given away
> in a wholly unexpected and startling manner, and then the clever joke elic-
> its roars of laughter from everyone. The film is intensely comic in itself,
> quite apart from its interest as a topical parody.[67]

The Unclean World follows *Cheese Mites*'s two-shot format: in the first shot
the "quasi-scientific gentleman" eats a meal, tries some cheese, and, after ex-
pressing his displeasure, places a small bit of the cheese onto the stage of a
microscope. The point of the joke emerges over the course of the second shot,
when hands appear within the "microscopic" image to reveal the microscopic
creatures as mechanical wind-up toys (Fig. 1.7).

The joke has a double edge. On the one hand it functions as an ostensible
demystification. As the "bunkum" and "guyoscope" in the subtitle indicate,
The Unclean World questioned the validity of what *The Unseen World* made
visible. When the hands intrude on the frame, the film is revealed as a fake
scientific view. In this sense, *Unclean* invoked the nineteenth-century tradition of "visual scientific performances" that questioned or probed the reliabil-
ity of science's revelation of new worlds.[68] On the other hand, the joke is
reflexive; the bugs' clockwork mechanism resembles the mechanism of the
cinema.[69] In this sense, the clockwork toys serve as a reminder that microcinematography is itself a mechanical contrivance. This is the sense in which the
film presumes "to burlesque a popular application of itself." The discovery,
made in the mode of fun, is of a machine that mimics life. *Unclean* thus points

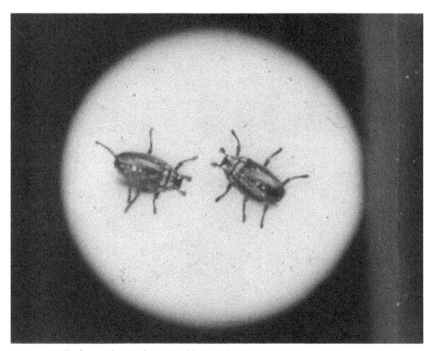

FIG. 1.7 Stills from *The Unclean World*. British Film Institute.

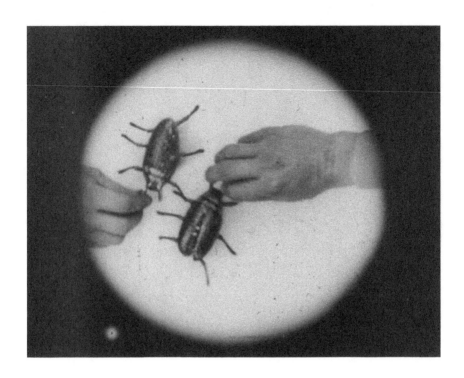

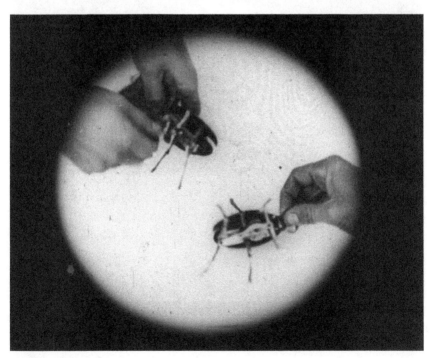

FIG. 1.7 Continued.

to a similarity between the trick film and the science film that involves their mode of revelation: "Just as in the scientific films, there presides in these films [trick films] the desire to show, in the spectacular mode, to be sure, that which the eye cannot see, to understand what escapes from knowledge."[70] Another instance of this affinity appears in the nearly identical mottos of Urban and Méliès: Urban's films were sold with the words, "We Put the World before You," while Méliès's slogan for the Star-Film company was "*le monde à la porté de la main*" ("the world within hand's reach").

Popular-science films and trick films can be understood as examples of what Tom Gunning, borrowing from the Russian Formalists, has called "cine-genres." Gunning writes of wanting "to offer a theory of cine-genres which is less rooted in narrative and editing and more related to those elements which Piotrovskij probably intended by the term 'photogeny.' . . . a new experience phenomenologically . . . [that has] little to do with the actual content of the films, but rather relate[s] primarily to the cinematic illusion itself."[71] So while "nature's closest secrets" designate amazing views of unfamiliar phenomena—cheese mites, the chameleon's tongue, the inside of a beehive—in another sense "nature's closest secrets" are also the cinema's unique representational possibilities, especially the ability to expand or compress time and scale. For popular-science films, the sources of nature's closest secrets are indebted as much to the revelatory powers of cinematographic representation as to nature itself.

The Unseen World and the Program Format

The Unseen World inspired rapt attention: "more extraordinary than are the publications of these secrets of nature is the absorbing interest with which they are examined by the audience. During this 'turn' the bars are deserted, the promenaders are all facing one way and every eye in the house is riveted on the screen."[72] Another account also picked up on the show's ability to draw the audience's attention to the screen:

> Success was, in fact, so pronounced that the picture display was eventually given the last place in the bill, for the reason that if they had been presented earlier the audience would leave, having seen all they wanted, in which case the exchequer would have suffered, for small audiences mean small re-freshment returns. It was noticed, with varying feelings of pride and regret—according to the aspect—that whenever scientific or educational pictures appeared upon the screen, the bars automatically emptied and the treasury lost commensurately.[73]

As the mention of *The Unseen World*'s relocation to the end of the bill indicates, it was part of an entertainment program, and its status as one part of a larger show is crucial to understanding how it functioned.

Before considering *The Unseen World*'s place within a program, it is worth first bearing in mind that it also had its own internal structure.[74] Accounts of *The Unseen World* emphasized the microcinematographic films to the point that the program sometimes has been described as consisting only of microscopic views.[75] This emphasis has led to a valorization of the films shot through the microscope; as an example, McKernan writes, "The 'pugilistic' toads showed the tendency toward trivial anthropomorphism, while the circulation of the blood was unquestionably a cinematic revelation."[76] In the first program, however, the microcinematic films and the "comical" films about animal life were interspersed, and to dismiss *The Pugilistic Toads and the Tortoise Referee* or *The Meal of the American Toad* discounts a crucial aspect of the program's appeal (Fig. 1.8). Contemporary audiences responded with as much interest and delight to the films about reptiles as to the microcinematic films' unusual aesthetic. The review in *The Era* takes note of the microcinematographic films but reserves its strongest praise for the other films:

> Then [after *Cheese Mites*] we are introduced to the great American toad, who takes his dinner of worms in sight of the audience. The smaller worms are snapped up in an instant; but the fun comes in when the toad tackles an extra long one. Bit by bit it disappears between his lips, until with a final gulp he absorbs it into his interior. . . . An amusing picture is that of two "pugilistic" toads, who paw each other about very comically, the supposed "referee" being a tortoise, who agitates his fore-limbs and moves his head languidly. . . . The feeding of the chameleon is undoubtedly one of the most wonderful and diverting representations of the series. Two of these

American Toad catching Worms.

FIG. 1.8 Catalogue illustration for *The Meal of the American Toad*. Courtesy of Stephen Herbert.

lizards are perched upon a branch and a hand is seen offering them a fly at the end of a pair of tweezers. There is an instantaneous flash of a long white tongue—as long almost as the animal itself—and the fly has simply disappeared. Those present at the Alhambra on Monday thoroughly enjoyed the awe-inspiring depiction of a fine boa-constrictor in company with a white rat, who exhibited not the least fear of his beautifully-marked companion.[77]

For this viewer, the "wonderful" and "awe-inspiring" activities of the toads, tortoises, chameleons, and the boa constrictor were more noteworthy than the views through the microscope.

Furthermore, while the often-comic activities of macroscopic animals could provide a counterpoint to the abstraction of the microcinematographic views, the films about reptiles and bees also could evoke wonder, and there were gestures toward humor in the microcinematic films as well. In *The Fig Mites and Maggot*, for example, two boys eating figs pull out a magnifying glass and discover the eponymous creatures living on the dried fruit. Their initial reaction of distress, which recalls the response of the character in *Cheese Mites*, changes abruptly: "Both boys evince surprise and alarm at the sight revealed by their magnifying glass; but their consternation gives place to broad smiles at the curious antics of the inhabitants of the figs."[78] The microscopic views, then, were capable of provoking a range of responses, and while the microcinematographic films received a considerable amount of attention, other films played a significant role in the overall program. The *Daily Telegraph* concluded its review of *The Unseen World* with the following comments: "Mr. Douglas Cox thinks that natural history has a future at the halls. If so, he might do worse than give us some pictures of the monkeys at the Zoo as part of his Christmas entertainment. Beside the ever gesticulating and clambering simian, the rotifer and his efforts to solve the housing problem would pale into insignificant interest."[79] The reviewer would not have long to wait. The 1905 catalogue contained a troop of monkey films: *The Monkeys of Borneo*, *Within the Monkey's Cage*, *The Monkey and the Strawberries*, *The Monkey and the Dates*, *Educated Monkeys in Costume*, *An Old Philosopher (Monkey Portrait)*, *The Thirsty Monkey and the Tea-Cup*, and *Lemur and Monkeys with Keeper*. The fig mites and *Educated Monkeys in Costume* both had a place in Urban's vision for cinema as an educative amusement.

The alternation between the micro- and the macroscopic illustrates the ambivalence of the show's subtitle, "Revealing Nature's Closest Secrets by Means of the Urban-Duncan Micro-Bioscope." On the one hand, "closest" refers to proximity, to the literal distance that the microscope bridges by bringing human perception to the level of the previously invisible. The closeness, however, also refers to a sense of an intimacy with nature, an observational proximity that the camera makes possible. In this sense the viewer of

The Unseen World became acquainted not only with microbes but also with the habits of the frog, the chameleon, the boa constrictor. The closeness, in other words, was not solely a matter of magnification but also a method of observation that promised a better understanding.[80]

The Urbanora Matinees

"Twenty-five minutes, the length of the exhibition, is a long time to give to a Bioscope turn," remarked *The Daily Telegraph*, a comment that underscored how *The Unseen World* was unusual not only for its subject matter but also for its duration.[81] Film programs lasting around thirty minutes were not unique, of course, and boxing films, passion plays, and travel lectures all had significant durations, frequently constituting standalone programs.[82] *The Unseen World* was an initial example of Urban's interest in longer film programs, and following upon its success, popular-science films at Urban went from a variety turn to a self-sufficient, long-format film program.

The Urbanora matinees began at the Alhambra on January 9, 1905, and were a hallmark of Urban's filmmaking enterprise. The daily shows lasted from 3 p.m. until 5 p.m. The film program lasted ninety minutes, and musical interludes filled the remaining time. A number of special features distinguished these shows from the typical film exhibition of the time. One significant difference was how they targeted a different clientele than the audience for the nightly music-hall show: "As an encouragement to the ladies and children, smoking will not be permitted in the auditorium, and afternoon tea will be served, while half prices are to be charged to all parts of the house save the gallery, which will not be opened."[83] Another review provided additional details: "The promenade will be converted into an afternoon tea-room, the bars will be closed, and there will be no smoking in the auditorium. The entertainment, which will last from three till five o'clock, will consist of a display of Urban Bioscope pictures, with two sets of scientific, geographical, and historical interest. In the ten minutes' interval between the two sets musical selections will be given."[84] Urban targeted a new public with these shows, aiming to draw school-age children accompanied by their caregivers or teachers, an audience that several press reviews mentioned: "The management of the Alhambra has also done its best to amuse the dear children, inasmuch as the programme at the series of Urbanora matinees, which started on Monday, was not only devised to amuse and entertain the younger generation, but also to give it 'Object Lessons' in the pleasantest and most interesting manner possible."[85]

The two series that constituted the initial Urbanora show were *Voyage to New York* and *Wild Beasts, Birds and Reptiles*. *Voyage* was a travelogue shot by Urban himself, who had been instructed in the use of the camera by G. A. Smith. It consisted of seventy scenes detailing Urban's trip from Southampton to New York and back to Plymouth harbor in October and November 1904 aboard the Norddeutscher Lloyd steamer *King Wilhelm II*. The total footage exceeded 2,300ft. *Wild Beasts* was shot primarily at the London Zoo in Regent's Park, with a few scenes courtesy of Lord Strathcona, whose Manitoba ranch provided the opportunity to photograph elk, buffalo, and moose. It consisted of fifty-eight "pictures," measured 1,950ft, and lasted almost forty minutes (Fig. 1.9). *Wild Beasts* included films by several filmmakers (Duncan, Joseph Rosenthal, H. M. Lomas, J. G. Avery, and "others"), and it included films about the chameleon, boa constrictor, giant tortoise, snake, and rat, which were likely taken from *The Unseen World*.[86]

FIG. 1.9A Poster for the Urbanora series *Wild Beasts, Birds, and Reptiles*. Courtesy of Stephen Herbert.

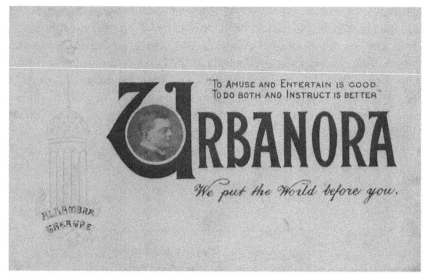

FIG. 1.9B Cover for an Urbanora program at the Alhambra Theatre. Charles Urban Papers, National Media Museum, Science & Society Picture Library.

The program for this series emphasized its scientific qualities: "For the first time since its invention, the Bioscope has been seriously and scientifically applied in obtaining a record of the ways and habits of Wild Animals." The program explained in detail what this serious and scientific approach entailed:

> The greatest patience, care, thought and resource has to be employed, so as to successfully show the creatures in their natural and characteristic movements, for they are very easily disturbed and alarmed, and when frightened their whole aspect becomes changed to unnatural. In obtaining this unique series of Natural History Films, many long hours and even days have had to be spent in patient waiting, ere the characteristic picture could be procured. For much of the work special costly apparatus had to be designed and constructed, and many elaborate and delicate experiments carried out, but the results have yielded the highest standard of perfection that has ever been gained, and these wonderfully realistic pictures of Wild Animal Life are the admiration of all.[87]

These claims about the importance of "natural and characteristic movements" indicate an attitude toward observation that Daston and Galison call "truth-to-nature," a mode of natural knowledge prior to "mechanical objectivity."[88] Also noteworthy in this description is the awareness both of how the cinematographic apparatus changes animal behavior as well as an appreciation of the amount of time and care that had to be invested into the production of these films, which both have become fundamental to accounts of wildlife filmmaking.

Several reviews referred explicitly to the length of the program. *The Sunday Times* commented, "The principal feature is the presentation, in a more synthetic form than is practicable in the evening program, of some of the latest achievements of the bioscope."[89] The "more synthetic form" of the presentation was made possible by the exhibition context, since an evening variety program would not accommodate a film show any longer than twenty or twenty-five minutes. The length of the programs was singled out for praise as well: "Both sets of pictures are splendid examples of their kind, while their continuous character—the one show lasts over an hour, and the second over thirty-five minutes—adds to their effectiveness."[90]

Urban's catalogue published in 1905 contained other long programs fashioned out of preexisting films. The catalogue contained a section of listings and descriptions for complete programs, which included *Quaint Denizens of the Insect World* (700ft), *The Story of the Moth and Butterfly* (550ft), and the revamped and renamed *The Life of the Bee* (550ft as opposed to the 450ft of the previous version). There also were multipart programs: *The Animal Kingdom* aka *Noah's Ark* (1950ft), *A Visit to Birdland* (1,000ft), and *Amongst the Reptiles* (825ft). The catalogue listed these programs by breaking them down into sections that ranged from 300 to 450ft, "supplied in separate sections as specified, to suit the requirements of our patrons."[91] *The Animal Kingdom*, for instance, was subdivided into seven sections, and exhibitors could lend the series a theological touch with the inclusion of *Noah's Ark* (75ft): "Showing the wooden animals of the Children's Ark, descending the gangway in pairs. This section is adaptable to precede the 'Animal Kingdom' series, thus carrying out the nature of the title."[92]

Urban's separate listings for these long programs are in one sense an attempt to wring every last bit of return from his footage by providing yet another configuration of titles. *The Busy Bee*, which made up the second half of *The Unseen World* program, was composed of fifteen parts, and the catalogue noted that the series was "supplied only in its complete length of 450 ft."[93] But the catalogue also listed shorter films that seem to derive from the series: *Making Foundation of the Honeycomb and Examining the Combs in the Hive* (150ft), *Primrose and the Bee* (60ft), *Bee Culture (Four Views)* (50ft), *Bee Life out and in the Old Skep* (75ft), *Bees Preparing to Swarm* (50ft), *Preparing the Comb for Honey* (50ft), *Enlarged Views of Honeycomb and Bees* (50ft), *Special: The Brood Comb in Various Stages* (100ft), and *Special: Drone, Queen and Worker Bee Cells on the Comb* (150ft). With the exception of *Primrose and the Bee*, all the individual titles seem to be made up of scenes contained in *The Busy Bee*.[94] This duplication of footage could be seen as a way to pad the number of films available in the catalogue, but it also could be understood as a concession to contemporary exhibition practices. In a period

when exhibitors often selected titles and fashioned the program, Urban
would not have been well served by offering longer films exclusively. Indeed,
the catalogue often suggested links among titles, noting that *The Naturalist
at Work with the Microscope* "forms an admirable introduction to No. 2505
[*The Fresh-Water Hydra*] or any other of the Microscopic series."[95]

However, the long programs also, and perhaps primarily, provide evidence
of Urban's desire to promote his particular vision of cinema. By creating a
film show that could not be accommodated in the music-hall variety format,
Urban was attempting to change how film was exhibited. The long-film
format demanded its own venue and method of exhibition, which in turn
supported its claims for educational value. Urban, in other words, tried at first
to promote his vision of cinema within existing exhibition practices, as with
The Unseen World, but he then sought alternative modes of exhibition for his
products, a tendency that would culminate with the establishment of the Urbanora house in 1908, a trajectory that presaged the creation of nontheatrical
cinema.[96]

With the establishment of the Urbanora matinees, Urban moved away
from the mixed appeal of the early Alhambra shows and toward the promotion and elaboration of nonfiction cinema on its own terms. Urban's ideas
about the possible and preferable uses of cinema were indebted to the pro-
grammatic statements of W. T. Stead, a pioneer of the New Journalism whose
"The Mission of the Magic Lantern" (1890) and "The Mission of the Cinematograph" (1902) argued for the importance of visual media in education.[97]
Duncan's article written on the occasion of the first Alhambra show attributed arguments for the relative unimportance of the entertainment aspect of
the cinema to Urban: "The reproduction for the amusement of music-hall
audiences of interesting spectacles will before long, Mr. Urban declares, be
the least important of the uses of the bioscope."[98] The catalogues echoed this
rhetoric:

> The Ideas embodied in Urban Films are original, our Staff of Photographic
> Operators are Experts, and we do not hesitate to incur any expense in order
> to produce novel, high class, and interesting results from all parts of the
> world. Our aim is to maintain a high standard of excellence, accuracy, and
> quality of production, the subjects being of an elevating or educational
> character. We do not cater to degenerate tastes. All films herein catalogued
> preclude senseless frivolity, suggestive or immoral tendencies, the depict-
> ing of criminal or depraved subjects.[99]

The most elaborate expression of Urban's thoughts about the cinema's nonfiction mission appeared in a self-published pamphlet entitled *The Cinematograph in Science, Education, and Matters of State*.[100] In this manifesto, Urban
envisioned a future for the motion picture where its entertainment role constituted only a small part of the medium's duties. The first paragraphs of the

pamphlet alluded to the Alhambra shows but announced another goal—to liberate the cinematograph from its enslavement to the interests of the entertainment industry:

> Former Cinematographic exhibitions of individual scientific subjects in places of amusement were intended as an introduction, and served their purpose in attracting and compelling the attention of scientists and experts. Possibilities, as demonstrated in the displays of three years ago, are now accomplished facts in prepared educational and scientific series of subjects. The entertainer has hitherto monopolised the Cinematograph for exhibition purposes, but movement in more serious directions has become imperative, and the object of this pamphlet is to prove that the Cinematograph must be recognised as a National Instrument by the Boards of Agriculture, Education, and Trade, by the War Council, Admiralty, Medical Associations, and every Institution of Training, Teaching, Demonstration, and Research.[101]

Urban wrote about the merits of visual education, making claims about the efficiency of film as an educator, "A series of living pictures imparts more knowledge, in a far more interesting and effective manner, in five minutes, than does an oral lesson of an hour's duration." He wrote that film could perform "the work of text books without their dryness," thus invoking a concept that the French producers of popular-science films also used.[102] The subjects he saw as suited to the cinematograph included geography, cultivation and production, history (both through reenactments and as records of current events), industrial knowledge, and the demonstration of trades and industries. Urban also addressed the cinematograph's importance in matters of state, by which he primarily meant such military applications as recording artillery tests, taking aerial films of maneuvers, and using film as a recruitment tool.

More than half of the pamphlet was devoted to the uses of the cinematograph in science. This section begins with a long discussion of film as a record of surgical procedures that includes excerpts from a lecture delivered at the International Congress of Medicine at Madrid in 1903 by Doctor Eugène-Louis Doyen.[103] This discussion advances a number of arguments in favor of film: its ability to allow for better views of rare operations, its ability to preserve the skills of the finest surgeons for posterity, and its ability to allow practitioners to critique their own procedures after the fact. The section on physiology introduces an argument for film as a method to reduce the necessity for vivisection that concludes with the following sentence: "I am sure, could the question be put to the vote, the animal world would unanimously declare in favor of the sacrifice of one of their number under the perpetuating eye of the Cinematograph, rather than to the destruction of so many with no lasting result."[104] The pamphlet's final section considered Urban's achievements in bacteriological science, horticulture and agriculture, industry and commerce, physics, anthropology (for the preservation of civilizations threatened by the onslaught of modern civilization), zoology, and botany (especially time-lapse films of plant growth). This document represents the most extended articulation of Urban's arguments for nonfiction filmmaking.

A final example of the long-film format at Urban that demonstrates the development of Duncan's work is *The Empire of the Ants* (Urban/Duncan, 1904?), a 600ft series that consisted of sixteen "pictures" illustrating various aspects of ant life (Fig. 1.10). Empire remains indebted to previous insect iconography in some ways. The following description of a lantern slide comes from the lantern lecture *Ants and Their Ways* (1893):

> Slide No. 18. ANT SUPPORTING 1,649 TIMES ITS OWN WEIGHT. An average specimen of an Ant was carefully weighed, and the amount registered at one sixteenth of a grain; it was then held between the finger and thumb by the body, and the cord suspending the wooden ring brought into contact with it, which it immediately seized with its jaws and supported without any assistance. The ring was then weighed and by this means it was conclusively proved that the Ant had lifted 1,649 times its own weight.
>
> So tenacious is its hold that if the weight were increased beyond its strength it would allow its head to be pulled off sooner than relinquish its grip.[105]

This lantern-slide description is strikingly similar to illustrations of ant strength from *Empire*. The catalogue description for the tenth scene reads, "10—Lifting a Half-Sovereign. The champion weight-lifters of mankind are mere infants compared with the ant, who will grasp with its jaws a half-sovereign, and hold it firmly while hanging by one leg from a pair of micro-forceps." The description of the next picture reads, "11—A Modern Atlas. Not content with holding a golden coin, the ant must act the part of a modern Atlas, and bear the weight of the Globe, not upon its shoulders, but suspended from its jaws."[106] In terms of subject matter, natural-history films at Urban like *Empire* remained aligned with the traditions of scientific showmanship established over the second half of the nineteenth century.

In other ways, however, *Empire* was a harbinger of developments in film style, indicating a development away from the predominant intertextuality of the earlier programs. Underneath the title of the series in the catalogue, the following note appears, "Titles preceding each Picture," referring to the fact that the shot descriptions duplicated the text of the film's intertitles. With the replacement of the lecturer by intertitles, *Empire* was participating in the more general shift away from reliance on intertextuality to make films comprehensible and toward self-contained form.[107] As we will see in the next chapter, this film's demonstration of insect strength forms a link to Duncan's successor at Urban, Frank Percy Smith.

FIG. 1.10 "A Modern Atlas" and "Drawing a Silver Coach," from *The Empire of the Ants. Illustrated London News.*

The End of Duncan's Filmmaking Career

A cartoon from a 1906 issue of *The Optical Lantern and Cinematograph Journal* indicates how Duncan had attained a degree of prominence alongside Urban and how his persona as the head of the natural history department was sufficiently well known to serve as a visual emblem (Fig. 1.11). In the cartoon, Urban is pictured in a pose that imitates his company trademark. The cartoon's context is that "legitimate" producers were attempting to combat dupers of footage; under the "Ball of Reformation" is a man, possibly Walter Gibbons, who says, "My little game of copying films is all up this time."[108] The text on Urban's banner comes from a letter he wrote to the journal, "Although extremely preoccupied with the many details of our business, I shall, nevertheless, be pleased to 'start the ball rolling' [toward a better understanding between the serious minded members of the trade]." Duncan is the figure to the right. Urban's appearance apparently has startled Duncan into dropping some lantern slides. In his other arm he carries a microscope and some other apparatus, upon which a chameleon is perched.

Having become a recognizable part of the firm's public image, Duncan's days at Urban were numbered, however. In an interview with a trade journal, Charles Urban mentioned that Duncan was on his way to South America in late 1904, presumably on behalf of Urban and in order to make natural-history films: "Professor Duncan is just off to South America for a two years'

FIG. 1.11 Cartoon from *The Optical Lantern and Cinematograph Journal*, 1906. British Film Institute.

tour, which we expect will reap some wonderful achievements for future use."[109] Duncan's South American journey lasted only a fraction of the announced two years, though: "Mr. Martin Duncan has returned from his South American expedition. Mr. Duncan was a victim of fever during his travels; but the homeward voyage was a good one, and had restoring effect on the invalid, who, we trust, will rapidly regain his normal health."[110]

By 1908 Duncan had stopped working at Urban for unknown reasons. The company underwent significant changes in 1907. Eclipse, the French wing of the company, which Urban founded to produce fiction films to replace the waning output of Georges Méliès's Star Company, gradually took over Urban's company. Instead of contesting the takeover, Urban founded Kineto Limited, a company dedicated to the production of scientific, travel, and actuality films, in September 1907. He also was intensely occupied with the natural color process that would come to be known as Kinemacolor, something he had pursued since 1901, and he founded the Natural Color Kinematograph Co. Ltd. in March 1909.[111]

Whatever the reasons for Duncan's departure from Urban, he remained actively engaged in bringing science to the public, giving numerous public lectures on natural-history topics that often used films.[112] On February 4, 1908, Duncan gave a lecture at the Zoological Society entitled "Cinematograph Demonstration of Results of Natural Colour Photography with Zoological Subjects," which was probably still using Urban material.[113] On May 7, 1908, Duncan gave a presentation at the Linnean Society about "the movements of Peripatus and other invertebrate animals by means of a Newman fireproof kinematograph," which was an analytic projector that allowed, in conjunction with nonflammable film, the operator to slow down the movement of the film through the projector and to stop on individual frames.[114] Duncan's use of this projector may indicate that he no longer was associated with Urban. On May 20, 1908, Duncan spoke at the Royal Society of Arts on "Industrial Entomology: or the Economic Importance of a Study of Insect Life." His name appears sporadically in *Nature*'s listings of lectures for the next few years: in a lecture series at the London Institution in 1910–11, his announced topic was "autumn and winter, the web of life," and on March 20, 1912, he spoke before the Royal Society of the Arts about "The Work of the Marine Biological Association."[115]

In addition to his public lectures, Duncan never ceased working in the field of popular-science publishing; in his lifetime he wrote numerous articles and over seventy books, which included *Denizens of the Deep* (1907), *Our Insect Friends and Foes* (1911), *The Book of Animals* (1927), *Plant Traps and Decoys* (1930), *The Monkey Tribe* (1946), and *The Book of the Countryside* (1959). Many of the books he wrote together with his wife Lucy, a close collaborator for his entire life. His *Wonders of the Sea* (1912) was a series of books for children that consisted of six brief volumes: *Wonders of the Shore, The Lobster and His Relations, The Starfish and His Relations, Dwellers in the Rock Pools, Life in the Deep Sea,* and *The Sea Birds.* Each volume contained color drawings and colored photographs, which derived in part from Duncan's film subjects at Urban, particularly *Denizens of the Deep*. Duncan used images made during his time at Urban in other publications as well; the 1913 edition of *Cassell's Natural History* contains a number of photographs—of a boa constrictor; a "freshwater infusorian," which in *Cassell's* is called the "ceratium"; a freshwater hydra; and a porcupine—all of which are identical to the catalogue photographs in the 1903 catalogue.[116] And he continued his association with the chameleon; an image in *Cassell's*, which was also used for a London Zoo postcard in 1922, used a nearly identical image to the emblematic shot of the chameleon reproduced in Urban's catalogues (Fig. 1.12). Duncan's involvement with still photography, both monochrome and autochrome, continued during his time at Urban and afterward, particularly through his membership in the Royal Photographic Society, and this aspect of the career of this long-lived and versatile popularizer deserves further attention.[117]

FIG. 1.12A Photograph of a chameleon from Urban's catalogue. Courtesy of Stephen Herbert.

FIG. 1.12B Photograph of a chameleon from *Cassell's* (1913).

Duncan worked briefly with doctors at the Lister Institute during World War I, when he aided with research on trench fever.[118] And in 1919 Duncan became the Clerk of Publications and the Librarian to the Zoological Society, a position he held until his death in 1961[119] (Fig. 1.13). He remained interested in using film while working for the Zoological Society; in a 1922 letter to a supplier of cinematographic equipment, he refers to his current camera as "this box of tricks," and he goes on to write, "In my old Williamson-Darling Camera which I had before the War, I had none of these troubles."[120] He also is listed as the "compiler" for a "Secrets of Nature" film, *Betty's Day at the Zoo* (1923), which indicates that he may have remained in contact with Percy Smith, who also worked for the "Secrets of Nature" series.

The lack of a sustained filmmaking career is fitting, however. Duncan was a late-Victorian/Edwardian popularizer for whom film was an interesting secondary means by which to provide instructive entertainment.[121] His

FIG. 1.13 F. Martin Duncan near the end of his career at the London Zoo.

engagement with and subsequent abandonment of cinema is in keeping with the patterns of this era of film history, where pioneers often were left behind by a rapidly developing industry. Urban soon found a replacement for Duncan in Frank Percy Smith, a young clerk at the Board of Education with an avid interest in nature photography.

Smith proved a talented filmmaker with exceptional gifts for the patient tinkering that his delicate and difficult subjects often demanded. Smith's reputation has so outstripped Duncan's that a correction is necessary, however. To an extent, Smith's fame is due to his long career and association with the "Secrets of Nature" series. A major reason Duncan has been put so completely in Smith's shadow has to do with how few of Duncan's films survive, and those films that do exist are incomplete and often in sorry shape. McKernan, for instance, argues, "[Smith] went further than Duncan had done in combining investigative science with showmanship, and demonstrated more effectively than anyone else associated with Urban how a film might genuinely educate and amuse at the same time."[122] Smith's films may well be more appealing in certain respects, but this appeal is due more to the fact that his films are from a later, more familiar era in film history.

The point that bears emphasis is how indebted to and continuous with Duncan's foundational work Smith's achievements are. A syllogism that expresses this position in film history is: F. Martin Duncan is to Percy Smith as Edwin S. Porter is to D. W. Griffith. Smith built on Duncan's achievements while also developing popular-science filmmaking into new domains, becoming one of the first people to take on the identity of a popular-science filmmaker completely.

Chapter 2

Juggling Flies and Gravid Plants
F. PERCY SMITH'S EARLY POPULAR-SCIENCE FILMS

In popular science the world's market is practically supplied by an
English company, Kineto, Limited. This fact is due mainly to Mr. F.
Percy Smith, who possesses the happy faculty of investing his subjects
with a quaint fascination which compels appreciation.[1]

He devotes his life to putting the public into magically close intimacy
with the thrilling marvels of ordinary small life.[2]

In a combination of self-deprecation and defiance, F. Percy Smith once
described himself as possessing "no scholastic qualifications and no technical
training." This assertion distanced him from higher education and profes-
sionalized science, and thus implicitly aligned Smith with the traditions of
amateur science.[3] Although Urban's publicity at times presumptuously referred to him as "Dr." or "Professor," Smith's name never was followed by the
bevy of acronyms that accompanied Duncan's—F.R.H.S. (Fellow of the Royal
Horticultural Society); F.R.P.S. (Fellow of the Royal Photographic Society);
F.R.M.S. (Fellow of the Royal Microscopical Society); F.R.Z.S. (Fellow of the
Royal Zoological Society).

Smith's autodidacticism was distinct from Duncan's more learned up-
bringing, which brought with it a mode of access to the sphere of science popularization via *Cassell's*, lectures, and societies. And Duncan's father, after all,
was a Fellow of the Royal Society. Duncan, in other words, was connected in
ways Smith was not. Furthermore, popular-scientific filmmaking represented
only one episode in Duncan's career while for Smith it became a lifelong avo-
cation. For Duncan, filmmaking was an offshoot of preexisting popularizing
activities, constituting at most a five-year span of intensive engagement with
the new medium, whereas for Smith filmmaking became a consuming and
lifelong passion. Indeed, the transition from Duncan to Smith at Urban can

serve as an indication of a wider transition within film culture, from a period characterized by intertextuality to a period that developed its own strategies particular to the cinema's representational possibilities.

The sociocultural differences that distinguish the two men should not over-shadow the profound continuities that unite them and their filmmaking prac-tice, however. Their involvement with the Quekett Microscopical Club, an amateur-friendly alternative to the Royal Microscopical Society, is emblem-atic of their position in the cultural hierarchy of science at the beginning of the twentieth century.[4] Duncan and Smith participated in a mode of scientific practice that was becoming marginalized, as the modern disciplines of biology and zoology distinguished themselves from the prior "natural history" model of knowledge about nature.[5]

Smith's work joined a tradition of those "excluded from elite biological sci-ence and finding common cause with the artisan classes, which had often been the intended audiences for improving entertainments."[6] This "twilight world," to borrow Boon's evocative phrase, while being marginalized by such figures as Thomas Huxley and his promotion of methodological naturalism, was not marginal. As Boon notes, "these individuals simply belonged to older, not lesser, lay traditions," and J. V. Pickstone has pointed out that "even when natural history was being denigrated by exponents of analysis or experimenta-tion, it remained a major element of *popular* science, an important means by which professional biologists could extend their work and influence, and a key to public understandings of nature."[7] Furthermore, even in this era of harden-ing disciplinary boundaries, the distinction between professional science and popular science remained somewhat fluid.[8]

Smith was not the only filmmaker who contributed to Urban's popular-science films. Others included the brothers Richard and Cherry Kearton, who provided Urban with a number of films about bird life, including *Wild Birds at Home* (1907/08) and *Sea-Bird Colonies* (1907/08); and C. N. Mavroy-ani, who worked in Greece on insect films for Urban.[9] And there were other popular-science filmmakers in this period who did not work for Urban. Oliver Pike produced *In Birdland* in 1907, which enjoyed a successful run at the Palace Theater in London; Pike went on to make many films, primarily about birds, for Pathé.[10] J. C. Bee-Mason, E. J. Spitta, and James Williamson also made popular-science films in England during this period.[11]

While Smith was only one filmmaker among several working in the field of popular-science filmmaking at the turn of the 1900s, his best-known films epitomize the developments in the genre during this transitional period.[12] The two film subjects for which Smith is best known during this period—the "ac-robatic fly" films and time-lapse films of plant growth—exemplify changes in popular-science films, as the intertextuality of the early 1900s gave way to the more self-contained filmmaking that began to emerge in the latter half of that decade. In terms of the popular-science genre, this transition involved a move away from the emphasis on optical magnification, as in the fly films, and an embrace of the cinema's specific representational possibilities, as in the "speed magnification" of the time-lapse plant-growth films.

A familiar formula for popular science consists of two parts, as in "instructive amusement." Smith had his own version of this formula, writing, "I have always endeavoured to administer the powder of instruction in the jam of entertainment."[13] Amalgamating pleasure and instruction was always Smith's goal. The editor of the *Photographic Journal* appreciated Smith's work in this sense:

> The work of such men as Martin Duncan, the Kearton brothers, Oliver
> G. Pike, and now F. P. Smith (whose remarkable cinematograph studies
> of performing insects, given at the R. P. S. last week, have to be seen to
> be believed), opens the doors of the ordinary imagination to a world
> hitherto undreamt of, and arouses an appreciation for the wonders of
> Nature that surround us, as no mere printed books have ever been capa-
> ble of. The facts disclosed by the cinematograph in these cases are not
> new. They have been common property for many years. Yet how few
> fully realized the works and actions going on around us until the living
> picture made them plain for all to see.[14]

This appreciation begins by locating what is special about Smith's films, how they gave access to the "a world hitherto undreamt of," a world of the "wonders of Nature that surround us." Mortimer also makes the point that the knowledge being produced is both new and old; while the facts have been known for some time, the perceptual experience is something new. The novelty is how the "living picture" makes facts "plain for all to see." This mixture of new and old is central to an understanding both of Smith and of early popular-science films more generally.

Juggling Flies

Smith kept a notebook of his daily activities during the earliest period of his employment at Urban. Since he was not yet a contract employee, many entries in the notebook record expenses, the receipt of film stock or equipment, and requests for more stock or equipment. The notebook also contains terse descriptions of Smith's filmmaking activities. Beginning in May 1908 Smith's notebook recorded footage of dragonflies, wood ants fighting, ants milking aphids, green tree frogs, smoke, giraffes, jackals, gnus, and rhinos.[15]

In August 1908, Smith's notebook contained several entries about work that would result in his first notable public success. On August 9, an entry noted "head of a blow-fly."[16] Smith already had experience with microphotography through his involvement with the Quekett Microscopical Club, where he served as secretary from 1904 to 1909.[17] In an oft-repeated story, Smith was

MICRO-CINEMATOGRAPHY: BLOW-FLY EATING HONEY.

FIG. 2.1 Percy Smith photograph of a blowfly being fed from the tip of a needle. From F. A. Talbot, *Moving Pictures: How They Are Made and Worked* (1912).

called to Urban's attention by a photograph of a blowfly's tongue; a more elaborate version of this story has Urban asking Smith whether he had ever taken such a photograph of a fly's tongue and, if so, whether he could make that photograph move[18] (Fig. 2.1). Entries for the rest of the month included "acrobatic blow fly," "acrobatic flea," and "more acrobatic film," and on September 16 Smith noted, "Saw Bfly ready for market."[19]

The fly film that Smith saw to market was *The Balancing Blue-Bottle*, a title that appeared in Urban's catalogue supplements in late 1908:

THE BALANCING BLUE-BOTTLE.

DISCOVERY BY ACCIDENT OF AMAZING JUGGLING POWERS IN A COMMON BLUE-BOTTLE FLY.

The original Fly, accidentally anchored by its wings to a sticky fly-paper, instantly suggested, by the play of its legs, humorous and educative possibilities to the scientific kinematographer by whose patient efforts the following marvelous results were secured:—

Order of Pictures:

1. **A magnified fly performs with a rope-walker's pole**—a wisp from a coat broom.
2. **Experiments with a circus ball**—a pilule of bread—which he quickly twists with his feet.

3. **Further demonstration of the fly's marvelous muscular power** in manipulating a log of wood, a shell, a cube, a cork ball, and a dumb-bell made from two bread pills and a small splinter, occasionally pausing to rub his hands.

4. **The fly's most remarkable display** is that of rapidly twirling a ball of cork with another fly perched on the top. The second insect maintains his position by simply walking over the surface of the moving sphere, and shows no disposition to fly away.

5. **A very miniature Chippendale chair**—made from a penholder—is occupied by the upright fly, whose wings, protruding from the rails, absurdly resemble the tails of a morning coat. In this position he again performs cleverly with the dumb-bell.

INCONCEIVABLY INTERESTING, UNDOUBTEDLY ORIGINAL and HUMOROUS.

A VALUABLE NATURAL HISTORY DEMONSTRATION.

No. 2246 Code "Muscular"   Length 200 feet.[20]

This description, the first public account of Smith's fly footage, introduced tensions that figured prominently over the course of the film's initial exhibition history (Fig. 2.2).

The framing of this footage in terms of a circus performance is a motif that organized the film's reception. One component of this framing is the deliberate anthropomorphism contained in the phrases "occasionally pausing to rub its hands," the "absurd" resemblance of the fly's wings to "the tails of a morning coat," and the fly's "clever" performance with the final dumbbell. But the descriptions of the individual scenes make an additional move, activating an analogical process whereby the circus prop is revealed as a commonplace object. So "a rope-walker's pole" becomes a "wisp from a coat broom," "a circus ball" is revealed as "a pilule of bread," and what looks like "a dumb-bell" is in fact "two bread pills and a small splinter." The description thus performs an unveiling whose first step posits an analogical resemblance and whose second step undoes that resemblance by way of an explanation. The description alternately indulges in the fanciful invocation of the flies as circus performers and then has recourse to a demystifying explanation. But these two parts of the film were separable, which was at the crux of is varied reception.

The Balancing Blue-Bottle was screened at the Palace Theatre sometime in late September or October 1908.[21] As Smith recalled, "It . . . was, I found, looked upon as a clever 'faked' picture."[22] A newspaper account indicated one reason for this impression, "Some of us have been amazed by pictures of the educated fly. They were so remarkable that we were more than half inclined to fancy them 'just fakes.'"[23] In other words, the images in the film were a little too amazing, and hence they were suspected of being trick films, a suspicion

FIG. 2.2 Video stills from *The Acrobatic Fly*. British Film Institute.

FIG. 2.2 Continued.

that was amplified by the context of the Palace Theatre, a site of commercial amusement, where trick films were frequently screened.

Unhappy with this response, Smith availed himself of an opportunity to exhibit his work in a different venue.[24] Smith's lecture at the Royal Photographic Society (RPS) took place on November 11, 1908. Entitled "Flies and Their Foes, Through Microscope and Camera," the lecture covered a number of topics, including fly physiology; the fly's role in spreading disease; and the ways spiders, geckos, wall lizards, and frogs hunt and capture flies. It was illustrated throughout with lantern slides and concluded with "a cinematograph display." The change in exhibition venue triggered a reaction that far exceeded expectations; within a week of the lecture, over 150 press notices appeared.[25]

A commercial release in an established entertainment venue generated skepticism, but when Smith showed the film at the RPS, it became a media sensation. What about the change of venue effected such a significant change in reception? One factor that distinguished the Palace Theatre presentation from the RPS lecture was the presence of Smith himself as an interlocutor. By embedding the juggling fly film in a contextual discussion, Smith provided it with a veracity that it lacked when screened at the Palace. Additionally, while the RPS is not exactly a learned society, there was nonetheless a difference in the venues' social standing. In the Palace, images of juggling flies were seen as an optical entertainment; however, when placed within the context of a lecture at a respected institution of technical knowledge, these same images became fascinating in a different way. No longer just a photographic trick, the cinematographic images of juggling flies became instead a device that provided access to an actual natural phenomenon; a fantasy created by technology was replaced by fantastic access to nature via a technological device.

The attention that the RPS lecture garnered was not entirely to Smith's liking, either. As he recalled, "So, like an idiot, I came out of my shell, and exhibited it before the Royal Photographic Society. Then the reporters came!" The aftermath of the RPS lecture took a toll on the shy and retiring Smith, who told of a "fortnight's nervous breakdown" as a result of the publicity.[26] In addition to the disruption caused by the sheer volume of articles and letters, Smith also was troubled by how the film was being understood. In an effort to exert some control over the meaning of his films, Smith provided a number of detailed accounts about how he obtained the images.[27] One aspect of the reception that Smith contested was the Urban catalogue's account of the film's origin. Instead of an "accidental discovery," Smith insisted, "The juggling fly was not an inspiration—it was evolved. For some considerable period I had been studying insect anatomy with a view to working out some problems connected with the functions of certain organs."[28] He insisted that a scientific process underlay the film, invoking the trajectory of another technology that went from the laboratory into mass-cultural use, the phonograph: "Just as the omnipresent phonograph, which to-day grinds out its eternal music for the delectation of tens of thousands of human beings, was the result of deep research in the laboratory, so that unconscious little laughter-raiser, the juggling fly, was brought into prominence purely as the result of a technical scientific experiment."[29] He gave detailed accounts of his process of discovery, explaining how it arose from his investigation of the fly's respiratory system, which made it possible for the fly to generate the enormous amounts of energy that his visualizations demonstrated. Smith repeatedly emphasized that the film arose from preexisting investigations into the question of how to make the fly's strength visually accessible.

Smith also had to defend his film from suggestions that the scenes had been acquired by various inauthentic means, such as gumming the objects or feeding the flies iron filings and then magnetizing the objects that they juggled. To counter these suggestions of fakery, Smith explained his use of objects like dumbbells instead of more "scientific" scales in the following manner: "It was very obvious, however, that to show upon a screen a fly registering its pull, in grains, upon a dial would lay one open to the suggestion, so readily put forward by the man in the street, that the indicator was incorrectly graduated or otherwise 'faked.' The fly was therefore induced to juggle with articles of comparatively enormous size and weight, and thus to demonstrate, in the most graphic manner possible, its great strength and power of endurance."[30] This recourse to "the most graphic manner possible" opened up a field of associations that also contained pitfalls, however.

The most prominent association was that the flies had received some kind of "education," and this was a topic that Smith took pains to clarify. He repeatedly downplayed the importance of the "training" that the flies received, writing, for instance, "The 'training' consisted merely of inducing the insects to temporarily refrain from flying, not so much to evolve new tricks as to render them a little less erratic whilst being photographed."[31] He gave detailed explanations of the device he used to make the flies "perform," which consisted of a box with a glass door that was linked to an escapement that would give the fly a tap each time it tried to escape, a method adapted from the glass bell method used for conditioning performing fleas.[32] After being confined in this contraption for an extended period, some flies were more or less tractable, which permitted the feats of strength that Smith filmed. Smith theorized that the "juggling" was, in fact, something much less unusual: "It is not quite clear, however, . . . why it juggles with an object, but an examination of the enlarged pictures from the film shows that the action of the legs is exactly the same as when the insect walks, and it is only reasonable, therefore, to suppose the creature believes it is actually walking."[33]

While Smith took care to use the terms "acrobatic" or "juggling," by introducing the iconography of the circus, he nonetheless introduced the specter of an "intelligent" insect. A newspaper cartoon demonstrates how the film's

FIG. 2.3 *New York Herald* cartoon. From the George Kleine Papers, Manuscript Division, Library of Congress.

suggestive elements could lead to a more elaborate and fantastical scene (Fig. 2.3). The caption for the cartoon mentions that the "witty" cartoonist "draws somewhat on his imagination," and that while "the film shows the fly juggling with the ball, with another fly on top of it," "the other acts differ from the film" (as do the depictions of the flies with human expressions and of a beetle with a cello, for that matter).[34] A number of the press commentaries took a similarly tongue-in-cheek approach that expanded on the anthropomorphic prompt. *The Daily Mirror* proclaimed, "The performing flea had better look to his laurels!" and the next day the *Mirror* continued, "But the great lesson for flies, the lesson of *keeping away*, is not yet taught to any of them. Let them begin it at once. And in order to teach them this it would be well, we think, to instill into them the principles of some deeply pessimistic and life-denying philosophy such as Schopenhauer's. . . . And then let all the flies go out into an open place and kill themselves."[35]

Some of the footage Smith showed at the RPS lecture was not part of *The Balancing Blue-Bottle*. Images of flies on putrid meat, a fly walking on a watch gear, and a fly as a nursemaid soon were released by Urban as *Blue-Bottle Flies Feeding*, "a companion picture of the *Balancing Blue-Bottle*—the sensation of London."[36]

The catalogue description employed the rhetoric of education:

Synopsis: **The Uneducated Method:** Future Performers engaged upon putrid meat. **The Educated Insect,** after a few days' training, eats honey from the point of a needle—a wonderful picture, showing the action of the trunk-like tongue. **A Free Fly** climbs a revolving wheel, evincing no signs of coercion; in fact he (or she) enjoys the experience. **A Nursemaid Bluebottle,** in cap and apron, plays with a miniature doll—made from the handle of a tooth brush.[37]

As this description makes clear, it was not simply a matter of Smith versus the writer of the Urban catalogue blurb and the press. Particularly the shot that occurs at the conclusion of *Blue-Bottle Flies Feeding*, where a fly wears a nurse-maid costume and holds a tiny doll "carved from a chip of the handle of a tooth-brush," came to serve as a prominent emblem of the juggling fly films[38] (Fig. 2.4). Smith himself characterized this shot as a "novelty," and elsewhere he wrote about the necessity of the novelties: "[I]t was clearly seen that in introducing educational pictures to the public, a certain element of novelty or humour was often a great assistance, as tending to ensure a far wider range of exhibition and consequently increased usefulness."[39] On the one hand, Smith defended the films' scientific validity, but on the other hand he also insisted on the importance of his approach that introduced novelty, an attitude that is itself something of a juggling act. Smith's attempt to keep more than one thing in the air at once is

FIG. 2.4   *Daily Mirror* image of fly as nursemaid. Charles Urban Papers, National Media Museum / Science & Society Picture Library.

evident in the structure of the first sentence of his account of the films that he wrote for *Pearsons Magazine*: "The training of insects to perform striking feats (or, more strictly, the adaptation of the natural powers of insects to produce results which appeal strongly to the human mind) is always a matter of interest."[40] The oscillation between the literal and the rhetorical is typical of the aesthetic of curiosity, where the fanciful and the real are often intertwined.

A similar dynamic occurs in an interview where Smith discusses the curiosity whipped up by the fly films:

> The whole of the time I was bombarded with letters asking for information as to how the thing was done! The British public is very much disposed to enquire as to the means by which trick or novel films are produced. I often wonder whether the makers of patent medicines are pestered by anxious enquirers as to the components of their concoctions. A "trick" idea, especially one which can be worked out without the expense of actors, scenery, or elaborate appliances, is a valuable asset, which one can hardly be expected to impart to every curious enquirer.[41]

Smith's reticence to divulge his "trick" seems unusual, since at the time of this interview he had already detailed his methods, both in his lecture and in print. Although elsewhere taking recourse to the claim of scientific demonstration, here he maintains a showman's coyness regarding his methods, even indirectly comparing his film to a patent medicine. This pose represents a particularly clear example of Smith's split allegiance between professional science's mandate for transparency and the showman's proclivity toward the surprise and the trade secret.

Nowhere is this tension more evident than in the resonance the fly films have with the flea circus, whose venerable history includes many "juggling" fleas. Smith explicitly mentioned the flea circus as a predecessor—"In the days of our grandfathers the 'wonderful performing flea' was quite a popular institution"—which suggests that he saw his demonstration as updating the familiar curiosity.[42] The flea circus was a prime example of the aesthetics of curiosity whose effects were produced using a variety of methods, some of which involved dubious techniques such as heating the fleas to make them appear to be playing musical instruments. On the one hand, the flea circus was embedded in an appeal to the wonders of nature, much the same gesture of looking more closely that Duncan's and Smith's films invoked. But just as the specter of the "trick" haunted Duncan and Smith, there also was a version of the flea circus in which no actual fleas were present, relying on clockwork devices or magnets to produce the illusion of fleas.

The juggling fly films also foreground the freakish or the monstrous. The notion of an educated fly mixes the human and the animal, or at least the insect with the higher mammalian orders, inspiring a similar sense of wonder as that attendant upon the deranging of the order of nature (indeed, my classroom screenings of this film have elicited student comments that label *The Acrobatic*

Fly a horror film).[43] The catalogue description of *The Acrobatic Fly* contains a number of comparisons that partake of a similar tendency toward strange mixtures. The fly is "seemingly as large as a fox-terrier," while its skills rival those of a "Japanese juggler." The fly's proboscis is compared to "an elephant's trunk," and "the hairs over its body resemble porcupine's quills more than

THE FLY THAT MAKES THE WHEEL GO ROUND.

REMARKABLE PERFORMANCE BY THE COMMONS UPPER-HOUSE FLY.

TWISTING IT ROUND.

FIG. 2.5 Political cartoons by Sir Frank Carruthers Gould for the *Westminster Gazette*. Courtesy of Luke McKernan.

anything else."[44] And in a further instance of the film's insistent hybridity, the *Motion Picture World*'s genre designation for *The Acrobatic Fly* was "Nature/ Vaudeville."[45] This dimension of Smith's images proved evocative enough to serve as the pretext for a political cartoonist, whose use of them also availed itself of the iconography of the monstrous (Fig. 2.5).

Smith's next major success at Urban also involved the cinema's ability to reveal a remarkable aspect of the natural world. In this case, however, the revelation was based less on previous popular-science traditions and more on the representational capabilities specific to the cinema. With his films about plant growth, Smith took advantage of the cinema's ability to compress time, making the otherwise invisible movement of flowers blooming into a media sensation.

"Quite Spectacular and Almost Weird"

Smith recalled that he "started to photograph plant growth in 1907 in a rather uncongenial part of London" (i.e., Islington, where he lived with his parents) and that his "laboratory and studio consisted of a disused bathroom with its window obliterated with brown paper." His first time-lapse mechanism was "a small seesaw which carried at one end a cocoa-tin with a siphon and at the other a counterpoise. Water dripped slowly into the tin. As soon as the weight of water was sufficient to overcome the counterpoise the tin descended, shed its contents through the siphon with a painfully audible gurgle, and re-ascended with a bump. The impact of this bump, communicated by a clawed arm to a train of clock-wheels, provided ample power to drive the camera."[46] This device allowed him to make two films, one of opening flowers and the other of germinating seeds.

Although cinematography already had been used to visualize the growth and movement of plants around 1900, Smith's films were the first time-lapse plant-growth films shown widely to general audiences.[47] The time-lapse studies begun in 1907 did not result in film exhibitions until 1910, however. This delay had two sources. One reason was that this kind of filmmaking generally took a very long time: *From Bud to Blossom*, a Kinemacolor film, took 18 months to complete.[48] Smith reported, "one picture of the birth of a flower meant two months of ghastly disappointments, but it is only after repeated failures and experiments that success is achieved—especially in this work."[49] The other reason had to do with the introduction of Kinemacolor, which necessitated another version of the time-lapse device that included shutters controlled by a clockwork mechanism so that the films could be shot in daylight.[50] Smith had already completed time-lapse plant-growth studies using conventional 35-mm monochromatic film, but these films were not released until 1911 so that a Kinemacolor version could be made and exhibited first.[51]

Kinemacolor was a two-color additive color system that became one of the most successful episodes of Urban's career. The result of collaboration with

G. A. Smith, Kinemacolor's first test screenings took place in late 1907, and it was shown continually for selected audiences at the Urbanora House in 1908. It ran as a component of the program at the Palace Theatre from 1909 to 1911, and beginning in 1911 it was established as an independent, evening-filling program at the Scala Theatre where it ran until 1913.[52]

Urban differentiated his process from other methods for producing color film such as tinting, toning, and stencil coloring: "Kinemacolor is the only process in existence reproducing actual scenes in living, vivid colours. The real tints and hues of an object are secured at the moment of photographing; in all other processes colours are applied afterwards by hand or machinery—a crude and laborious method, possible only with the simplest of subjects."[53] This emphasis on how the process gave access to "reality" ("actual scenes . . . real tints and hues") was a central component of Urban's claims for the process. "It's just as if you're actually there" reads the caption of a Kinemacolor advertisement, depicting a film of a tiger emerging from some foliage that startles the audience (Fig. 2.6).

As with some of the reactions to Duncan's *The Unseen World*, Kinemacolor recalled the thrill of cinema's first screenings. The first public screening of Kinemacolor at the Palace Theatre consisted of twenty-one films. The film in the middle of the program, *Sweet Flowers*, was shown in a way that emphasized representational novelty. As the program notes, "This picture will first be shown as an ordinary Black and White Bioscope view. After an interval of two seconds for adjusting Colour Filters to the Urban Bioscope machine, **this same picture** will be shown in its natural hues and tints."[54] This showman's flourish recalls the Lumière practice of beginning their early presentations of the Cinématographe by projecting a photographic lantern slide of the first image of the film that then sprang into motion when the operator began to project the film, as a novel imaging technique invigorated the previous one. And as with first cinema exhibitions, the system itself was a scientific marvel that educated the public about the science of color. Urban billed Kinemacolor as a "scientific system of colour-reproduction."[55] A didactic paratext often accompanied the process. Thus, an "explanatory causerie by Charles H. Heydemann, Ph.D." was part of the presentation of Kinemacolor at the Scala Theatre.[56] A series of articles in the *Kinematograph and Lantern Weekly* described Kinemacolor and its potential, and the process generated articles in popular-science magazines as well, such as *Popular Mechanics*[57] (Fig. 2.7).

Beyond how Kinemacolor provided an intrinsic popular-science lesson about the reproduction of color, Urban claimed that it provided an ideal medium for conveying certain kinds of content. The rhetoric surrounding Kinemacolor was shot through with references to its educational powers:

> Hitherto the Kinematograph has been regarded chiefly as a means of amusement, but Messrs. Dick, Mark & Brock are bent upon developing the educational possibilities of Kinemacolor, and since the eye must

FIG. 2.6 Advertisement for Kinemacolor. Charles Urban Papers, National Media Museum / Science & Society Picture Library.

always be the greatest avenue of direct knowledge, the Urban Science Series, describing scientific facts in popular language and depicting them in natural tints, will lift the minds of millions from childish guessing to serious thoughts and study. When we went to school we were taught everything which it has since seemed easiest to forget; by the aid of these concrete illustrations of the World's wonders, explained not in the unintelligible jargon of the learned professor, but in simple words which all may understand, we may in ten minutes absorb as much real knowledge as a printed book could teach us in a fortnight.[58]

Kinemacolor's potent form of verisimilitude formed an ideal extension of the arguments for visual education.

FIG. 2.7 *From Bud to Blossom* on the cover of *Popular Mechanics* (1911).

The arguments for Kinemacolor's educational abilities were a central feature of the materials related to a special screening that Urban organized for
the Education Committee of the London City Council. The program for this
screening contained the following argument for Kinemacolor's qualifications
as an educator:

> Educationists agree that the surest method of appealing to the intelli-
> gence and memory of the student is to approach by of the eye. . . . How
> much more advantageous it will be, however, if pictorial methods of
> instruction can be carried a step further and instructive pictures of all
> kinds shown in motion, and, still more, in the actual colors of nature. If
> such a valuable aid to education as the animated picture is to be em-
> ployed it is only right that the most modern and improved form of this
> wonderful invention should be resorted to.[59]

The subjects noted as particularly suited to Kinemacolor were history, geography, natural history, science, and chemistry. In addition to *From Bud to*

Blossom, Percy Smith may have been involved in the production of other scientific subjects in Kinemacolor: a series on chemical action, where the signal
effects were changes in color (i.e., tests for known poisons, such as arsenic),
and a view through the spectroscope; the manufacture of aniline dyes; and the
repeated example of "protective coloration" in animals, a topic tailor-made
for the process.

Kinemacolor did have limitations and peculiarities—a perfectly pellucid
medium it was not. Criticisms of the process pointed to its difficulty with the
color blue and its tendency to be plagued by the phenomenon of "fringing."
Smith related a particularly memorable example of this latter issue in his rec-
ollection of some Kinemacolor work with mice, who posed a problem because
of their rapid and erratic movements: "I once took a full-face picture of a
mouse in which the whiskers shook to such an extent that he appeared to be
emanating red and green fire [the visual effect of the color-fringing]."[60] The
fiery mouse indicates color's dual potential. By appealing to the senses, color,
like popular science more generally, harbored the potential to detract from
the aims of education. As Tom Gunning has argued, color in the cinema can
enhance either verisimilitude or the "divergence from reality."[61] Indeed, the
two genres that most frequently received coloring in early cinema were fantasy films (e.g., Méliès' *féeriques*) and natural-history films (e.g., Pathé's
stencil-colored films)—a seemingly antithetical pairing that represents the alternative possibilities of realism and spectacle.[62]

As with the first exhibitions of cinema, the display of color could harbor an
uncanny dimension, a potential for estrangement that results from a new representational mode. Urban instructed exhibitors in how to manage this unfa-
miliarity, suggesting that they direct advertising appeals "principally to the
upper and educated classes in his neighbourhood, because for them this entertainment will have an all-powerful attraction." Instead of a single pianist,
there should be an orchestra. Finally, the construction of the program "calls
for discretion." It was important to provide a gradual introduction to the colored moving-picture world. The advice recommended beginning with familiar scenes; once these have been introduced, the audience's "interest and enthusiasm will be aroused as they see everyday things reproduced with such
fascinating realism on the screen, and they will be able, moreover, to appreci-
ate and believe when Kinemacolor shows them unfamiliar things and all the
marvelous colorings of eastern or tropic lands."[63]

When Kinemacolor debuted at the Scala Theatre on April 11, 1911, the
middle section of the three-part program was entitled "Urban Science" and
consisted of *Insects and Their Habits*, *Animal Studies*, *The Birth of Flowers*,
Reflections of Color, *The Soap Bubble and the Rainbow*, *Animal Studies*, and
Egyptian Sunsets.[64] The time-lapse subject of flowers blooming was a conspic-
uous hit of the Kinemacolor programs. One visitor to the Scala described the
experience in the following terms: "To see the birth of a flower shown upon

the screen is to enter into a new world, and I saw before my eyes many varieties open from the bud to the flower in Nature's own colours and perfection.
Small wonder that these pictures were received with much enthusiasm from
the audience present. Such instructive, novel, and educational films as these
provide food for thought and cannot but command the admiration of even
the most indifferent to Nature's beauties."[65] The film's catalogue description
foregrounded its scientific appeals: "This film admirably illustrates the possibilities of kinematography, and especially of natural color kinematography,
when applied to a specific scientific purpose. It is, undoubtedly, one of the
most remarkable subjects ever presented on the moving picture screen, and it
has done more than any other film to bring home to the minds of educated
people the fact that the kinematograph is not merely a device for providing
entertainment but an instrument of immense scientific value."[66] As with color,
however, the time-lapse technique also contained seeds of estrangement. One
commentator described the effect as "no less startling than beautiful," and another noted that "A feeling almost uncanny was produced by the unusual pictures."[67] An unattributed cartoon in Smith's scrapbook illustrates this state of
mind, as a spectator progresses from indifference through surprise to startled
fascination, his interest opening up in a manner that mirrors the process depicted on the screen. (Fig. 2.8).

From Bud to Blossom preceded *The Birth of a Flower* and was able to provide a more verisimilar experience of color, but since Kinemacolor required
specialized projection equipment that was installed in only a relatively small
number of venues, *Birth* was seen more widely.[68] *Birth* consisted of nine scenes
that showed the blooming of hyacinths, crocuses, tulips, daffodils, the Neapol-
itan onion, narcissi, the Japanese lily, anemones, and, as a finale, roses.[69] The
catalogue described it as follows: "The movements of opening buds made visible by means of a system of speed magnification. An absolutely unique phase
of educational kinematography. By means of elaborate specially-designed
mechanism the actual movements of developing flowers are made visible to
the eye, thus presenting a picture not only of great beauty but of immense scientific value."[70] Fritz Wolters, the resident manager of the Electric Palace in
Lewisham, wrote Urban to report an unusual occurrence during a screening
of the film: "A thing I think unprecedented in picture theatres is the calling for
an encore, which took place both last night and also to night."[71] This anecdote
became an oft-repeated item in the film's publicity, which was thenceforth
ballyhooed as "the film that was encored!"[72] Wolters was not entirely correct
in assuming that a film being encored was entirely unprecedented; although
rare, there were other examples of such a reaction. The first exhibition of the
Lumière cinematograph at the Société d'Encouragement pour l'Industrie Nationale was shown again at the insistence of its audience: "This animated view
[*La Sortie des Usines Lumière*], showing in complete motion all these people
hurrying into the street, produced the most striking effect, and a repeat of the

FIG. 2.8 Anonymous cartoon about *From Bud to Blossom*. Charles Urban Papers, National Media Museum / Science & Society Picture Library.

projection was demanded by the whole audience, filled with wonder."[73] *McKinley at Home, Canton, O.* (American Mutoscope and Biograph 1896) occasioned an encore when shown to an audience of Republicans at Hammerstein's Olympia Theater:

> The scene of the McKinley and Hobart parade at Canton called forth great applause, but when a few minutes later the audience caught sight of the next President himself, "in the flesh," pandemonium broke loose for five minutes. Men stood up in their seats and yelled with might and main, and flags were waved by dainty hands that would fain cast a vote on November 3, for the good cause. To satisfy the audience the Major [McKinley] was brought forth again with like result.[74]

The reactions of "wonder" in these accounts and the impression that cinema recreated reality ("'in the flesh'") are similar to the responses to *The Birth of a Flower*. The common denominator is their testament to cinema's amazing simulation of reality, and the prior examples, taken from some of the first audiences for cinema projections, underscore how *The Birth of a Flower* recalled the wonder of those initial screenings. The demand for an encore displays a mixture of disbelief and amazement, a response to an image that is so extraordinary that it almost cannot be believed and requires a repeat viewing. *The Birth of a Flower* also recalls the Lumière practice of running certain films, such as *Destruction of a Wall*, backward, which appealed to the sense of wonder at cinema's ability to manipulate time. Luke McKernan has made a similar point about how Urban's various innovations repeatedly took cinema "back to its roots" by reawaking the sense of wonder at the medium's representational capabilities.[75]

Other reactions drew on a variety of metaphorical registers. One notice compared the opening of the garden anemone to a "kaleidoscope"[76] (Fig. 2.9). The catalogue encouraged such analogizing, describing the scene of butterfly flowers blooming thusly: "In the first flower shown a distinct resemblance to a face may be distinguished; like that of a French clown. The second as it opens assumes the shape of a little Japanese doll, and the last is just like the golliwog."[77] A natural-theological reaction to this wonder of modern science also numbered among the responses: "It is impossible that the most thoughtless and miscellaneous audience should look on enacted miracles like these without having the sense of wonder stirred, and wonder, by consent, is the first step to religion."[78] Probably the most prominent reaction, however, saw the films as providing evidence of a greater kinship between plants and animals. The writer for the *Picture Theater News* declared, "By this process plants are transformed, as it were, into sentient beings."[79] This argument recalls Charles Darwin's comparison of the movement of the radicle, or root tip, to the brain of simple animals. The catalogue descriptions advanced the analogy between plant and animal in this manner: "Nature's processes are fundamentally the

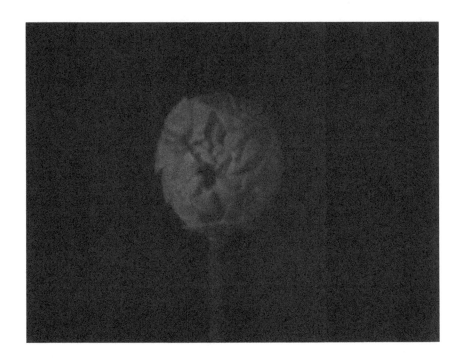

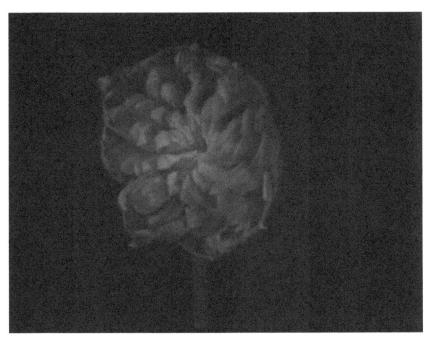

FIG. 2.9 "Kaleidoscope": the bloom of the anemone. Video stills from *The Birth of a Flower*. British Film Institute.

FIG. 2.9 Continued.

same, and this picture enables us to realise in a degree that would be impossible by any other means that growth in both the plant and animal worlds follows the same general principles, although this cannot always be detected by the unaided human vision."[80] This line of thought is behind the concept of the "birth" of the flower, which several reviews took quite literally: "The chief interest of the film, from a scientific point of view is undoubtedly that the pictures clearly demonstrate that in the plant world, as in the animal world, procreation is attended by effort. The petals of a flower gradually open, and then in a supreme moment, the bud becomes a blossom, a visible thrill or quiver passes through the plant and affects the leaves."[81] The notion of the flower giving birth even occasioned some slight embarrassment: "The effect is remarkable, and though it seems rather an impertinence to pry thus into the secrets of growth, the pictures are exceedingly fascinating."[82] Given this similarity between plant and animal, it was but a small step to see the flowers in relationship to humans: "The movements as the petals [of the Japanese tiger lily] are curved back are very similar to those of an athlete setting his shoulders and expanding his chest"[83] (Fig. 2.10). In a further instance of how early popular-science films evoked older traditions, here the sentient, anthropomorphized flower provides another example of a curiosity.

Another time-lapse, plant-growth film, *The Germination of Plants*, was released two weeks after *The Birth of a Flower*.[84] The catalogue's rhetoric similarly emphasized the aesthetics of astonishment and wonder: "Here the

FIG. 2.10 The Japanese tiger lily "expanding its chest." From *The Birth of a Flower*, British Film Institute.

FIG. 2.10 Continued.

Kinematograph acts as our interpreter and by showing in a few moments actions which have been spread over hours or even days, reveals to our astonished eyes the wondrous happenings, the struggles and the aspirations, ever upward towards the light. . . . The moving picture opens up a new world to our gaze and proves itself once more to be the hand-maid of science."[85] The film consisted of six scenes, and the catalogue descriptions continued the tropes introduced previously: The young shoots of scarlet runner beans curve "gracefully" and "rise from the ground like swans raising their heads," "blades of grass *jostle* one another in their struggles upwards," and in "a struggle for existence" a "more delicate fern [is] killed by peas which, planted near, exhaust the nutriment from the soil."[86] The reactions to this film also contained the recognition of the uncanny dimension that these images contained: "The various objects are shown in the film on a large scale so that the processes described are easily distinguishable. Indeed the film is quite spectacular and almost weird" and "The effect is, to say the least, both weird and wonderful."[87]

The term that Smith and Urban used for the time-lapse process was "speed magnification," which indicated a similarity in how the fly films and the time-lapse plant-growth films made their phenomena visible. This understanding of time-lapse, in other words, shifts the metaphor of the microscope from space to time. Some reviews of the time-lapse films made this analogy explicit: "What the microscope accomplished in bringing an object of minute size within the scope of human vision, increased speed in photography does in making visible to the eye movements which occur too slowly to be realized by ordinary means."[88] This extension of the concept of magnification to temporality links the fly films to the time-lapse plant films while also emphasizing how the use of time-lapse was unique to cinema.

Time-lapse, plant-growth studies continued as a significant category for popular-science films.[89] Smith also made many other films at Urban, and his filmmaking achievements before World War I go far beyond *The Acrobatic Fly* and *The Birth of a Flower*. These films do, however, exemplify Smith's work and demonstrate the development of popular-science films. The final section of this chapter will introduce an argument about the interrelations among popular science, the detective genre, and trick films, three areas in which Smith worked and that, instead of demonstrating a restless intellect hopping from one thing to another, constitute an interrelated set of concerns.

The Adventures of Percival Browne, Scientific Detective

"I never had any spare time," said Smith in 1911, referring to his years in the civil service. No wonder. While working at the Board of Education until sometime in 1909, he had begun his filmmaking tasks at Urban in 1908, while also editing the journal of the Quekett Microscopical Club from 1904 to 1909.[90] During this period, Smith also wrote a dozen detective stories for the *Civil Service Observer*. Using the pseudonym Maxwell Pyx, Smith's stories appeared between May 1909 and June 1912 under the general title "The Adventures of Percival Browne."[91] These stories may seem little more than a trivial sideline to Smith's filmmaking activities, a youthful foray into derivative fiction. In the attitude they embody toward knowledge, however, the detective stories are of a piece with Smith's film work. Their staging of the scientific detective's approach to solving crimes exemplifies a popular-scientific commitment to instructive amusement.

Smith described Percival Browne as "an obscure naturalist, with an inclination towards any problem of a scientific nature."[92] In this detail, as in many others, Browne bears a striking resemblance to a much more prominent fictional detective, Sherlock Holmes.[93] Smith's framing device is practically identical to Doyle's; instead of Watson relating Holmes's exploits, Smith has Maxwell Pyx serve as the admiring friend and chronicler of Percival Browne's acumen. Details of setting are also similar. Browne's house on Guilford Street near Russell Square looks likes Holmes's Baker Street apartment: "I found my friend in his den, surrounded by piles of papers, books, jars of pickled specimens, optical appliances, and miscellaneous paraphernalia of one kind and another scattered apparently haphazard on tables, chairs, and floor. I knew, however, from previous experience, that there was a definite system in this delightful muddle, and that the owner was quite familiar with the whereabouts of any particular article."[94] Watson describes Holmes's housekeeping habits in similar terms, "in his personal habits one of the most untidy men that ever drove a fellow-lodger to distraction," although Watson also notes that Holmes is always able to retrieve the relevant bit of information from his mass of papers when necessary.[95] By singling out the detective's peculiar approach to organization, this echo introduces a more thoroughgoing similarity.

Both characters exhibit a devotion to scientific methods that makes them seem peculiar, and their bodies provide a further marker of this peculiarity. Not only do Holmes and Browne share the physiology of the mental worker (Browne's "bony fingers" recall Holmes's "long, white nervous fingers"), but both characters also have similar constitutions.[96] Holmes is characterized by "outbursts of passionate energy when he performed the remarkable feats with which his name is associated . . . followed by reactions of lethargy." Browne similarly alternates between powerful activity and weakness: "I knew that, physically, he was by no means strong; that the occasional feats of strength and endurance were purely the result of terrific mental concentration, and were followed, as often as not, by a week or two in the bed room."[97] These physical similarities result from shared mental attributes; underlying these nervous, busy bodies are minds driven by incessant curiosity. While Browne does not share Holmes's taste for a seven-percent solution, their bodies are remarkably similar in their craving for mental stimulation. Neither Holmes nor Browne likes to eat when working on a case. Mental stimulation substitutes for physical sustenance; the detective is sustained by knowledge. As Andrea Goulet has noted, there is a pronounced tendency among detectives toward bibliophilia, where the desire for food is transferred to a desire for knowledge, as signaled by the locution "voracious reader."[98]

As Holmes explains to Watson in a justification for his drug use: "'My mind,' he said, 'rebels at stagnation. Give me problems, give me work, give me the most abstruse cryptogram, or the most intricate analysis, and I am in my own proper atmosphere. I can dispense then with artificial stimulations. But I abhor the dull routine of existence. I crave for mental exaltation.'"[99] This argument finds its most striking articulation when Holmes tells Watson, "My mind is like a racing engine, tearing itself to pieces because it is not connected up with the work for which it was built."[100] Browne describes a similar situation, "I am like a top. As long as I have a superabundance of interesting work on hand, as long as I keep in a state of rapid movement, I maintain a rigid equilibrium, and can enjoy life. Cut off the possibilities for thinking and investigating, deprive me of the opportunities for the expenditure of energy in congenial channels, and I become a weak, wobbling creature, a nuisance to myself and everyone around me."[101] In this commonality, the devotion to and aptitude for mental activity function as bulwarks against the terrors of boredom.

The frequently obsessive character of this relation to knowledge can bring the detective into proximity with the inhuman. Watson describes Holmes as "an automaton, a calculating machine"; Pyx describes Browne as "a thinking automaton."[102] Indeed, the scientific detective displays a definite tendency toward being an outcast. Although Holmes can be socially fluid, he also indulges in antisocial behaviors. While it might seem that Smith has smoothed out some of the more disturbing aspects of Holmes's character, such as his distrust for women (Browne is married), this distinction is without a difference. Browne's wife never speaks and appears only to serve Browne and guests hot drinks or to answer the door, thus playing an even more minor role than Holmes's housekeeper, Mrs. Hudson.

The epistemological attitude that underlies these similarities is indebted to a variety of late-nineteenth-century sources. Holmes famously described himself as the world's first "consulting detective," an epithet modeled on the established phrase "consulting physician." As numerous commentators have pointed out, this affinity between Holmes and medical knowledge is based on Doyle's admiration for Joseph Bell, the lecturer at the Edinburgh Royal Infirmary whose espousal of close observation made a strong impression on Doyle when he was a medical student.[103] Bell is only the most proximate source for Holmes's method, however. While Holmes's prominence has led some commentators to credit Doyle as the inventor or visionary prognosticator of various advances in modern criminology, Holmes reflected, rather than originated, advances in late-nineteenth-century scientific policing. As Laura Snyder has noted, Doyle created Holmes's methods from a blend of "certain images of science that were popular in mid- to late-nineteenth-century Britain." Snyder names three main components of the Holmesian methodology: Georges Cuvier and Roger Owen, who modeled the "historical" sciences of paleontology, geology, and archeology (via Thomas Huxley); Francis Bacon (via T. B. Macaulay), from whom Holmes inherits the idea of "eliminative induction" (i.e., the notion of fact-gathering as preceding the formation of theories); and William Whewell, for the importance of a certain kind of imagination that follows inductive chains.[104]

This amalgamation represents a certain strand in scientific thought that Carlo Ginzberg describes as a "model of medical semiotics," which became prominent around 1870 to 1880. Ginzberg describes this tradition as "venatic, divinatory, conjectural or semiotic" and distinguishes it from the Galilean mode of systematic, nonparticular knowledge where mathematics is the abstract language of nature and science.[105] This type of science demystifies by reading clues, divining moments of clarity in a general opacity. The detective's mode of thinking is tantamount to a training that allows him to see what others overlook; as Holmes famously remarked to Watson: "You see but do not observe."[106] Thus, Browne possesses "the power of careful observation" and follows a "chain of facts," which leads him to "deductions."[107]

Doyle's Holmes stories are peppered with topical references to technological developments in criminology: in *A Study in Scarlet*, Holmes invents a blood test; "A Scandal in Bohemia" involves the importance of photography as evidence; and "The Adventure of the Cardboard Box" and "The Adventure of the Norwood Builder" both hinge on anthropometric methods of individual identification (ears [which is to say Bertillonage] and fingerprints, respectively). Browne's exploits similarly include instances of Smith drawing on his immediate experiences as a filmmaker when writing the stories, which are replete with details that point to the close relations among filmmaking, detective stories, and popular science. These instances demonstrate how certain proclivities for intellectual puzzles and spectacular display unite the stories and his films.

One group of details relates to cinema exhibition practices of the 1910s. "The Adventure of the Namarobi Extension" incorporates an insider's knowledge of the phantom-ride genre and the relationships between railroads and film producers. The story concerns "a photographic puzzle" brought to Browne's attention by a certain Pickering, who owns a small railway in East Africa and has entered into an exclusive contract with "a noted cinematographic firm" for rights to film the scenery along the railroad route.[108] Before the firm can produce the phantom ride, however, another film depicting the scenery along the very same route appears on the market. Pickering is baffled because, as he explains, the way his locomotives are built makes it impossible to mount a camera surreptitiously on the front of the train. Pickering consults Browne, who takes the film to the "Electric Theatre" to have it screened. After the screening, he proceeds to solve the enigma by pointing out a small detail—a duck that "flew *tail first*," which leads him to conclude that the film was taken from the back of the train and then projected tail to head.[109] By deciphering a fleeting clue left by the manipulation of the apparatus, Browne proves himself a canny viewer, demonstrating an exemplary understanding of this new medium.[110]

Another example of how details from the world of cinema exhibition figure in the Browne stories appears in "The Adventure of the Black Crag." Here Browne goes on holiday with "a cinematograph, two cameras, a box of blasting powder, hundreds of feet of rope, a portable dark room, and a host of boxes."[111] His destination is Elliston, a seaside town plagued by poachers who steal the eggs of rare sea birds. Browne catches the egg poachers by deploying an automatic photographic trap, a device that recalls the special camera rig that Oliver Pike and R. B. Lodge devised for bird photography whereby birds tripped the camera shutter themselves, thus taking their own portraits.[112] The setting of the story also invokes the investigations of Pike, the naturalist and cinematographer whose *In Birdland* (1907) was a milestone of wildlife filmmaking and whose early films included *Cliff Climbing—The Egg Harvest of Flamborough Head* (Cricks and Martin, 1908) and *St. Kilda, Its People and Birds* (Williamson, 1908).[113] Furthermore, this story illustrates the confluence of certain kinds of leisure activity (birdwatching) and an ecological bent, where filmmaking and photography take the place of the more exploitative hobby of egg poaching.

A final cluster of details that indicates similarities between Smith's stories and his film work relates to chemical knowledge and trick devices. Smith made several films in which he performed experiments that demonstrated chemical principles, and Browne also employs his knowledge of chemistry to solve several mysteries. "The Case of the Stepney Doctor" involves arsenic, precise weights and measures, and other poisons (morphia); "The Adventure of the Mysterious Incendiary" hinges on how a certain constellation of typical household chemicals, including battery acid and kitchen matches, creates a mysterious conflagration. In "The Adventure of the Crack-Shot Colonel" Browne exposes an American Army officer by using a combination of tricked-out devices of his own design that allow him to simulate a gunshot.[114]

"The Adventure of the Knight's Nose" provides not only the most extended and impressive example of that particular group of intellectual skills that constituted the detective's signature ability but also a prominent instance of how Browne's abilities inspire astonishment and wonder. In this story Browne displays two instances of fine forensic reasoning. The first involves a single piece of paper that he is able to subject to numerous methods of scrutiny. He identifies the type of pen ink (a stylographic pen), the kind of paper (blotter paper), the type of inscription (an impression of a receipt), and the impression of a stamp. Taken together, these bits of information let him identify the part of the city from which the receipt came. In a second and culminating demonstration of his detective prowess, Browne conducts an examination using a magnifying lens. This scene provides a paradigmatic image of the scientific detective searching for clues. "'What a history is written here,' he [Browne] said, as he searched the debris with the aid of a pair of fine forceps and a lens, 'if only one could read it.'"[115]

This act of scrutiny reveals a minute substitution—a tiny piece of a figure, the titular knight's nose, has broken off. This observation allows Browne to conclude that the original chessmen had been replaced by copies; the originals, which contained valuable jewels, are then retrieved. As Pyx puts it, Browne's detective work here is "one of the most brilliant strokes of deductive genius that it has ever been my good fortune to witness," a response to Browne's methods that indicates the proximity of the scientific detective to the cultures of scientific display and scientific magic.[116]

Yoked to this showman's flair for producing astonishment is a commitment to the accessibility of the modes of analysis the detective practices. Displays of astonishing virtuosity, in other words, are counterbalanced by gestures toward openness and access. The literary detective tradition contains a powerful component of audience participation, of which Watson's character is a prominent example. The implicit promise, improbable as it may be, is that you, too, can solve these puzzles, if only you learn how to observe. Browne's refusal to accept payment for his services "other than incidental expenses," a trait he shares with Holmes, is an extension of this precept, highlighting an ideal of intellectual self-sufficiency and a proclivity for excluding scientific knowledge from the commercial marketplace.[117]

An ethic of observation that values precise observation and simplicity is at work here. At one point Pyx mentions Browne's interest in "the simple but ingenious devices so dear to him."[118] A specific example of these devices is Browne's solution of a problem for the engineers of the Central Subway Extension Works, who needed to get a cable through a z-shaped channel. Browne recommends that the engineers tie fishing line to the tail of a mouse and send it through the channel.[119] More generally, however, simplicity and ingenuity serve as keywords for Smith's approach not only to detective literature but also to popular-scientific filmmaking.[120] Fittingly, the last words Smith puts into Browne's mouth are, "Simple, isn't it?"[121]

In an article on the juggling fly films, Smith insisted that scientific knowledge should be accessible: "There are some people, however, who seem to consider that the Sciences, and Natural History in particular, should be treated as subjects which the uneducated man has no right to enjoy. They would raise a wall around themselves and a few of their own following, demanding as a shibboleth of admission a knowledge of their own advanced methods and abstruse terms."[122] Or, as Percival Browne puts it, "Nowadays almost everyone hates a simple explanation of anything, preferring to clothe an incident with a tangled mass of intricacies rather than observe it in all its natural simplicity."[123] The emphasis on simplicity underscores the confluence of scientific knowledge and accessible explication and demonstration. This attitude underlies Smith's filmmaking as well, where knowledge is made available in much the same manner as in a boy's science magazine or home experiment kit. Melanie Keene has found similar links between popular science and the detective genre in her discussion of the Construments sets of science toys, which linked science, education, and the detective genre. An accompanying publication, *Construmag*, contained a series of detective stories written by Capt. Frederick Annesley Michael Webster, a prolific author of children's fiction. As Keene writes about the relationship between detective fiction and scientific reasoning:

> [T]he skills of scientific observation and deduction . . . were the two faculties most prized in the *Construmag*'s detective fiction. . . . In these ways, the journal emphasized the power of Construments' practical scientific education to train the mind. The rhetoric of detective fiction, which emphasized the rational processes of reasoning followed to reach a logical conclusion as to who committed a crime, was invoked by writers like Webster to demonstrate the similarity of these mental processes to scientific skills inculcated through using a Construments set.[124]

As McKernan notes, "Audiences were not merely lectured to by Smith's films, but were invited by their observant method to become discoverers themselves."[125] These similarities in method form common ground shared by detective fiction and popular-science films, too.

Popular Science and Eccentricity

In his restless curiosity, Browne bears a strong resemblance to Smith himself; not for nothing did Smith share a barely concealed version of his first name with his scientific detective (Percival/Percy). In addition to other similarities, such as the chronic busyness that exemplified the tireless, ever-curious investigator, Smith also was like his detective protagonist in how his knowledge marked him as unusual. Stories about Smith frequently commented on details of his life that were seen as odd: his house that doubled as a filmmaking studio, complete with time-lapse alarms; trout in the bathtub; black mold that had escaped from a set; or his love for animals that fell outside the bounds of traditional petdom. These similarities suggest not only that Smith saw Browne/ Holmes as an extension of his own personality but also that what was at issue was a question of how Smith fashioned his scientific persona.

"Smith's was a strange personality," noted the writer of Smith's obituary in *Nature*.[126] This strangeness, if not simply taken at face value, fits neatly into the profile of the eccentric, which, as Victoria Carroll has established, was "an historically and culturally specific phenomenon" that, in the British context, "became established only in the early nineteenth century, within a specific, formative social and cultural context." "Natural knowledge was a particular focus for eccentricity," Carroll notes, and indeed, the eccentric persona was a clever branding strategy for Smith.[127] Carroll also points out that "eccentricity could be construed as self-conscious affectation—as a cloak of appearances which could be put on or set aside at will, and which could, if carefully considered, be well received."[128] And, indeed, inconsistencies in Smith's persona indicate just such a self-conscious adoption and laying aside of a particular set of traits. The *Nature* obituary mentioned his "retiring and shy disposition," a character trait mentioned by Smith himself, as in his claim that the furor occasioned by his juggling fly films had caused him to have a nervous breakdown. But for someone supposedly shy and retiring, he was remarkably willing to be in the public eye, frequently appearing in the films he made for Urban (Fig. 2.11). While Smith's persona had an antisocial aspect to it—he was said to be most comfortable tinkering with his gadgets and tending to the creatures he was observing—he continually attended meetings of scientific organizations and gave lectures. And although some sources mention that Smith only ever worked together with his wife, for a period in the early 1930s, Smith had another female assistant.[129]

FIG. 2.11A Percy Smith performing a demonstration. Video still courtesy of Jay Schwartz.

MR. F. PERCY SMITH.

FIG. 2.11B Percy Smith portrait. Charles Urban Papers, National Media Museum / Science & Society Picture Library.

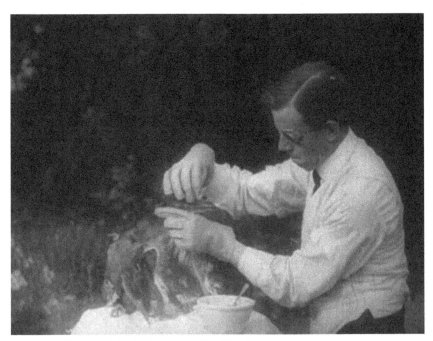

FIG. 2.11C Percy Smith with herons. British Film Institute.

Some of the better-known anecdotes about Smith emphasized his exceptional devotion to observation—so, for instance, as a child, he froze to the
ground watching insect life in winter; and he was alleged to have taken motion-
picture equipment with him on his honeymoon.[130] Smith recalls the Enlightenment naturalist, who cultivated what Lorraine Daston has termed the "cult
of attention." The process of making films was unthinkable without this concentrated attention; multiple anecdotes detail how Smith's subjects required
years of patient observation before the final record could be secured. This form
of attention frequently led Enlightenment observers to what Daston terms
"creature love," which she describes in the following terms: "Attention infused
its objects with affect: the naturalists came to regard their bees and aphids and
even insects extracted from horses' dung with wonder and affection."[131] An
article Smith wrote about spiders illustrates his participation in this attitude.
Beginning the article by noting the "distaste, and sometimes horror" that spiders arouse, he continues, "to say he studies spiders because he likes them is to
court unbelief." But he then makes this reproof: "we ought to remember that,
like the spider, we prey upon helpless creatures, though, by reason of the cultivated delicacy of our feelings, we may demand that our victims shall be slain
by proxy and outside the range of our senses."[132] This defense of a "loathed"
creature is typical of Smith's attitude toward nature.[133] Smith's response to his
colleague Mary Field's question about how to control pests in her barn exemplifies the transformative powers of attention: "If I think anything is a pest,

I make a film about it; then it becomes beautiful."[134] Smith's cultivation of both unusual creatures and unusual relationships with creatures further speaks to his adoption of an eccentric persona.

Eccentrics, notes Carroll, indicated boundary transgressions, whether between the professional and the amateur, between science and nonscience, or between elite and popular. Smith embodied the eccentric persona in this way, too. His films drew on venerable traditions of scientific display while also embracing the newest media technology. Smith's allegiance to prior modes of natural-historical knowledge in an era when professional science increasingly was moving into the laboratory and hence away from the public sphere made him, like many popularizers, both a relic and a pioneer. Thus, Smith's social position is similar to earlier eccentrics, especially in his relation to technology. His ability to fiddle patiently with the various configurations of the microscope/camera/time-lapse apparatus gave him access to knowledge production while also consigning him to the margins of mainstream scientific culture. Here the boundary that appears is one introduced by a novel imaging device, the cinema, and the new forms of knowledge it creates.

Finally, Smith's technical expertise underscores again the proximity of the popular-science film and the trick film. Smith made several successful trick films in his time at Urban, including *Animated Putty* (1911), an early example of stop-motion clay animation, and *The Dissolving Government* (1912), where an unfixed photographic image was heated, which caused the gelatin emulsion to slide down the plate (Fig. 2.12). In *To Demonstrate How Spiders Fly* (1909), Smith used stop-motion animation to illustrate how spiders use their silk as a kind of parachute.[135] Smith later created animated war maps that illustrated a series of World War I military engagements.[136] Beyond demonstrating Smith's polymath sensibilities, his movement between popular-science films and trick films is indicative of the circulation of cinematic technical knowledge.

Smith continued to make popular-science films after World War I, becoming particularly well known for his involvement in the popular "Secrets of Nature" and "Secrets of Life" series.[137] By the end of his life, Smith's work had attained recognition among the professional scientific community; the obituary that appeared in *Nature* went so far as to call him a "scientific genius." The obituary also made the following point: "Although much of Smith's work was shown in the theaters, many will remember the weird beauty of his *Plants of the Underworld* and the drama of *The Life of a Plant*, yet his main work was rather in the scientific film. Here he was undoubtedly in a class by himself, especially in the field of Biology."[138] This mention of Smith's involvement with "the scientific film" emphasizes his involvement with professional scientists, referring to Smith's collaborations with Julian Huxley and the botanist E. J. Salisbury, but it distorts the ethos of instructive entertainment that characterized Smith's work in the pre-World War I period.

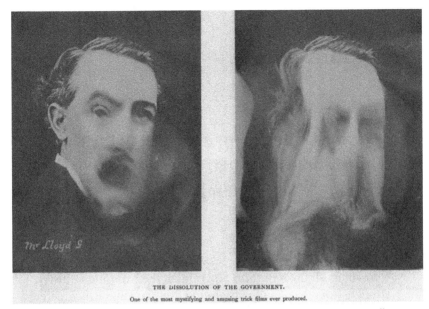

THE DISSOLUTION OF THE GOVERNMENT.
One of the most mystifying and amusing trick films ever produced.

FIG. 2.12 The *Dissolution of Government* (Urban/Percy Smith, 1912). From Talbot, *Moving Pictures: How They Are Made and Worked* (1912).

During Smith's time at Urban Jean Comandon began his filmmaking career, In late 1909 he sparked a remarkable expansion of popular-science filmmaking in France with a series of microcinematographic films. The flourishing of popular-science filmmaking in France in the early 1910s signaled a concentrated expansion of the genre. Although Comandon came from a different background, having been trained as a laboratory microbiologist, his filmmaking career followed similar contours as Smith's. Indeed, Duncan's and Smith's work at Urban established a gamut of subjects that subsequent filmmakers repeated; a great many of the animals, vegetables, and minerals that figured in the French films were already present in Urban's catalogues. In part relying on the traditions of nineteenth-century scientific display culture while also developing new, cinema-specific representational methods, the popular-science filmmakers at Urban developed the medium's methods for generating curiosity and wonder.

{ Chapter 3 }

"A Drama Unites Them in a Fight to the Death": The Flourishing of Popular-Science Films in France, 1909–1914

> [T]he composition of the film programs at the Exposition differed strongly from the popular fairground film showings which were tracing their way across France at this time. The underlying elitist project to instruct more than entertain strongly inserted itself into the major orientation of the Exposition, which was intended as a gigantic national "school."[1]

> By 1911, when the eleven-year cycle of Paris world expositions came to an end without a new world fair, the renovated Gaumont-Palace, as a kind of symbolic replacement, opened its doors to seat up to 3,400 spectators and quickly became the premier cinema in France.[2]

There is something more than symbolic in the replacement of the cycle of expositions with a cinema. The Gaumont-Palace was an apt "symbolic replacement" of the Parisian world expositions because central features of those expositions, and especially the belief in public spectacle as an educative force, were central to the Gaumont-Palace as well. The notion that the exposition was "a gigantic national 'school'" was present in the Gaumont-Palace in a number of ways. While the projector was no longer on display in the central hall, the foyers and galleries of the Gaumont-Palace displayed the latest modern technologies, from electric guns to advances in photography, in an ongoing commitment to the operational aesthetic.[3] The popular-science displays that characterized the expositions did more than maintain a presence at the periphery of the French cinema of this era, however; they also claimed a place on the film program.

The establishment of such cinemas as the Gaumont-Palace exemplified the French motion-picture industry's attempt to garner middle-class respectability. This movement to "uplift" the cinema is another connection to the "elitist project" of the exposition, and the widespread production of popular-science films formed a major component of this campaign to bring the bourgeoisie back to the cinema. The sudden increase in popular-science films on French screens was well under way in 1911. There were 2,300 *documentaires* produced in France between 1909 and the end of July 1914, when World War I began to interrupt film production.[4] Thierry Lefebvre has counted over four hundred popular-science titles for the period 1910 to 1914, with Pathé producing 230, Gaumont seventy-six, Éclair sixty-one, Eclipse and Kineto thirty-one, and many other companies—Edison, Cinès, Cosmograph, Ambrosio, Instructic, Kalem, Raleigh—also producing a handful.[5] In all roughly twenty percent of the nonfiction films produced were popular-science films, a significant increase over their negligible presence in the field of French nonfiction prior to 1910.

For all the novelty of this sudden emergence of popular-science films onto French cinema screens at the beginning of 1910, there was nonetheless something familiar about these images. The rhetoric of the cinema as a medium of instruction struck a familiar chord, resonating with a refrain that often accompanied the first cinema projections, calling for the cinema as an educator and as a force of enlightenment. The optimism of this vision of the cinema contains a note of melancholy as well, the sadness of a dream deferred, an oft-repeated but unfulfilled fantasy.

The flourishing of popular-science films in France at the beginning of the 1910s resonated with Charles Urban's vision of the cinema. Popular-science films absorbed some of the functions of such established genres as the trick film while opening up new cinematic territory, especially in terms of the manipulation of time and scale. In the attempt to address a popular audience and to create a market for a scholastic audience, these films ultimately encountered significant problems, however. To see this efflorescence of popular-science films simply as a failure, however, would mean discounting its impact on fictional genres, both in terms of style and content, a legacy that is arguably as important as its status as a precursor of educational cinema.

This chapter will focus on the two primary producers of popular-science films in France from 1909 to 1914, Pathé and Gaumont, with some attention to exemplary films made by Éclair. It also will account for the flourishing of popular-science films in the years immediately before World War I by positioning this surge in production at the confluence of several factors: the systematic extension of cinema into new markets, advances in imaging techniques, and the elaboration of a discourse about the role cinema could play in education. While high-minded rhetoric furnished much of the ostensible rationale for the flourishing of the popular-science genre, the films themselves were often far from dignified, appealing to audiences with precisely those devices of melodrama that cinema reformers considered harmful.

The Commercialization of Popular-Science Films in France:
Jean Comandon and Pathé

The emergence of popular-science films in the early 1910s in France resulted from an alliance formed between a young biomedical researcher and the era's most powerful cinema studio. Working on his dissertation under Dr. Paul Gastou at St. Louis hospital's central laboratory, Jean Comandon was investigating syphilis (Fig. 3.1). The microorganism responsible for syphilis, the spirochete *T. pallidum pallidum*, had been discovered by Fritz Schaudinn, in conjunction with Erich Hoffmann, in 1905. Diagnosing syphilis remained a difficult task, however, not only because the disease, nicknamed "the Great Imitator," mimics other diseases but also because it typically has a long latency period that occurs after the primary and secondary stages during which the infected person exhibits no outward signs of infection.

Comandon was searching for a reliable diagnostic method for identifying the syphilis spirochete.[6] Under the guidance of Gastou, Comandon became an expert in the use of the ultramicroscope. Invented in 1902 by the Austrian chemist Richard Zsigmondy, in collaboration with Heinrich Siedentopf and the Zeiss corporation, the ultramicroscope initially was used to study colloids, and it allowed for the observation of particles whose dimensions were smaller than the wavelength of light. Its dark-field illumination technique

FIG. 3.1 Jean Comandon (seated) and Albert Dastre. Courtesy of Thierry Lefebvre.

meant that it also was particularly suited to the observation of certain micro-organisms, like syphilis, that were difficult to see with conventional micro-scopes.[7] While examining over five hundred specimens of blood, semen, phlegm, and other bodily fluids under the ultramicroscope, Comandon no-ticed that the syphilis spirochete had a distinctive way of moving, which per-mitted its positive identification. Film's capacity to record this movement and to make it available to share with other researchers made it the optimal method with which to document these observations.[8] Comandon had trouble obtaining satisfactory results with the equipment he had at his disposal at the hospital, however. As a result, Gastou put him in touch with Charles Pathé, who agreed to provide technical assistance on the condition that Comandon move his experiments to Pathé's buildings (Fig. 3.2).

Thanks to the resources, both technical and human, afforded him at Pathé, Comandon was able to achieve better results, which resulted in a series of films shot through the ultramicroscope that showed the syphilis spirochete and other bacteria; serological phenomena, such as the observation of hemoconia, parti-cles in the bloodstream that were also known as "blood dust"; and details of cell biology.[9] On October 22, 1909, Pathé and Comandon filed a patent that described the modifications to the instruments Comandon had undertaken, an action that protected Pathé's investment before the public debut of film produced by the device.[10] The first public description of the technology and the first public

FIG. 3.2 A staged Pathé publicity still of Comandon's studio, circa 1910. Collection of Maurice Gianati.

exhibition of the films took place at the Académie des sciences on October 26, 1909, and the films were screened after Professor Albert Dastre presented Comandon's paper. The films' function was to accompany the verbal presentation, providing a visual record of ultramicroscopic preparations. As Comandon wrote about the films, "These are documents that permit the study of movements of microscopic organisms. The cinematograph is the only instrument that truly gives us the means to conserve the images reproduced by ultramicroscopic preparations."[11] Beyond providing a visual record of movement, however, the films also allowed Comandon to count the microorganisms and particles he was observing as well as to measure their rates of movement. To make the films provide this sort of information, Comandon added "a scale of 1/100 of a millimeter and the shadow of a clock pendulum marking the seconds" to the image field. These measurement devices allowed for a "quantitative" approach that "materializ[ed] time and space."[12] These additions to the microcinematographic image placed Comandon's work within the Mareyian tradition of visualization, as Comandon acknowledged when he wrote that "In thus studying each image individually, one can analyze the movements of microorganisms, as Marey has done so successfully with the human gait and the flight of birds."[13]

As is often the case in the scientific employment of visual media, however, the films' spectacular aspects were as prominent as the analytical framework. This tendency was most obvious in the attention the presentation received in the press: *Le Matin*, *Je sais tout*, and *Lectures pour tous* all covered the presentation; *Le Matin*'s headline proclaimed "Man Has Succeeded in Cinematographing the Invisible!"[14] By describing the presentation as an instance of making the invisible visible, the popular press invoked an aesthetic of wonder, a reaction that constituted a return to the aesthetic of the first film screenings.[15] The *New York Times* noted that "His [Comandon's] work was duly reported to the Academy of Sciences at its last session, causing more open wonderment than is usually expressed by that body of cool-blooded savants"[16] (Fig. 3.3).

The celebratory rhetoric surrounding these screenings is largely responsible for the persistent myth of Comandon as the father of microcinematography. This technique, however, is as old as cinema itself. In 1891, Marey and Alfred Nachet made microchronophotographic series of daphnia, vorticella, and other microorganisms.[17] Victor Henri's studies on Brownian motion in 1908 provided the motivation for Comandon's recourse to film, and Lucienne Chevroton's and Fred Vlés's account of their time-lapse film of the sea urchin's egg also was published before Comandon's presentation.[18] Comandon was not even the first to make ultramicroscopic films, since he was preceded by Dr. Karl Reicher, physician at the second Royal Clinic in Berlin, who at the end of July 1903 shot and exhibited a number of these films.[19]

FIG. 3.3 Press coverage of one of Comandon's public lectures, given at the Académie de médécine. From *Je Sais Tout,* May 15, 1914.

FIG. 3.3 Continued.
A screening of Jean Comandon's films at the King's College Hospital Medical Society
Illustrated London News 137, no. 3733 (5 November 1910)

The ultramicroscope provided a different sort of image from that of the conventional microscope, reversing the typical contrast between the object and the background by making the things being observed appear luminous against a dark background. Comandon wrote about the appearance of the images, "Everyone who has worked with this mode of examination, against the black background, knows how beautifully certain preparations can appear. They doubtlessly have regretted not being able to preserve these images that are almost magical and often of the highest scientific interest [*ces images presque féeriques et du plus haut intérêt scientifique*]"[20] (Fig. 3.4). The ultramicroscopic image displayed a formal similarity to the background of certain trick films that were based on the black-box magic illusion.[21] This similarity to an established entertainment genre, in conjunction with the films' own perceptual novelty, may have contributed to their popularity. The fact that the subject matter of one of the films, the syphilis spirochete, was a somewhat taboo subject may have contributed to the general interest as well. Also contributing to the considerable interest the films generated were the efforts of Pathé's publicity department as well as Comandon's own skills as a lecturer and self promoter.[22]

While Comandon's status as the first scientist to provide access to, in the terms of an oft-repeated phrase at the time, the "world of the infinitely small" (*le monde de l'infiniment petit*) cannot be sustained, his films do mark an important moment in the history of popular-science films, inaugurating a remarkable boom in their production that for the first time involved numerous studios. Comandon's films fulfilled certain crucial roles for an expanding cinema industry, allowing Pathé to integrate popular-science films into the studio's increasingly rationalized output. The films provided an important element of Pathé's conversion from an artisanal endeavor to a full-fledged industrial concern with a mass-market business model. Whereas French film companies had done well by selling their prints to the itinerant showmen of the *fêtes foraine*, in July 1907 Pathé began to rent films instead of selling them.

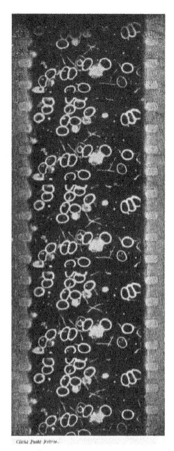

FIG. 3.4 From Jean Comandon, "L'Ultramicroscope et la cinématographie," *La Presse Médicale* 94 (November 1909).

Pathé also inaugurated changes in exhibition, chiefly through the establishment of permanent cinema venues.[23] From the vantage point of these economic factors, the flourishing of popular-science films in France was tied to Pathé's interest in diversifying its products and the concomitant interest in reaching new sectors of the audience, specifically the bourgeoisie. Popular-science films fulfilled both requirements, providing a new film genre that appealed to the tastes of the better-educated classes.

Alongside the attractive prospect of appealing to the bourgeoisie lay the possibility of an entirely new market, France's educational system. Comandon's comments about the Académie presentation indicate that he thought of his films as destined for this market: "Projected on the screen at the same speed [at which they were taken—that is, 16fps], these photographs allow the real appearance [*l'aspect réel*] of the preparations to be reproduced. They can be therefore, we believe, of a great usefulness for teaching and scientific popularization."[24] An article announcing a special screening for the magazine's subscribers echoes Comandon's belief, opining that "the cinematograph will soon assert itself as a marvelous method of instruction."[25] These comments resonated with the growing prominence of movements that sought to include cinema in the educational system. The interest in visual education had been gathering momentum since Jules Ferry's educational reforms in the 1880s, which led to the institution of the *leçon de choses* (object lesson) in 1889.[26] The notion of the object lesson came from the theories of Johann Heinrich Pestalozzi, a Swiss educator and reformer whose ideas about learning were influenced by Locke and Rousseau. Pestalozzi's belief in the primacy of sensation led him to emphasize the importance of studying actual objects as an initial step in learning. He reversed the importance of the lecture, arguing that direct, concrete perception should precede verbal description. Only after an initial encounter with the object was the student encouraged to name it and identify its characteristics, such as its form. Some schools created "object lesson boxes," repositories of everyday objects such as plants and mineral specimens with which students could interact directly. The cinema fit neatly into these arguments for *education par l'aspect*; according to this line of thinking, vision was more intuitive than any other means of instruction and therefore an invaluable resource for educators. As François de la Bretèque and Pierre Guibbert have noted, the rhetoric surrounding cinema and the French school system as reformed under Jules Ferry had a number of things in common: They appeared almost simultaneously, they understood themselves as popular institutions, and they partook of the general attitude that embraced social progress and the education of the nation.[27]

The vision of the cinema as an ideal modern device for instruction represents another return to one of cinema's "forgotten futures." In the earliest days of cinema, numerous voices suggested that the new medium would find its destiny in the area of education. One of the most famous of these formulations occurred in Boleslaw Matuszewski's 1898 description of cinema as a "new form of history," which included a consideration of it as a new tool in the classroom:

> In addition it [animated photography] could become a singularly effective teaching method. How many vague descriptions we will abandon the day a class can watch, projected in precise and moving images, the calm or troubled faces of a deliberating assembly, the meeting of chiefs of state ready to sign an alliance, the departure of troops and squadrons, or even the mobile and changing physiognomy of cities! But it may be a long time before we can draw upon this auxiliary source for teaching history. First we must accumulate these exterior manifestations of

history so later they can be unfolded before the eyes of those who did not witness them.[28]

Charles Urban's interest in this area is an elaborate example of the commitment to this particular vision of cinema, but even Charles Pathé, whose interests were aligned more with fairground exhibition, demonstrated how widespread this trope was in cinema's formative period when he declared, "The cinema is the newspaper, the school, and the theater of tomorrow."[29]

The call for the incorporation of cinema into the educational system had sounded by 1905, but it only began to gain momentum around 1910.[30] At this point, the changes to the economic fundamentals of the French cinema industry and ongoing developments in the French educational system combined to make a screening of a research film a catalyst for the launching of a new commercial genre. Soon after the first screenings of Comandon's films for learned societies, Pathé began to distribute a film entitled *La Cinématographie des microbes*. Appearing in the catalogues in December 1909, the film premiered at the Omnia Pathé cinema in Paris on January 20, 1910. 165 meters in length, it was classified under the catalogue rubric *"scènes diverses"* and consisted of "12 tableaux." The catalogue describes the film as "the presentation at the Académie des sciences of discoveries made in the laboratories of the establishment Pathé Frères under the direction of Doctor Comandon."[31] Given this description, the film might be expected to follow the lantern-lecture format of many of the early Urban films made by F. Martin Duncan. Instead of returning to an earlier cinematic style, however, *La Cinématographie des microbes* displays a number of notable differences from this format, embedding Comandon's scientific documents within more contemporary protocols of film as a commercial entertainment product. These differences become clear when considering the information about the film contained in the program of the Cirque d'Hiver from February 28, 1910, which begins with the same text as in the catalogue and then lists the film's intertitles:

Communication to the Academy of Sciences of discoveries made in the laboratories of the Pathé Frères Establishments under the direction of Dr. Comandon.

  Titles of the Tableaus
  Microscope serving for the examination of the preparation
  A healthy rat is going to be examined
  We cut the tip of the tail to remove a drop of blood that we place between two [strips] of glass under the microscope
  What one sees in the drop of blood from the healthy rat
  We inoculate the rat with the sleeping sickness by injecting under the skin some blood that comes from a sick rat.
  Third day after inoculation.

We see in the blood of the animal numerous trypanosomes that move around and knock against the red blood cells, of which we can note their elasticity.

Fourth day after the inoculation.

The parasites multiply in an extraordinary manner, considerably increasing in one day the seriousness of the sickness.

Fifth day.

The quantity of trypanosomes is such that the rat succumbs.

This terrifying sickness is transmitted by the sting of the Tse-tse fly that originates in Central Africa.[32]

The intertitles illustrate how the film motivates the use of the microcinematographic views via a frame story. Instead of a series of views of different microorganisms explained by a lecturer, the film is internally coherent and narrates the progression of a single illness, interspersing six microcinematographic views with other shots that give contextual information (the microscope, the rat, the inoculation, etc.).

A surviving print of another Comandon film, *Le Microbe de la fièvre récurrente* (April 1910), allows for a more concrete understanding of the changes wrought by the shift from research film to popular-science film.[33] The scale and the chronometer are no longer present in the image. As with *La Cinématographie des microbes* the ultramicroscopic shots are embedded within a narrative framework. The film's opening intertitle after the title card reads, "This sickness causes terrible plagues in Russia that are propagated by flea bites." It then cuts to a shot of fleas on a white background. The next intertitle reads, "It also occurs in Africa, where it arises from tick bites." Again, the film cuts to a shot of what was being discussed in the intertitle, ticks on a background of sand. After the intertitle "The African tick," there are two nicely photographed close-ups of a live tick, one from above and the other from below, which is achieved by placing the tick on a pane of glass.

After this introduction to the parasites that carry the disease, the frame story begins with a laboratory scene, possibly Comandon's laboratory at Vincennes, followed by the intertitle, "The laboratory technician [*Präparator*] takes blood from a healthy animal." We see how the technician takes blood from the animal in question, a monkey, and then a closer view shows how the blood is placed on a glass slide. At this point, the film cuts to an intertitle that introduces the view through the microscope, "Blood from an uninfected animal." This view then alternates with a shot of the laboratory, which is interrupted by the following intertitle, "After the animal has been injected with the relapsing fever, one can see some spirochaetes in its blood. These are the bacteria of the sickness." The film continues to alternate between laboratory views and shots taken through the microscope that demonstrate the progression of the disease—how the fever microbes multiply quickly, causing the monkey to become gravely ill, and how they then disappear, leaving "the young patient" seemingly recovered. Finally, the film shows the monkey "obediently taking his medicine," which allows him to "escape death." Whereas the research film requires certain features, such as the chronometer and scale, these aspects of the image are not necessary for a commercial product. The popular-science film benefits from the addition of other elements, primarily the frame narrative.

Comandon made numerous further microcinematographic films for Pathé. In July 1910, Pathé released a special brochure, addressed to "all levels of instruction," entitled "La Cinématographie ultramicroscopique—vues prises sous la direction scientifique de M. le Docteur J. Comandon," which listed, in addition to the previous two films, fifteen new titles.[34] These films were relatively short and followed a similar pattern of narrativization as the films already discussed. *Faites bouillir votre eau* is exceptional both in its length (270m, almost three times as long as the longest of the other films) and in its attempt to do something other than demonstrate the appearance of a microorganism. After shots of the many types of microorganisms that can live in water and demonstrating how to avoid illness by boiling and filtering water, the film's concluding intertitle exhorts, "Boil your water or drink mineral water!" This intertitle is followed by a shot of a bottle of Badoit mineral water against a black background.[35]

Judging by the subsequent acceleration of production, these films were successful, and the scientific service at Pathé expanded (Fig. 3.5). The first film to appear in the catalogue under the rubric of *vulgarisation scientifique* that does not feature microorganisms was *Pisciculture pratique: La Truite* (August 1910; 150m).[36] The remaining titles produced during 1910 represented the wider range of subjects that were typical of the production at Pathé and its competitors. First and foremost were natural-history films, frequently featuring exotic or unusual animals. *L'Axolotl* (September 1910) is a study of the Mexican salamander.[37] *Le Dytique et sa Larve* (December 1910) presents the ferocious water beetle that appeared repeatedly in popular-science films of various producers.[38] *Examen de l'estomac par les rayons X* (October 1910), a Comandon film that he made together with his partner in radiological imaging, Dr. A. Lomon, represents the extent to which scientific imaging is itself a constant source of content.[39] *Le microscope de Jacques* (December 1910) stages microscopic views via the frame story of a young boy receiving a microscope as a gift, which underlines the importance of the youth audience for this genre. *Comment jouent les muscles chez un athlete* (December 1910) provides an anatomy lesson, isolating and labeling muscle groups.[40]

Pathé's production of popular-science films picked up rapidly after 1910, with twenty-seven titles in 1911, fifty-one in 1912; fifty-nine in 1913; thirty-five in 1914 (of which only thirteen appeared from July to December, a

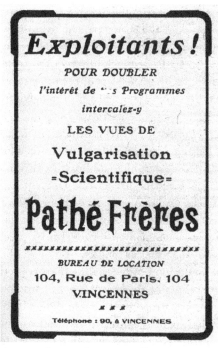

FIG. 3.5 Pathé advertisement for popular-science films, *Ciné-Journal* 96 (June 25, 1910).

drop-off due to the mobilization for World War I). In 1912, the rubric "*scène instructive*" appeared in the catalogue to designate a series of films targeted at children.[41] Pathé's production typifies the French popular-science film and provides the model that the other studios copied. Nonetheless Gaumont, Pathé's main rival, displayed certain noteworthy differences in its popular-science films.

In the Shadow of the Rooster: Popular-Science Films at Gaumont

Given Gaumont's secondary position in the French market, the appearance in its catalogues of a number of science titles in the second half of 1910, shortly after Pathé's release of the Comandon films, might seem little more than an instance of competitive imitation dictated by market logic. To see Gaumont's foray into popular-science films as simply a reaction to Pathé would mean overlooking Gaumont's longstanding commitment to scientific popularization, however. The studio was involved in collaborations with prominent scientists from its very beginnings, and Léon Gaumont's first-hand experience with popular science allows an understanding of why

Gaumont as a corporate entity was committed to cinema's documentary mission and to scientific popularization in particular.

Léon Gaumont's interest in and devotion to scientific and technical pursuits stand out even among cinema's inventors, a group characterized by a strong strain of technophilia. Born to a relatively poor family of low social standing (his parents were servants for the Count and Countess of Beaumont), he nonetheless received an education more proper to a member of the petit bourgeoisie. Attending primary school as a boarder in the town of Dreux, he was an excellent student, showing a special aptitude for geography. Gaumont then went on to the second level of schooling, an unusual feat principally because *secondaire* education was not free. Although it is not clear who paid his tuition fees, he enrolled at the *collège* Sainte-Barbe-des Champs from 1876 to 1878, and then in October 1878 until the end of the school year of 1879–1880 at the *collège* Sainte-Barbe in Paris.[42] He continued to distinguish himself, receiving numerous prizes. At the age of sixteen, Gaumont was forced to leave school because of a change in his family's financial situation.[43]

The end of his formal education did not stop the young Gaumont's pursuit of knowledge, however, which found an outlet in public courses at L'Institut popularie du Progrès, founded and run by Léon Jaubert. There he continued to study physics, biology, and astronomy in courses that were run by prominent members from such institutions as the Muséum d'histoire naturelle, the Sorbonne, the Collège de France, and the École des beaux-arts. Afterward attendees of the courses could use a collection of microscopes arranged by Jaubert where they could "observe the circulation of blood, microbes and bacteria of certain contagious diseases, the animalcules of freshwater plankton, infusoria, etc."[44] Meusy and Faugeron stress that these public courses were a major component of the popularization of scientific knowledge in the latter part of the nineteenth century: "You can never emphasize enough the progressive role that the societies of popular education played, particularly in this second half of the nineteenth century where studies are still reserved for the privileged classes."[45] Gaumont also attended courses at the Observatoire popularie du Trocadéro, another of Jaubert's projects. The presence of this type of education in Gaumont's life provides one likely source for his company's commitment to popular science.

Gaumont appeared to display a genuine intellectual interest in the material—an image that several recollections recount is of Gaumont as boy scientist, assembling his own chemistry laboratory with funds he slowly saved. Of course, it is difficult to separate any interest in these subjects themselves from the fact that scientific expertise also offered the promise of social advancement; Gaumont's attraction to the sciences was in part due to how they functioned as a social equalizer.⁴⁶ As mentioned, Gaumont's ability to attend secondary school represented a coup in a society where education was closely tied to class: "The [free] primary school was the school of the people; the *lycées* and the *colleges*, with their fee-paying elementary classes, were the schools of the bourgeoisie."⁴⁷ These two aspects of the acquisition of scientific proficiency—the desire for knowledge and the desire for status—are, in most cases, inextricable, and the relation between popularization and class is crucial.

For Gaumont, in short, education opened the door to higher social status. The favorable impression Gaumont made on Jaubert led to a position at Jules Carpentier's precision machine and optics shop (Carpentier later fabricated the Lumière Cinématographe). After his military service and further employment at Carpentier's shop, in 1894 Gaumont was able to take over as director of the Comptoir générale de photographie, a photographic supply company that also sold optical devices. He bought the business in 1895, at which point it became L. Gaumont et Cie.⁴⁸ His position at the head of this company put him in a position to meet with Georges Demenÿ, whose research he would develop in a commercial direction with the manufacture of the Chronophotograph Demenÿ beginning in 1896.⁴⁹

Of course, the film industry during this period had a strong relationship to scientific popularization since cinema itself was seen as a scientific marvel. Even during this technophilic period, Gaumont's commitment to technological innovation was extraordinary, however. His company was dedicated to pushing cinema's representational possibilities, spending significant amounts of time and money developing a sound system (Chronophone) and color systems (Gaumontcolor and Chronochrome). These interests are similar to Charles Urban's involvement in color experiments, and of the French production companies, Gaumont most closely resembles Urban's understanding of the cinema's documentary mission.

Even after the importance of the entertainment aspect of his business had become predominant, Gaumont continued to devote time and resources to various scientific applications:

> The company was interested in all scientific areas. Films were made for the improvement of deaf mutes. Dr. François-Franck came often to film his experiments in comparative physiology. Cailletet studied an underwater device ["underwater" crossed out and replaced with "device for taking aerial views"]. We filmed the life of bees with Académician Bonnier. [...] We equipped explorers such as André, lost in a polar expedition, scientific missions like those of Dr. Yersing [sic].⁵⁰

A comparison of Gaumont's support for François-Franck with Pathé's employment of Comandon provides a telling contrast. In the *Comptes rendus des séances de la Société de biologie* in 1906 François-Franck thanks

Gaumont for "his inexhaustible kindness." When François-Franck stopped researching in 1908, Gaumont continued to support Chevroton's research. She thanked Gaumont publicly as well in her report to the Acadèmie des sciences: "That we may be permitted here to bear witness to our gratitude to the house of Gaumont, whose generosity has allowed us to pursue to the very end these delicate and costly experiments."[51] Whereas Pathé countered Comandon's request for technical assistance with a business proposition that involved the rights to the films produced and resulted in widespread commercial screenings, Gaumont's role in similar research remained that of a benefactor who provided "a form of industrial patronage."[52]

Another way to distinguish between Pathé's and Gaumont's approach to popular-science filmmaking is to consider how the films fit into the companies' internal classificatory schemes. Pathé's film catalogues were organized according to rubrics, a system that emerged in 1902–1903 and changed very little until 1914. The one significant change to those categories, however, is the addition in 1910 of popular-science films, which appeared initially in the *"scènes de vulgarisation scientifique"* and then also composed the majority of the *"scènes instructives."* The addition of new rubrics within the entertainment catalogue instead of, for instance, creating a separate area of the catalogue, as at Gaumont, or a special logo, as at Éclair, indicates that Pathé saw popular-science films as a product that was not fundamentally different from the other films in the company's inventory.

By contrast, Gaumont's organizing metaphor for its documentary production, the *Encyclopédie*, provided a different conceptual framework and relied at least in part on the company's early interest in cinema as a scientific and educational medium. Not just one series of films among others, the *Encyclopédie* envisioned a documentary project that could claim to inherit the mantle of such venerable undertakings as Diderot's encyclopedia. The first mention of the *Encyclopédie* appeared in internal company documents in 1912–1913.[53] The majority of Gaumont's *documentaire* films eventually were collected in the *Encyclopédie*, a catalogue that first appeared in 1921, although the definitive version did not appear until 1929. It used a classificatory system that it claimed was taken from the "decimal classification system of the *Répertoire Bibliographique Universel*," encompassing a broad range of films that included "Astronomie," "Physique," "Chimie Minéralogie," "Géologie," "Botanique," "Zoologie," "Médecine—Hygiène," "Chirurgie," and "Pisciculture—Chasse—Pêche."[54] With the creation of the conceptual framework of the *Encyclopédie*, Gaumont articulated an idea that differed in scope from Pathé's understanding of its popular-science products.

There were, of course, ways the *Encyclopédie* at Gaumont fell short of the goals that its ambitious name implied. Delmeulle enumerates the project's myriad "incoherences," which included its tendency toward ahistoricity, the way the catalogue's authors padded content by listing some films under more than rubric, thus inflating the number of titles, and the inclusion of certain films that stretched the limits of a collection of educational cinema to the breaking point, such as *Oxford contre Martigues*, a Jean Durand burlesque that was classified under the rubric of "culture physique/sports diverses." Instead of continually updating the collection's contents, the films were allowed to exist in the inventory indefinitely, leading to a stratification that gave "the insistent impression of bric-a-brac," giving the collection the appearance of a "dump" [*fourretout*] for old material.[55] Delmeulle's assessment of the *Encyclopédie*'s shortcomings concludes that "certain films of this *Encyclopédie* are of an ineptitude that is frankly surprising. . . . In short, a minimum of information drowned in an ocean of parasitic noise."[56]

Although Delmeulle's analysis helpfully isolates shortcomings, by evaluating the *Encyclopédie* primarily according to its own educational rhetoric, Delmeulle discounts how the films that constituted it served different purposes at different times (in this sense it is important to emphasize the collection's retroactive formation).[57] Like all popular-science films produced before World War I, the Gaumont productions served several masters. While on the one hand the films were produced with a view to an eventual incorporation into a scholastic environment, on the other hand, they were released as products destined for commercial cinemas, where they were expected to fit into the program format that defined the mode of exhibition at the time of their release.

The first popular-science film produced at Gaumont was *Petites anguilles* (September 1910), which, judging from the images that survive, was a straightforward aquarium film.[58] As such, it was uncharacteristic of many of the early Gaumont science films, which highlighted the genre's spectacular aspects, and especially the importance of the company's ongoing experiments with color processes, which were competing with Pathé's stencil-color system. Gaumont produced a considerable number of films about flowers, which were remarkable for their unique mise-enscène. *Études des fleurs*, which was announced in *Ciné-Journal* on September 24, 1910, as "colored film, magnificent stereoscopic effect," is the first example of this subgenre.[59] The film consisted of a number of shots where a vase of flowers was placed on a rotating pedestal, a method of display that was familiar from store windows and that again recalls the aesthetic of the earliest films (instead of a living photograph, a living autochrome).

Although the initial push for the adoption of cinema in schools failed, the interest in a scholastic cinema had tangible results, including governmental recognition. In late 1915 Paul Painlevé proposed an extra-parliamentary commission for the investigation of "the means to generalize the usage of the cinematograph in the different branches of education." The commission, which consisted of sixty-seven members, was established early in 1916. Partly as a result of this commission, a number of institutional collections of educational cinema were established—the Musée Pédagogique de l'Etat, Cinémathèque de la Ville de Paris, Cinémathèque Centrale d'Enseignement Professionnel, and a collection of films at the Ministère de l'Agriculture.[60]

Intertextuality and Violence: Recurring Themes in French Popular-Science Films

The subjects for popular-science films were diverse, encompassing fields from zoology to chemistry to hygiene, but some general tendencies run through the various topics and fields. One tendency, which we have already seen in Urban's productions, is the prominence of intertextuality. *[L'Air Liquide]* is a film in the collection of the Cinémathèque de la Ville de Paris that is assembled from footage from several films.[61] Compilation films are not unusual in the collection of the Cinémathèque, which was equipped with an editing studio where films were cut to meet the needs of classroom teachers.[62] There were several films on the topic during the period: *L'Air liquide* (Eclipse, January 1910), 124m; *Air liquide et ses applications* (Raleigh, December 1911), 180m; *Une leçon sur l'air liquide (1er serie)* (Pathé, February 1912), 155m; *L'Air liquide et les applications du froid intense* (Pathé, May 1912), 205m; and *Expériences sur l'air liquide* (Pathé, January 1913), 185m.[63] The catalogue description for this final Pathé film mentions a number of scenes that are in the first part of the archival print—the normally supple metal zinc becoming brittle after immersion in liquid air; a rubber ball being broken into fragments after being frozen; lead being formed into a spring that can sustain weight when frozen, until it heats up again and becomes soft; the freezing and subsequent breaking apart of a steak; and the same procedure performed with a bouquet of roses.[64]

The demonstrations in these films were familiar from popular-science shows. The engineer and entrepreneur Georges Claude had a booth at the Luna Park in Paris in 1910 where he demonstrated the properties of liquid air and neon tubes.[65] Illustrations from various editions of Claude's book about liquid air make clear how common certain demonstrations were (i.e., the transformation of metals, freezing roses, demonstrators taking liquid air into their mouths, the hammer made of mercury) (Fig. 3.6).

The film's initial lesson about liquid air involves how it transforms substances, mostly by making them fragile, progressing from mineral to vegetable to animal. This trajectory culminates in the film's most startling sequence,

FIG. 3.6 Demonstrating the effects of liquid air in print and film. The first image is from Georges Claude, *Liquid Air, Oxygen, Nitrogen* (1913); the next three images are from *[L'Air liquide]* (Pathé, circa 1913). Cinémathèque de la Ville de Paris.

FIG. 3.6 Continued.

the final demonstration in the first part where two live eels are subjected to the effects of liquid air. The catalogue description notes that the exposure to liquid air can "suspend life without stopping it," a characteristic demonstrated when one eel is revived in a bowl of water after being frozen. In the next act, the demonstrator takes the second eel out of the liquid air container and breaks it into pieces, which is unnecessary from the point of view of the description, since we have already seen the supposed point of the demonstration, the revival of a frozen animal[66] (Fig. 3.7).

The destruction of the frozen eel does, however, fit into a predilection for spectacles of violence that constitutes another theme. *Deux escargotphages: La Glandia et L'Ophisaurus* (Éclair, November 1913) exemplifies these films' fondness for scenes where animals eat one another. The mollusk that eats snails, the glandia, is fed for the camera. After the initial shot of the glandia invading the snail's shell, the film cuts to a closer framing of the *escargotophage* fully involved in its meal, where the emphasis is on the frothy liquid that has formed at the junction of the two shells, visual evidence of the one animal's consumption of the other (Fig. 3.8). *Deux escargotphages* is an example of how popular-science films were particularly interested in species that were little-known, peculiar, or violent.[67]

FIG. 3.7 Breaking apart the second eel. Video stills from *[L'Air liquide]* (Pathé, circa 1913). Cinémathèque de la Ville de Paris.

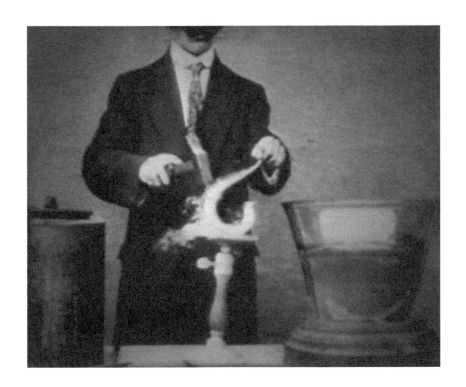

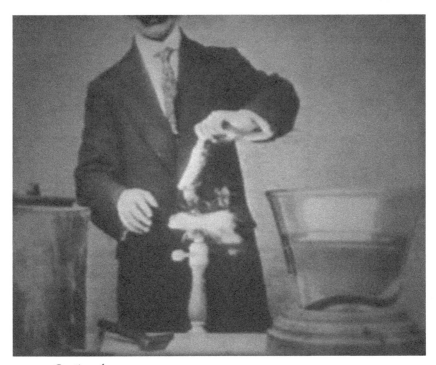

FIG. 3.7 Continued.

FIG. 3.8 The consumption of a snail by a mollusk. Video stills from *Deux escargotphages: La Glanida et L'Ophisaurus* (Éclair, November 1913). Cinémathèque de la Ville de Paris.

FIG. 3.8 Continued.

The following catalogue description of *Un Bandit des grands chemins, la larve de fourmi-lion* (Pathé, May, 1912) provides another example of how the rhetoric employed by the production companies framed the films not only as violent spectacles but also in terms that highlighted their links with melodramatic genres:

> The study of the world of insects reveals to us their ferocity. We will see in this film the ant-lion for whom life is nothing but a succession of dramas and massacres. One remains stupefied by the activity, the incomparable ingenuity and the aggressive boldness of this insect that, from the bottom of its funnel-shaped hole in the sand, a marvel of construction, lies in wait for a victim and mercilessly captures all prey that falls in. The ant-lion demonstrates itself as the master of the art of highway robbery.[68]

The other notable strategy in this description is the relentless anthropomorphization—ingenuity, boldness, mercilessness—of the ant-lion. Nor is anthropomorphism reserved for the animal kingdom, extending to the vegetable kingdom as well. In *La Sensitive* (Éclair, March 1914) a mimosa plant is subjected to a number of experiments that demonstrate its unusual sensitivity to stimuli. The culmination of this film is the anesthetization of the plant with ether, which proves that it can also be rendered insensitive[69] (Fig. 3.9).

FIG. 3.9 Demonstrating the sensitivity of the mimosa. Video stills from *La Sensitive* (Éclair, March 1914). Cinémathèque de la Ville de Paris.

Jean-Henri Fabre and *Le Scorpion Languedocien*

The writings of Jean-Henri Fabre constituted an important source for French popular-science films. A letter from Georges Orléans, who ran the scientific service at Gaumont, to Charles Gaumont, Léon's oldest son, contained the following request: "Please check the table of contents of the five volumes of Fabre that you have. If you find a chapter related to the white cabbage butterfly, please send me the volume as soon as possible."[70] This reliance on Fabre is not an isolated instance: French popular-science filmmakers frequently had recourse to Fabre's writings, which were collected in the ten-volume magnum opus, *Souvenirs entomologiques*.

Although modern science usually rejects anthropomorphism as an affective clouding of objectivity, Fabre's entomology frequently had recourse to anthropomorphizing turns (as well as lyricism and metaphor).[71] While Fabre's work certainly enjoyed scientific credibility—many of his observations resulted in articles published in professional journals—he nonetheless cultivated a certain bias against professional science. This critique was couched in the context of his involvement with science education; he wrote a number of widely used textbooks on various natural-history topics. Fabre's estimation of the problems of contemporary scientific discourse contains an echo of Percy Smith's objections to learned discourse: "Others again have reproached me with my style, which has not the solemnity, nay, better, the dryness of the schools. They fear lest a page that is read without fatigue should not always be the expression of truth. . . . Well, if I write for men of learning, for philosophers, who, one day, will try to some extent to unravel the tough problem of instinct, I write also, I write above all things for the young."[72] This emphasis on an educational approach that appealed to the young was one affinity between Fabre's writings and popular-science films.

Éclair was another prominent French production company during the late 1900s and the early 1910s. Éclair's popular-science series, Scientia, "was aimed towards a young public, 10 to 12-year-olds to be exact—just the ones who, ready to leave elementary school, had acquired the basic knowledge of the three rules of Nature thanks to those famous 'general science' classes which the Ministry of Public Education imposed and systematized during the 1880s."[73] One of the Scientia films, *Le Scorpion Languedocien* (Éclair, October 1912), can serve as a case study for the continuing importance of intertextuality for popular-science films, and Fabre's impact in particular.[74] A reading of *Le Scorpion Languedocien* requires an understanding of Fabre's writings, the fields of entomology and ethology, and early nonfiction film style.

The film's topic is the subject of a section in *Souvenirs entomologiques*, where records his observations of the "yellow" or "Languedoc" scorpion (*Buthus occitanus*), which lives southern France. Pathé already had produced *Le scorpion* (January 1911), so perhaps Éclair sought to distinguish its film from its predecessor, but the film borrows more than just its titular animal from Fabre, however.[75] A comparison of the intertitles in *Le Scorpion Languedocien* with Fabre's chapters about the same species of scorpion in *Souvenirs entomologiques* reveals that fully half of the intertitles are direct quotations or paraphrases of Fabre's text. The issue of fidelity to Fabre is vexed, however. The second half of the film culminates with a "fight" between the rat and the scorpion that does not take place in Fabre. Although Fabre is not above staging battles himself, there is nonetheless a question of whether the film violates the spirit of ethological observation to which it pledges indirect allegiance. Ethology counts Fabre among its founding fathers. The obvious problem with seeing these films as ethological is that they are, at least for a careful observer, obviously staged. Thierry Lefebvre has remarked that, because of technical limitations, in the Éclair films, the ethologist's credo of observing life in its natural habitat, in vivo, gives way to in vitro recreation.[76]

After the opening title, two further intertitles follow, which is in keeping with the tendency in popular-science films to recreate the illustrated lecture format. Indeed, Lefebvre notes how intertitles provide meanings for "ambiguous images."[77] As we will see in *Le Scorpion Languedocien*, however, there is often a gap between image and intertitle. As Mark-Paul Meyer has noted, in early nonfiction film "Image and text . . . continue pointedly to exist *alongside* one another."[78] The film's first images show a man wearing a suit and a hat turning over a rock and then using tweezers to collect and place some scorpions in a small box. A match-on-action cut to a closer shot of the man placing the scorpions into the box follows (Fig. 3.10). This action contains an incongruity. Fabre writes about the scorpions, "Excessively intolerant and passionate about their solitude, they are constantly alone in their shelters. In vain I have visited them, but it never occurred that I found two under the same rock; or, to be more precise, when there were two, one was in the process of eating the other."[79] Either the film has captured a moment so rare that it eluded Fabre in his months of observation, or the scene has been staged without concern for the details of Fabre's account. Perhaps the filmmakers thought two scorpions would be more interesting visually than a solitary scorpion, in any case, this discrepancy is an initial, minor example of how spectacle takes precedence over entomological accuracy.

The next shot of the film disrupts the spatial unity established in the prior two shots. While the first two shots take place outdoors, this shot, taken from directly overhead, seems to have been taken in a terrarium, since one of the scorpions repeatedly bumps into the left edge of the frame and cannot move beyond it. Additionally, this shot breaks with the logic of the scenario thus far presented; it is unrelated to the story of collection. In a similarly achronological way, the next shot, a medium close-up of a single scorpion, is seen from the side through the glass of a terrarium. The scorpion assumes an attack

FIG. 3.10 Picking up the second scorpion. Video still from *Le Scorpion Languedocien* (Éclair, October 1912). Cinémathèque de la Ville de Paris.

posture, raising its tail to a striking position. After this action, there is a camera stoppage, then the scorpion moves forward a little bit.

An opening scene of a scientist figure collecting samples is familiar, as is beginning with a sequence of the capture of the animals to be observed. These framing sequences are not simply scenes illustrating the intertitles; rather, they employ the same type of editing found in fictional films to create a coherent space, especially through match-on-action editing. The opening of *L'Ecrevisse* [The crayfish] (Éclair 1912), for example, contains two examples of a match-on-action cut, the first from a long shot to a close-up on the net being baited with cod, which is similar to the cut to a closer framing in *Le Scorpion Languedocien*. The second match-on-action is more remarkable since it knits together the exterior space of the initial shots with the aquarium in which the remainder of the action will take place (Fig. 3.11). This editing pattern enhances the believability of the ethological fiction that the observations are of animals in their natural habitats. It is also an example of the interpenetration of the techniques of fiction and nonfiction and qualifies the thesis that the style of the nonfiction film was stagnant.[80] Popular-science films, in other words, could create diegetic space similar to what was being established in fictional filmmaking of this period.

FIG. 3.11 A match-on-action cut. Video still from *L'Ecrevisse* (Éclair, June 1912). Cinémathèque de la Ville de Paris.

The third intertitle is a compressed paraphrase of Fabre's anatomical description of the scorpion's unusual head: "In the middle of this bizarre part that is the head and the stomach shine two very convex eyes."[81] Besides the unsurprising streamlining of Fabre's literary language to better fit the limitations of an intertitle, the film here follows Fabre's text relatively closely. This section of the film, which could be called the anatomization, occurs frequently in animal films, and the circular mask close-up, familiar from the lantern-slide tradition, is its signature composition. The anatomization continues with a masked close-up of the pincers and two separate close-ups of the tail, one full-frame image in which the tail curls into an attacking posture, and another masked close-up on the end of the tail, the stinger (Fig. 3.12). In this section, the distribution of the intertitles and shots is almost 1:1 (the exception being the two shots of the tail, where the second shot is a close-up of the "prismatic articulation"). This section of the film most closely resembles an illustrated lecture, and it is the section that holds most closely to Fabre's text.

The rest of the film is devoted to depictions of scorpion behavior. This section departs from Fabre's account, which is ironic since his reputation is due to his observations of behavior, not his contributions to the study of insect morphology. Indeed, at the beginning of the scorpion chapters, Fabre

FIG. 3.12 Detail of the scorpion's sting. Video still from *Le Scorpion Languedocien* (Éclair, 1912). Cinémathèque de la Ville de Paris

criticizes the focus on anatomy: "Disemboweled after being steeped in alcohol, it is quite well known; acting in the domain of its instincts, it is almost unknown."[82] However, what a spectator of the film learns about the instincts of the scorpion is questionable.

The next intertitle reads, "Friend of the darkness, deploying its pincers and its tail, it clears a space under the rocks to escape the heat of the sun," which describes the behavior that follows and corresponds to Fabre's observations, although, again, there are multiple scorpions in the shot. One scorpion performs the burrowing action described in the intertitle when another scorpion appears in the frame from screen right; an interruptive cut follows, and then the two scorpions seem to chase each other offscreen to the right. The appearance of the second scorpion is unexpected given the preceding intertitle. Why this second scorpion? It may be another instance, as in the first scene, of livening up the action by introducing more animals. Perhaps the filmmakers felt that more scorpions were necessary to make the film more exciting. Another possibility is that the shot may anticipate the information contained in the next intertitle, which reads, "Not social, it evicts the unfortunate [le fâcheux] that comes to trouble its solitude." The shots that follow this intertitle all illustrate this proposition, but with a degree of equivocation.

In the first shot, one scorpion is already installed under a rock. Another scorpion enters from the right of the frame and also seeks refuge under the rock. Then a camera stoppage occurs, and the "intruder" leaves. It is, of course, impossible to say what has happened during the ellipsis, although a plausible explanation is that there was simply too much "dead time" between the moment that the second scorpion entered the space under the rock and the moment when it was expelled.[83] After this initial compromise, the next shot depicts exactly the behavior the intertitle describes—the second scorpion approaches and then immediately leaves the frame after sensing the presence of the other scorpion under the rock. However, there are two further shots in this sequence (and the transition to both shots, as before, is a cut or perhaps just a camera stoppage). In the third shot, a scorpion is clearing a small rock from the entrance to the space under the larger rock (the small rock was not present in the prior shots). Another scorpion approaches and, in contrast to the previous two "intruders," does not seem at all inclined to leave. In fact, this intruder seems bent on ousting the prior scorpion, but the action is halted abruptly via another cut that introduces a completely different kind of insect into the film, a large black beetle, possibly from the set of Les Carabes, auxiliaries du cultivateur (Éclair, November 1913). It enters the frame from the right and tries to find a place underneath the rock as well, but when it senses the scorpion, it makes a quick exit, in part climbing up the glass wall of the terrarium, which makes the glass visible for a moment (this type of event, a functional equivalent for the returned gaze in the travelogue or industrial film, occurs with some frequency in popular-science films).

The behaviors in this sequence repeat an activity described in the preceding intertitle, but with varying degrees of fidelity.

The next intertitle reads, "They leave their dens at night, the encounters giving way to playful fights (*luttes amicales*)." Fabre mentions these playful fights as well, but situates them in the context of courtship rituals, an issue that the film occludes. The shots of "playful fights" depict behaviors that Fabre describes. But they are problematic for a number of reasons: One is that Fabre's observations took place at night, which was technically not feasible for the Scientia team. Second, Fabre's accounts were the result of hours if not days of careful observation. The film provides scenes where animals are thrown together in situations that seem like the "playful fights" that Fabre describes, but they also demonstrate a degree of inauthenticity, whether because of a lack of patience on the part of the filmmakers or perhaps as a result of production schedule pressures. In the first two shots of the sequence, the action between the two scorpions appears to involve nothing more than a quick encounter and separation, as both animals rush out of the frame in different directions. In the third shot of the sequence, there is indeed a behavior that could be described as a "playful fight," as two scorpions engage each other by rubbing their tails. Following Fabre's description, however, this example of playfulness is not a fight so much as a euphemism for the mating dance (Fig. 3.13).

FIG. 3.13 A "friendly fight." Video still from *Le Scorpion Languedocien* (Éclair, October 1912). Cinémathèque de la Ville de Paris.

A climactic battle as a finale is a common occurrence in these films.[84] The following quotation describes the concluding struggle in *Le Dytique* (Éclair, September 1912):

> What are a water beetle and a newt to us? At first glance, nothing. An insect like any other, an amphibian without further interest. However, should a waiting Cinematograph be able to surprise them, once projected on screen, the interest and emotion win us over and increase prodigiously. Here are two characters: the water beetle, carnivorous insect, clad like a medieval warrior and terribly armed; the newt, graceful and harmless. A drama unites them in a fight to the death. The one attacks, the other defends itself.
>
> At this point, not only the imagination but also the sight of such real suffering become of the greatest interest. And those spectators laughing a little while ago at an epileptically comic spectacle become suddenly serious and are soon gasping in distress before the horrible feast that takes place before them.
>
> However, the dramatic element should not constitute the sole interest. That is only the immediate dynamic effect. The result of that would be more harmful than useful. In this popularization the artist as well as the thinker, the comedian as well as the scientist, find their due, and this enlargement of the conception of cinematography must be the object of deeper study whose resources are infinite.[85]

The rhetoric of animals caught unawares by the gaze of the camera is responsible for the initial "nothing" being transformed into "interest and emotion" that increases "prodigiously." The prodigy here, a word that Maurice uses repeatedly, indicates the transformation of the animals into two characters by their representation on the screen, the metamorphosis of a water beetle and a newt into a medieval warrior, terribly armed, and a graceful and harmless innocent. Equally striking in this passage is the lack of conviction conveyed by the final gesture. All the drama that has been evoked is only "the immediate dynamic effect," but the passage's rhetorical energy is invested in precisely the process that Maurice tries to qualify as "more harmful than useful."

The final two scenes of *Le Scorpion Languedocien* represent two battles, first an attempt to recreate a battle that Fabre observed (and instigated) between the scorpion and the millipede, and the other a staging by the Scientia team of a battle between a scorpion and a rat, presumably because the Fabre-inspired battle did not prove spectacular enough. The appeal of the millipede battle is evident in Fabre's description: "I have seen many entomological battles; I know of none that are more horrible than that between these two monstrosities. It gives you goose bumps."[86] The scene actually captured in the film, however, falls considerably short of providing the creeps that Fabre mentions. An echo from Fabre's text returns in the intertitle that introduces the failed battle with the millipede: "The tail arched, the pincers open, the scorpion is ready to receive the powerful millipede (*scolopendre*) with venomous spikes that refuses to fight and flees."[87] The scene is, in fact, one of the shortest in the film, consisting of a single shot without stoppages.

The encounter between the scorpion and the rat provides a prime example of the more unsettling aspects of popular-science films. An intertitle introduces the scene: "What lightning rapidity and what virtuosity in the attack! Despite its fury, even the rat succumbs to its blows." The images that follow, however, tell a different story, one rather more filled with pathos and cruelty than "virtuosity" and "fury." The rat sits at the bottom left corner of the frame. The scorpion appears from the right side of the frame and heads in the rat's general direction. The rat seems oddly subdued, almost asleep, but the scorpion, after turning around once on the way to the rat, strikes at it without hesitation (Fig. 3.14). At first the rat occupies itself with the shock and pain of the sting (it has been stung in the face), and rubs its snout with both paws. The scorpion, meanwhile, continues to attack the rat, striking numerous times. After a number of further stings, the rat grabs the scorpion in its paws and attempts to bite it, but drops it, apparently after being stung even more. Then there is an interruptive cut to a point when the venom has begun to affect the rat, which digs jerkily in the sand. Following this scene, the film's final intertitle appears, "A few hours later."[88] The

FIG. 3.14 Rat meets scorpion. Video still from *Le Scorpion Languedocien* (Éclair, October 1912). Cinémathèque de la Ville de Paris

film's final scene shows the rat in its death throes, and the scorpion wandering over to inspect the rat. Some animals may have been more cooperative than the scorpion, but the tendency toward overt manipulation, especially through camera stoppages, is a recurring feature of popular-science films.

There is a gap here between the rhetoric of the intertitle, whose anthropomorphizing brio transforms the rat and the scorpion into characters in a

FIG. 3.15 "If some intruding hand takes them from their element where they reside, their fragility is such that they break." Video stills from *Les Animaux transparents de la mer* (Éclair?, 1920?). Cinémathèque de la Ville de Paris.

melodrama, and the dubious spectacle of a rat being placed in a position to be stung to death by an animal that it would normally avoid. In this sense, *Le Scorpion Languedocien* belongs to the tradition of animal fight films, a few examples of which are *Fight between Spider and Scorpion* (Biograph, 1900) and *Een Strijd tusschen wilde dieren* ["A Fight between Wild Animals"] (Kalem, 1912). In the latter case, which features a bull and a tiger, what might seem a fair fight is, in fact, a terrible mismatch that is decided after the bull's initial charge, after which the tiger desperately and unsuccessfully seeks refuge for the rest of the film.

In *Les Animaux transparents de la mer* (Éclair?, 192?), a hand enters the frame to remove a transparent sea creature from its aquarium (Fig. 3.15). An intertitle explains, "If some intruding hand takes them from their element where they reside, their fragility is such that they break." In popular-science films, hands frequently appear in the image, poking, prodding, manipulating, breaking, dissecting, and marking the distance between this mode of scientific cinema and other practices. These hands can function as an emblem of popular-science cinema's embrace of the cultures of demonstration and scientific showmanship.

Popular-Science Films and the Program Format

The primary way a spectator would have seen a popular-science film in France in the early 1910s was as a part of a program. The program format designates the mode of exhibition that was predominant from the beginnings of cinema until the early 1920s, where short films were combined to create an evening's entertainment.[89] There were, of course, many different types of programs during this period, which could range from the Urbanora shows at the Alhambra; to the mix of genres that characterized a nickelodeon show, where comedies and dramas would alternate with nonfiction films, especially travelogues, but also actualities, newsreels, popular-science films, and sports films; to parascholastic programs organized by a religious or educational organization, and often accompanied by a lecturer, that would contain comedies and dramas but whose primary emphasis was on the nonfictional components of the program.

Lefebvre explains the position that popular-science films tended to occupy in French programs during the early 1910s:

> The majority of the large halls in effect adopted a tripartite structure for their screenings. The first block is linked to what we can term the archaic tradition of cinema: centered on monstration and specifically designed for the attention of children, it was composed of "curiosities," short burlesques and "instructive films." The second block was generally assembled around a comedy and a short drama, to which was attached a weekly actuality film. As for the final part, it was dedicated to a longer film, generally a drama, which could last up to half-an-hour, sometimes a little longer.[90]

This type of program cordons off the popular-science film from the surrounding films, aligning it with child spectators and the cinema of attractions. In other configurations, popular-science films might appear in the middle of a show, following a comedy and preceding a drama, and therefore the potential for interaction with the contingent films could be more pronounced.[91] Of course, direct contiguity is not the only way viewers could make connections; a film in an early part of the program might just as easily resonate with a film screened later.

The watchword of the program format, in any case, was variety. When viewed in succession, films could affect one another, and these coincidences could be intentional or a matter of chance. As Yuri Tsivian has remarked, "Before then [mid-1910s] the text of cinema was still largely perceived as a potentially endless series of randomly juxtaposed units with blurred boundaries between them."[92] Although there were instances where this proximity of diverse films led to problems (Tsivian notes criticism of how newsreels of the royal family were exhibited in Imperial Russia, which led to strict rules about how such films could be shown), these sorts of situations were unusual. The instances of what Tsivian calls "cultural incompatibility" were not sufficiently problematic to put an end to the program format.

One reason for the persistence of the program format was the acceptance of similar forms of variety programming in other media. Vaudeville was not, after all, the only model for the program format.[93] Other cultural forms provided models for how the cinema program's mix of fiction and nonfiction functioned. The illustrated magazine was one source of the taste for juxtaposition that the program format served. As Ian Christie has noted, "the contents of any issue of *The Strand Magazine* in the mid-1890s read remarkably like a film program of the decade to come, in which adventure fiction, travel and scientific reports would be increasingly fully realised, while the magazine's graphic satire and humour trade in exactly the same anecdotal currency as early 'made-up' films."[94] The organization of *La Nature* and *Je Sais Tout* provides models for how popular-science films functioned in the program format. *La Nature* provided a high-minded vision of popular-science cinema. *La Nature*'s sober tone, its devotion to a single type of article, and its lack of color illustrations all mark its difference from the more entertainment-oriented content of *Je Sais Tout*. As much as *La Nature* may represent the type of public discourse about science that popular-science films aspired to emulate, a glance at issues of *Je Sais Tout* from the era before World War I establishes that magazine as more similar to the program format in terms of its range of contents. Delmeulle notes, "Such projects [as the Gaumont encyclopedia] inscribe themselves, more or less consciously, in a perspective of a democratization of knowledge and the illusory domestication of global learning. This is, for example, the era where a magazine like *Je Sais Tout*, the 'major magazine for scientific popularization' (but also technology and economics) founded in 1906, could flourish."[95] *Je Sais Tout* contains the mix of fiction and nonfiction that characterizes the program format, with profiles of heads of state or members of royal families and accounts of current events that resemble newsreels, comic stories and cartoons, and such popular-science content as an article on the "conflagrations of the heavens" by Camille Flammarion occasioned by the approach of Halley's comet, or an article on Dr. Doyen's microscopic research, illustrated with color plates.[96]

Another staple of *Je Sais Tout* was serialized fiction by such authors as Arthur Conan Doyle and Maurice Leblanc. As the final chapter will argue in more detail, the cinema serial offers an experience that is similar to the program format, combining drama, comedy, and documentary moments. Part of the reason for the rise of the multireel film in the early 1910s in France was its ability to continue to provide the experience of variety that the program format offered, and the presence of popular-science moments in the serial film was an important aspect of this continued appeal. The familiar mode of address that encompassed both education and amusement foreshadowed the two major ways popular science was incorporated into the feature film—as an explanatory sequence and as a special effect.

The persistence of the program format also emerges more prominently when we consider the skeptical reaction to the introduction of longer films, or, as Georges Dureau dubbed them, *films kilométriques*: "I do not believe that the use of these films will become a general condition, and I think that cinematographic shows are essentially short shows [*des spectacles coupés*] whose appeal is constituted by diversity."[97] As a contemporary exhibitor commented:

> A view of 900 meters makes a program unbalanced. We must not forget, and all exhibitors know this, that the public demands a variety of views: according to the town, ten, twelve, or fourteen views are required, which means 1800, 2000, or 2200 meters of film. If you introduce a single film of 800 to 900 meters, for example, there remains no more than the insignificant amount of 1000 meters to show the week's actualities, the sensational drama, the bare necessities, and the indispensable comedies, without counting the *féerie*, dear to children, who enliven a show, and the scientific or instructive view.[98]

The introduction of the multireel film implied a change in the audience's relation to the film show. The audience for the program format was one that "enters and exits during the show"; "Our usual spectators are people who go to the cinema just because they are passing by, in order to experience, in one hour, diverse emotions and the rapid satisfaction of their curiosity."[99] Exhibitors were concerned that longer films would exhaust their patrons' attention. The multireel film did catch on quickly, however, so audiences not only were willing and able to pay attention to longer narratives but also did not find the multireel lacking in variety. One reason for the acceptance of the multireel film was that instead of providing an entirely new experience, features incorporated key aspects of the variety program.

The rise of the feature film often is associated with the decline of the cinema of attractions. As the cinema's monstrative abilities were yoked increasingly to the purposes of narrative, popular-science films, with their emphasis on display and demonstration, might be expected to wane or even disappear. As Ben Singer suggests, however, "classical narration amplified the stimulating capacity of attractions by endowing them with strong dramatic and emotional significance."[100] To expand this argument, narrative and attractions can enhance one another not only in terms of drama and emotional impact but also in terms of the nonfiction film's appeals. And indeed, popular-science films did not decline over the course of the 1910s but proliferated. One story of this proliferation involves the development of presentational strategies that led to the institutionalization of the educational film, the medical film, and the industrial film. On the other hand, however, popular-science films also contributed to the various pleasures of the multireel fiction film. As the last section of this chapter has indicated, the confluence of entertainment and instruction that characterizes popular-science films recurred in how the films fit into an entertainment program. This understanding of popular-science films not as self-contained units but as combinable modules provides a model for discerning a similarity with how popular-science moments functioned in narrative feature films.

Gaumont's *Encyclopédie* project provided an example of how popular-science films circulated in a manner distinct from fiction films. The final chapters consider two other forms of circulation: George Kleine's collection of nonfiction films and the circulation of popular-science moments in the serial films of Louis Feuillade. The idea of a film collection that would function as a pedagogical repository followed along a path of making cinema an ideal modern educator that had been plotted by Urban and Gaumont. Kleine envisioned a storehouse of educational moving pictures that would allow for knowledge to circulate in a novel form. The transit of popular-science moments into fiction films, by contrast, requires a conceptualization of the boundaries between fiction and nonfiction as porous, whereby the fantastical exploits of scientific supercriminals contain documentary elements.

{ Chapter 4 }

A Modern Cabinet of Curiosities: George Kleine's Collection of Popular-Science Films

The future has an ancient heart.

−CARLO LEVI

Louella Parsons remembered George Kleine in 1923 with an analogy: "George Kleine in the old days was to the motion picture industry what John D. Rockefeller is to Standard Oil."[1] Unlike the billionaire industrialist, however, Kleine has not remained a household name. His reputation has dwindled even within cinema history; if he is remembered at all, it is for distributing Italian epics in the early 1910s (*Quo Vadis*, *Othello*, *The Last Days of Pompeii*) and for negotiating between Edison and American Mutoscope and Biograph in the patent wars that led to the establishment of the Motion Picture Patents Company.[2]

Part of the reason for Kleine's neglect can be gleaned from another part of Parsons' encomium: "He was a conservative, one of the pioneers who had joined hands with Thomas Edison to help make the motion picture recognized as a universal form of entertainment." It is unsurprising that a fixture of the Hollywood publicity apparatus characterized the bond between Kleine and Edison as having made the motion picture into "a universal form of entertainment." While the pairing of the two men is apt, it is misleading to compare them on the grounds of their contributions to the development of Hollywood cinema. In fact, the rise of Hollywood and the concomitant understanding of cinema as "harmless entertainment" relegated Kleine's vision of motion pictures to what Christian Metz termed the medium's "border regions."[3] Kleine's most significant contribution to cinema history lay not in his involvement with entertainment cinema but rather in his consistent attempts to establish another form of cinema, which he termed "educational."

Parsons' description of Kleine as a "conservative" also should be modified in another sense, for Kleine's approach to cinema incorporated a mixture of radicalism and conservatism peculiar to progressivism.[4] While certainly a representative of the status quo in many ways, he nonetheless championed a reformist agenda for the use of motion pictures in education. This advocacy for the cinema as an educative medium aligns Kleine with Charles Urban and Léon Gaumont, for whom, not coincidentally, Kleine was the sole U.S. distributor. Kleine's interest in and efforts toward making the cinema into an educational device have remained obscure even though they constituted a major part of his career and formed the centerpiece of his vision for the future of cinema.[5] Kleine's interest in cinema's ability to educate gave a prominent role to popular-science films.

Popular-science films drew from a wide variety of nineteenth-century sources for visual strategies and content, including lantern-slide culture, as in *The Unseen World*, or written sources, as in Éclair's reliance on Jean-Henri Fabre's entomological writings. Popular-science films also tapped into traditions that extended beyond the latter half of the nineteenth century. Kleine's educational-film catalogue provides an example of popular-science films' relationship to earlier display practices, in particular cabinets of curiosity. This chapter's underlying assertion is that popular-science films drew on both contemporary contexts and more venerable traditions.

Centuries separate cabinets of curiosities and Kleine's catalogue, during which time the display traditions involving education and entertainment underwent many changes. Emphasizing the similarities between Kleine's catalogue and cabinets of curiosity is not meant to discount the developments of the intervening centuries, most notably the development of the museum.[6] Clearly there are important differences between the individual, private collections of Renaissance gentlemen and national, public collections of the predominately nineteenth-century institutions that embody the modern image of the museum. In many ways, nineteenth-century traditions can account for the form and content of Kleine's catalogue. For example, P. T. Barnum's American Museum is an important precursor to Kleine's collection, as are other spaces of display, including world's expositions, amusement parks, freak shows, medical amphitheaters, zoological and botanical gardens, Chautauquas, and physiological demonstration halls.[7]

The aim of insisting on links to the cabinet tradition is to highlight overarching continuities, and particularly to emphasize the incomplete hegemony of certain modern epistemological formations, most prominently scientific objectivity. Accounts of the cabinets of curiosities trace their demise to the Enlightenment's replacement of a taste for the bizarre with the dispassionate investigation of the normal.[8] The wonder generated by the cabinet came to be seen as inimical to rational inquiry, and the inheritors of the cabinet, particularly the museum, would increasingly eschew the cabinet's proclivity for the curious.

The cabinet's particular constellation of affect, where rationality and enchantment stood in a complementary relationship to one another, does not vanish, however. While no longer the cultural dominant, this aesthetic of curiosity persisted.[9] In a number of ways—the centrality of the collecting impulse, organizational logic, the importance of certain genres (i.e., travel), and the centrality of wonder and curiosity—Kleine's catalogue tapped into a "cabinet culture" display tradition that emphasized variety and novelty, curiosity and wonder. Dubbing Kleine's catalogue a *modern* cabinet points to its mixture of the rational and the wondrous while also indicating that a central feature of the catalogue's appeal was how the films it contained updated the technological basis for these effects.

Gathering Fragments for a Cinema of the Future

In April 1910 Kleine released his first *Catalogue of Educational Motion Pictures*. The scope of Kleine's catalogue was considerable; it ran to 336 pages and contained over a thousand titles. Taken simply as a list of nonfiction titles produced before 1910, the catalogue constitutes a valuable source of information, but it provides much more than a list of titles. Early catalogues also can "provide important evidence about the social and cultural attitudes prevalent in American society at the turn of the century."[10] A more or less detailed description accompanied each title, usually, if not always, taken directly from the producers' catalogues.[11]

While these descriptions make up the majority of the catalogue, it contained three other significant components. The front cover functioned as an emblem for the entire project, creating an iconographic précis of Kleine's educational venture. An introductory section contained a number of texts that set out the catalogue's aims and procedures, constituting a kind of preface whose message had as much to do with its form as its content. At the end of the catalogue, several indexes showed how Kleine sought to organize the catalogue's disparity; his categories constituted a working system of nonfiction genres circa 1910.

The catalogue boasted high production values, which were nowhere more evident than in its color cover that encapsulated the project's ethos[12] (Fig. 4.1). The Latin motto "*disce videndo*" presented a didactic imperative: "learn by seeing." This exhortation contained two, somewhat contradictory, facets. The fact that the message was in Latin aligned it with a traditional conception of education that privileged classical philology. The content of the statement, however, represented a more modern line of thought about the importance of the senses, especially vision, in education. In terms of the history of education, these two discourses were frequently antagonistic; visual education's rhetoric often targeted textually centered philological methods associated with the teaching of Latin and Greek.[13]

FIG. 4.1 Cover of *Catalogue of Educational Motion Pictures* (1910). Billy Rose Theatre Division, The New York Library for the Performing Arts, Lenox and Tilden Foundations

This unresolved tension between the old and the new was typical of Kleine's approach. The image's outer frame, formed by Ionic columns and amphorae placed in niches, also participates in a duality that mobilizes aspects of the classical as well as the modern. These architectural references suggest a kinship between the catalogue's project to collect knowledge and the nineteenth-century boom in museums and libraries, sites characterized by precisely this kind of neoclassicism. More proximately, the image references the architectural idiom of the American Renaissance, which found a prominent venue in nineteenth-century expositions, beginning with the Philadelphia Centennial Exposition of 1876 and reaching a pinnacle in the Chicago Columbian Exposition of 1893. The Chicago exposition's gigantic temples to progress, such as Machinery Hall, provided an excellent example of the style's mixture of classical allusions (Greek democracy, Roman law, Renaissance humanism) and embrace of modernity (plaster-of-Paris construction illuminated by electric lights). The catalogue's edifice forged an iconographic link to this institutionalization of culture that installed erudition as a cornerstone of a novel American identity.[14]

The green velvet curtains that form a second frame inside the image's neoclassical proscenium invoke a theatrical tradition, suggesting a conception of education linked to certain affective appeals, an educational experience that involved a degree of showmanship. The image of the waterfall that forms the centerpiece of this mise-en-scène is probably taken from one of the catalogue's travelogues, possibly of Niagara Falls. It participates in the picturesque tradition of visualizing nature that frequently was conscripted by educational rhetoric.[15] The waterfall is also a natural occurrence whose essence involves movement, which constitutes a specific appeal to cinema's verisimilitude illusion. The image at the heart of the catalogue's cover is part of a nineteenth-century tradition that extolled the virtues of sightseeing, as embodied by the phenomenon of the picture postcard, while also invoking the novelty of the cinema's ability to present such images in a new way by bringing them to life.

The assortment of national flags from France, Switzerland, Great Britain, and Italy emphasized the catalogue's internationalism, which was embodied by the considerable number of travel films, while the prominence of the American flag in the center of this cluster indicates an integrationist logic at work, with America as the hegemon or perhaps the container of various national identities. The ribbons spiraling up the columns inscribed with the names of various branches of knowledge resemble subject headings in an encyclopedia and suggest a systematic organization underlying the project. Finally, the image also resembles the stage of a school auditorium or a town meeting hall, and could thus be seen as an attempt to visualize a scene in which this new educational cinema would be deployed.

As the cover image indicates, the catalogue had a tendency toward syncretism that allowed it to appear both ahead of its time, a precursor to an educational cinema movement that flourished beginning in the early 1920s, and outmoded, both in terms of its system of distribution and its positioning versus the mainstream entertainment cinema. Individual aspects of this introductory image—the appeals to classicism and internationalism, its foregrounding of movement, and the showman's gesture of the revelatory curtain—will return in more detailed discussions of other aspects of the catalogue. Ultimately, however, the cover image created an edifice for a monumental ambition, emblematizing the catalogue's aspirations for a grand launch of a new era of cinema culture. The catalogue was at once commemorative and anticipatory, archival and futuristic. By gathering the remains of the first fifteen years of nonfiction cinema history, it necessarily reflected on the past while elaborating a vision of a cinema to come. In this sense, the catalogue functioned as a hinge, a collection of fragments in the service of its vision of the educative cinema of the future, which did not yet exist but that it would help create.

Whereas the cover image provides an iconographic announcement of Kleine's aims, the catalogue's opening pages contain a series of texts that make verbal arguments for cinema as an educational medium. The first text, "Plan and Scope," supplies an initial rationale for the use of motion pictures in education:

> The plan and scope of a work of this kind is not sharply defined. In a sense, all subjects are educational, but in classifying a mass of motion picture films for educational purposes the line must be drawn about a reasonable area. A dramatic or comic tale in motion pictures, laid in some foreign country, is educational in so far as it shows the manners, customs and environment of the people; an Indian tale, the habits of the aborigines. But there must be a halt before we reach fanciful ground, where there is danger of accuracy being sacrificed to dramatic effect. Here and there a subject has been included in this list which lies on the border, and perhaps outside of it. But there is an educational application in every instance. The word "Educational" is here used in a wide sense, and does not indicate that these films are intended for school or college use exclusively. They are intended rather for the education of the adult as well as the youth, for exhibition before miscellaneous audiences, as well as for more restricted use.[16]

The fundamental problem of classification with which Kleine begins vacillates between two basic propositions—on the one hand, that all motion pictures are educational, a widespread idea in the years of cinema's emergence; and on the other hand, the acknowledgment of a border, however vague, beyond which any appeal to the educational must appear "fanciful," where "accuracy" is "sacrificed to dramatic effect."[17] And yet, where a film in the catalogue might be seen as having crossed the line and departed educational territory, Kleine insists, "there is an educational application in every instance." This uncertainty about how, exactly, to recognize an educational film recurs in the discussion of audience. Kleine claims that the films are not for school or college use exclusively and are therefore suitable for "miscellaneous audiences," while later allowing that they are appropriate for "more restricted uses" as well.

One way to understand this imprecision is as a function of the vast number of films included in the catalogue; while some were indeed appropriate for more specialized audiences, such as the surgical films, most of them were pitched to general audiences.[18] Alternately, however, while this wavering definition of the educational field might seem a weakness born out of either imprecise thinking or an economic strategy that sought to include as many films as possible in the new market segment, it is a precise description of a protean object. In other words, Kleine's uncertainty about how to define an educational film attests to unsettled definitional protocols, which would begin to be formulated in a systematic way only in the early 1920s.

The discourse of visual education, already indicated by the cover's motto of "learn by seeing," made numerous appearances in the catalogue's prefatory materials. A brief statement entitled "An Educational System by Visualization" contained the following sentence: "[T]he public mind, and especially that part which is concerned with the development of the immature intellect, is awakening to the value of motography as an educational force."[19] This "awakening" referred to the various strands of Progressive culture that sought to provide "uplift," and that the catalogue explicitly addressed: "Progressive educators will welcome this opportunity to instruct their classes in any of the above subjects by means of first-class motion pictures."[20] Education figured prominently in these movements, and Kleine's invocation of "the immature intellect" was an indication of how the uplift movements saw cinema's "impressionable" audiences, usually understood as women, children, and immigrants, as the primary recipients for the new cinema's educational message. Ben Singer writes that the catalogue was "one indication of the transformation of attitudes toward the medium," and he characterizes this transformation as "a specific watershed moment in the socio-economic vicissitudes of the film medium," involving a shift in social status of the cinema as uplift movements attempted to remake the medium in the image of middle-class respectability.[21]

This understanding of cinema was allied with the advocacy of sensory experience in education. A prominent articulation of this discourse was the notion of the object lesson, which came from the theories of Johann Heinrich Pestalozzi, a Swiss educator and educational reformer. Influenced by his reading of Jean-Jacques Rousseau's *Émile* (1762), Pestalozzi believed in the primacy of sensation, which led him to emphasize the importance of studying actual objects as an initial step in learning. He reversed the traditional importance accorded to the teacher's lecture, arguing that direct concrete perception should precede verbal description. Only after an initial encounter with the object was the student encouraged to name it and identify its characteristics, such as its form.[22]

In the United States, Pestalozzi's ideas began to find a small audience by the 1820s, and they were popularized in the 1860s by Edward Sheldon's object-lesson plan (the "Oswego plan") and Francis W. Parker, whose "Quincy methods" included such natural-history lessons as taking field trips and planting seeds (leading some parents to complain that he had turned schools into "mud-pie factories").[23] Some schools created "object lesson boxes," repositories of everyday objects such as plants and mineral specimens with which students could interact directly.

In its popularized form, this educational movement represented an attempt to organize the curriculum according to what its proponents saw as the natural laws of human development. An ancient hierarchy of the senses placed vision above hearing, touch, taste, and smell. Since vision was seen, so to speak, as more intuitive than other means of instruction, it presented an invaluable and primary resource for educators, and the cinema's obvious visual appeals allowed it to fit neatly into arguments for "education by the eye." Visual learning via the newest technology was thus both efficient and modern. As the catalogue put it, "Education thus imparted is never likely to be forgotten, and pupils who are slow in memorizing text-book instruction absorb the same knowledge very readily and rapidly when conveyed by moving pictures, which teach as no words do."[24]

Visual learning was frequently opposed to "dry" book learning; this term was used as shorthand to refer to traditional approaches to pedagogy that involved book learning, rote drills, and memorization. The antonym for "dry" varied, although "vivid" was frequently used to distinguish visual education's special appeals. Herbert Spencer, for example, wrote that child-centered and self-directed learning methods lead to a "vividness and permanency of impression which the usual methods can never produce. Any piece of knowledge which the pupil has himself acquired, any problem which he has himself solved, becomes by virtue of the conquest much more thoroughly his than it could else be."[25] The "vividness and permanency of impression" that "learning by doing" imparted carried over from the domain of educational theory into the work of promoting cinema as an educational tool. While advocates for educational cinema most likely had not studied educational theory, the frequency of the dry-versus-vivid comparison indicates that these ideas had become part of the turn-of-the-century vernacular. Not surprisingly, the catalogue invoked this concept as well: "We have endeavored to provide life-motion pictures in sequences which give the work of text-books without their dryness, and yet impart a knowledge which cannot be gained by mere reading."[26]

"The Personal Activity of a Discriminating Collector"

The words from Kleine's catalogue quoted above were copied nearly verbatim from Charles Urban's 1908 Urbanora catalogue.[27] While Kleine made a special effort to acknowledge Urban's contributions to his catalogue, writing that "especial mention must be made of the work of Mr. Chas. Urban, whose unceasing efforts of the last ten years have been largely responsible for the motion picture films which are now at the disposal of educators," he was indebted to Urban in more immediate and material ways.[28] All of the film descriptions for Urban's films were taken verbatim from Urban's catalogues, a fact that seemed to displease Urban.[29] An Urban employee, Thomas Clegg, wrote a critical letter regarding Kleine's catalogue that appeared in a number of trade publications.[30] In a letter to Charles Rogers, the head of the French production company Eclipse, Kleine complained, "A vicious attack has been made upon me personally practically accusing me of stealing Mr. Urban's thunder. . . . I have seen a rather vicious article which was sent by a man named Clegg to an American trade paper."[31] Rogers' reply was entirely sympathetic to Kleine: "It is true that the description was done in great part by Mr. Clegg while in our employment, but during that time he was largely remunerated and his work was never considered a work of literature but a sensible description of our films, and I cannot understand the reasons of Mr. Clegg making this attack on you and indirectly attacking our mutual interests."[32] Kleine's response to Urban also emphasized the commercial nature of the catalogue descriptions: "In putting out the Educational catalogue we had in view the furtherance of the sale of films. This was looked upon as an ordinary commercial catalogue and not as a literary proposition."[33]

This incident can be characterized as a passing antagonism between two otherwise like-minded collaborators, a minor kerfuffle occasioned by Kleine's overzealous and somewhat injudicious use of Urban's catalogue texts. It does, however, raise a larger issue. As the opposition between the literary and the commercial introduced here indicates, this altercation involved the boundary between the cultural and the commercial. Urban wanted his films to remain recognizably his, whereas Kleine saw the catalogue blurbs as a generic, unauthored form of commercial description. As Kleine's mention that there is something "philanthropic" about the educational catalogue indicates, his endeavor seems indebted to an understanding of the knowledge that the films in his catalogue represent as free and public.[34]

Similarly, the assembly of other texts in the catalogue's introduction is not the activity of an author who seeks to transform disparate materials into a coherent, seamless product. Instead, the materials marshaled there indicate a collector's mindset, and, indeed, Kleine repeatedly referred to the catalogue as a "compilation."[35] The catalogue's prefatory pages contain a variegated collection of texts: a facsimile letter from Thomas Edison commenting favorably on page proofs of the catalogue; a reprint of Frederick Starr's article "The World before Your Eyes"; a page entitled "An Educational System by Visualization" that is signed and dated by Kleine, although it contains large chunks of text copied from the Urbanora catalogue; and a page entitled "Description of Educational Films," which also was copied directly from the Urbanora catalogue.[36] Over half of the first nine pages of the catalogue explicitly come from other sources, and half of the texts seemingly written by Kleine contain, to a greater or lesser degree, significant portions copied from Urban's catalogues.[37]

Cut and pasted into the first page of one copy of the catalogue was the sentence, "This is the first catalogue of educational motion pictures ever published."[38] This claim, a further example of Kleine's cut-and-paste aesthetic, places a misleading emphasis on the catalogue's priority, both in the sense that it is patently incorrect (Urban's Urbanora catalogue appeared in 1908) and in the sense that it tends to obscure continuities with previous display traditions. While the catalogue represents an early instance of visions of cinema as a modern educator, it also belongs to a longer tradition of instructive amusement. In the same way that the history of cinema is part of a history of screen practice that reaches back into the seventeenth century, so, too, the early educational cinema is part of a longer history of display practices.[39] The catalogue's similarities to cabinets of curiosities indicate the persistence of certain kinds of affect and traditions in the display of knowledge about nature. These similarities are divided between two levels. First, the catalogue as a whole resembled a cabinet, particularly in how it was assembled, its organizational logic, and its emphasis on certain categories of knowledge. Second, individual films also resembled individual cabinet objects, especially in their reliance on the affective appeal of wonder.

The cabinet of curiosities originated in the sixteenth century, developing on the one hand out of *Schatzkammern*, royal collections of treasures, and on the other hand from collections of apothecaries and naturalists.[40] These collections flourished in the first half of the seventeenth century and usually took the form of large rooms (Fig. 4.2). An initial similarity between the cabinet and Kleine's catalogue involves the method of acquisition. Kleine described how he assembled the films for the catalogue in the following terms:

> This collection is in no sense merely a commercial stock of moving pictures. It is comparable, rather, to a collection of rare books, paintings or etchings. Many of the negatives from which these subjects were printed are no longer in existence, making it impossible to replace the film should it be destroyed. The collection as a whole is the result, not of a sudden effort to acquire all the educational film possible, but of the personal activity of a discriminating collector, covering a period of a number of years. The subjects which make up this collection were selected with no thought as to the commercial value, but because they represented, educationally and artistically, the highest development in the art of making moving pictures.[41]

Affinities between Kleine's methods for building the catalogue and the cabinet tradition emerge here, beginning with the importance of the individual, idiosyncratic collecting impulse. By describing his practice as "the personal activity of a discriminating collector" Kleine recalls the tradition of the gentlemen collectors and early natural historians whose collecting habits constituted the core of the cabinet tradition. When Kleine asserts that his catalogue

FIG. 4.2 A cabinet of curiosities; frontispiece to Ole Worm, *Museum Wormianum seu historia rerum rariorum* (Leiden 1655).

contained only "the highest development in the art of making moving pictures," he evokes the *virtuosi* and their interest in the rare, expensive, and exotic.

Kleine's collector's mindset was in fact common among his contemporaries with an interest in early nonfiction. Despite Urban's irritation with the catalogue, his and Kleine's vision of what nonfiction film was and how it was to be used were similar. In particular, both men participated in the general tendency to recycle and repackage early nonfiction, which was treated as a more stable, reusable kind of material that did not age in the same way as fiction film.[42] Early nonfiction film did not display the same degree of stylistic innovation as fictional film, which might be construed as a lack of ingenuity or as an inherent conservatism.[43] Since nonfiction was less reliant on developments in editing and mise-en-scène that propelled the advancement of narrative style, its frame of reference was more stable, thanks in large part to its reliance on established, nineteenth-century demonstration cultures. As a result, a nonfiction film could be reused in ways that were inconceivable for a fictional film.[44] Indeed, this tendency toward recycling occurred with most significant collections of early nonfiction; Urban reused footage continually, and his last project, the "Living Book of Knowledge," drew heavily on his stock library;

Gaumont reissued the bulk of his nonfiction films from the 1910s in his encyclopedia of the 1920s; Pathé reissued the majority of their early nonfiction
titles in smaller formats (28mm, 9.5mm, Pathéscope). Similar practices took
place in other contexts, too, as in the pedagogical editing of existing nonfiction films undertaken at the Cinémathèque de la Ville de Paris.[45]

This tendency toward stability aligns these films with particular kinds of
knowledge production, which is usefully underscored by the British phrase,
"films of fact." Historians of science have detailed how the fact is historically contingent, and how its form—its tendency toward brevity, its seeming
authorlessness—allows it to circulate. The emergence of the modern fact
can be related to certain practices of reading, observation, and collecting,
which were visible in both the cabinets of curiosity and in other early
modern collections of knowledge such as the commonplace book.[46] Kleine's
assembly of the catalogue, both in terms of his textual practices and in
terms of his understanding of the kind of material the films themselves represented, recalls these earlier traditions.

The importance of travel is another similarity between the cabinets of curiosity and Kleine's catalogue. The cabinets were repositories for the unusual
materials that were being brought back from voyages to the New World,
housing objects that testified to the literal travels of Europeans who came into
contact with other civilizations, such as the mantle of Chief Powhatan, Poca-
hontas's father, which remains in the collection of the Ashmolean Museum in
Oxford, or the feather headdress of Montezuma now in the Museum of Ethnology in Vienna, which originally was part of the Habsburg collection.[47]
Travel facilitated and accelerated contact with unusual things. Indeed, the
category of anomaly and the interest in the unusual are prominent characteristics of cabinets. As one of the German terms for these collections, the *Wun-
derkammer*, indicates, the experience of seeing these materials incited wonder,
which is the reaction proper to troubled boundaries, primarily the boundary
between naturalia and artificialia, the cabinet's two major categories.

The cabinet also constituted a site of vicarious travel, providing a synoptic
view of the world, a world in miniature. This sense of the world in a box is
encapsulated by an alternate name for the cabinet as a *"teatrum mundi,"* a
theater of the world. In a later manifestation of this collecting impulse, called
the *Kunstkammer* or *Kunstschrank*, the collection or microcosm has shrunk
from the size of a room to the size of a large piece of furniture. The cabinets
were attempts to collect a representative sample of the world's knowledge in a
small space, to mirror the macrocosm in a microcosm. In their relation to
travel, the cabinets displayed two impulses: on the one hand, an emphasis on
the unusual, but on the other hand, an attempt to show all of human knowledge, all the wonders of creation.

An essay entitled "The World before Your Eyes" by Professor Frederick K.
Starr, an anthropologist at the University of Chicago, outlined how early

nonfiction cinema could be a form of travel. After a long paragraph in which Starr evoked scenes from locations as diverse as Niagara Falls, Australia, Europe, China, and Norway, he wrote, "and I didn't have to leave Chicago for a moment. No books have taught me all these wonderful things; no lecturer has pictured them; I simply dropped into a moving picture theater at various moments of leisure; and, at the total cost for all the visits of perhaps two performances of a foolish musical show, I have learned more than a traveler could see at the cost of thousands of dollars and years of journey."[48] The educational value of travel that underlay the cabinet's emphasis on voyages persisted as a major argument for the educational value of the early nonfiction film.[49] Travel was a predominant category in Kleine's catalogue; over 150 pages were devoted to travelogues.

A final category of resemblance between cabinets and Kleine's catalogue is related to organizational structure. A signature effect of the cabinets was an overwhelming profusion of items on display. The wealth of artifacts materialized the inquisitiveness that uncovered the unknown, whether geographical (the conquest of the New World) or visual (the views afforded by the telescope and the microscope).[50] This tendency toward spectacular display stood in contrast to the underlying attempts to order and classify the collections. As Daston and Park note, "The actual physical arrangement of many collections (in contrast to the more systematic classifications of catalogues and inventories) was often calculated to highlight . . . heterogeneity." The array of materials that could appear in a typical cabinet constituted a bewildering jumble of stuff: "coral, automata, unicorn horns, South American featherwork, coconut shell goblets, fossils, antique coins, turned ivory, monsters animal and human, Turkish weaponry, and polyhedral crystals."[51]

The catalogue demonstrates an inverse dynamic, whereby its veneer of order dissolves into the dazzling plenitude that typified the display spaces of the cabinet. The tenuousness of the attempts to organize the catalogue's miscellany is nowhere more evident than in its "Index to Subjects According to Classification," also called the "classified index." The main categories in the subject index—Agriculture, Allegorical, Applied Sciences, Aviation, Fine Arts, Fisheries, History, Military and Naval, Natural Sciences, Railways, Sports, Surgery, Travelogues—display a remarkable variance in their specificity. What, for instance, justifies the specificity of the categories "fisheries" and "surgery" versus the much broader categories "natural sciences" or "travelogues"? The subcategories make for an even more variegated mix of topics:

> Aeronautics (under Aviation); Apiculture (under Natural Sciences); Archeology (under History); Architecture (under Fine Arts); Army (under Military and Naval); Athletics (under Sports); Ballooning (under Aviation); Biology (under Natural Sciences); Bird Life (under Natural Sciences); Botany (under Agriculture); Chemistry (under Applied Sciences); Classics

(under Fine Arts); Dances (Civilized) (under Fine Arts); Dances (Barbaric) (under Travelogues); Entomology (under Natural Sciences); Ethnology (under Travelogues); Forestry (under Agriculture); Geography (under Travelogues and also Natural Sciences); Geology (under Natural Sciences); Hydraulics (under Applied Sciences); Hydrography (under Travelogues and Natural Sciences); Industrial (under Applied Sciences); Literary (under Fine Arts); Marine (under Travelogues); Mechanics (under Applied Sciences); Microscopy (under Natural and Applied Sciences); Mining (under Applied Sciences); Music (under Fine Arts); Mythology (under Allegorical); Natural History (under Natural Sciences); Optics (under Applied Sciences); Panoramic (under Travelogues); Patriotic (under Travelogues); Physics (under Applied Sciences); Pisciculture (under Fisheries); Physical Culture (under Sports); Political (under History); Religion (under History); Scenic (under Travelogues); Secret Societies (under History); Seismology (under Natural Sciences); Volcanoes (under Natural Sciences); Zoology (under Natural Sciences).[52]

This attempt to provide a comprehensive overview of the collection provokes not a sense of mastery but rather a host of questions. Where are the films about acoustics to go along with those about optics? Where are the films about astronomy to go along with those about microscopy? The answer to these questions and the many others that could arise here lies in a recognition of the fact that despite Kleine's gestures toward comprehensiveness, the collection was made up of films that were produced by numerous companies that had a variety of agendas, so there were simply no films to fill the aforementioned gaps.[53] In other words, despite gestures toward systematicity, the haphazard is a barely submerged characteristic of Kleine's collection.

Furthermore, the films themselves rendered attempts at categorization particularly difficult. An even more bewildering thicket of topics appears, in other words, at the moment the films are considered in terms of their specific content. For instance, the first rubric of the "classified index," "Agriculture," contains the film *Tulips*, which could just as easily be classified under "Natural Sciences." Beyond the issue of missing cross-references, some films simply fall outside of the given categories; *Tourists Riding Donkeys on the Banks of the Nile*, for instance, also is classed under the rubric of "Agriculture," but for no discernable reason.[54] Many more examples could be produced here, but suffice it to note that the catalogue's compilers were also aware of the unruliness of the films' content. The following warning was placed at the beginning of the general alphabetic index: "NOTE: To find any educational subject by title, see under the following General Alphabetic Index. Do NOT rely on titles as sufficient data to judge a film by. READ ALL LIKELY SYNOPSES VERY CAREFULLY."[55] This admonition clearly recognizes the presence of the contingent in these films.

Kleine wrote that the catalogue would provide "a library of motion pictures to which the educator will turn for illustrations as freely as to a library of books." He also described the catalogue as "the most complete list extant of Educational and Scientific Licensed Motion Picture Films," and a section of the catalogue's prefatory material was entitled "An Educational System by Visualization."[56] These verbal gestures—"library," "most complete list extant," "educational system"—suggest that Kleine saw his endeavor as continuous with other nineteenth-century knowledge projects. As this initial section of the chapter has shown, however, in its method of assembly, in its reliance on certain genres such as the travelogue, and in its organizational structure, the catalogue exhibits similarities with cabinets of curiosities. As the following section will show, these resonances also exist at the level of individual films.

"The Most Educational as Well as Most Revolting Motion Picture Film"

Cabinets frequently housed monsters. Ole Worm's cabinet, for example, included a Scythian lamb, a hybrid of an animal and a plant that was believed to sprout and grow, eating the food within reach until it was exhausted and the animal died. Other cabinets contained hydras, unicorns, and so on.[57] Alongside these creatures that from a contemporary perspective are clearly mythical, the cabinets also contained animals that exerted the fascination of the unusual. The chameleon, which featured prominently in cabinets, was also a recurring animal in early popular-science films.[58] Early popular-science films contained an abundance of extraordinary animals. Instead of a preponderance of films about dogs or cats or similarly mundane and ubiquitous creatures, the filmographies of this period are filled with such boundary-troubling critters as the axolotl, a Mexican salamander that spends part of its life cycle as an aquatic animal with gills and part of it as a terrestrial animal with lungs; and the dysticus, a carnivorous beetle capable of eating a lizard.[59] Even though professional science had turned away from an emphasis on singularities and monsters and toward the systematic investigation of the everyday and a production of the normative, the fascination with the unusual continued to constitute a central preoccupation of popular science.[60]

Alongside rare or exotic animals, cabinets also featured sights of things rendered unusual by the mode of visual access to them, such as peepshows, magic lanterns, telescopes, or microscopes.[61] The fascination with how magnification could reveal a strange world just beneath the familiar finds a potent form of expression in observations of flies, which was a prominent monster in the Kleine catalogue. There were four films about flies in the catalogue, *The Balancing Blue-Bottle*, *Blue-Bottle Flies Feeding*, *The Acrobatic Fly*, and *The Fly Pest*, all of which were produced at the Charles Urban Trading Company by Frank Percy Smith. The juggling fly films that were made in late 1908 celebrated the wondrous and amusing possibilities of the magnified world.[62]

The Fly Pest, however, represented a different attitude toward the fly. Percy Smith's presentation to the Royal Photographic Society that concluded with a screening of the juggling fly films contained an indication of this attitude. In that lecture he mentioned another way of regarding the fly: "The fly was sometimes spoken of as Nature's scavenger, but its proclivity for bacteria-infected meat and other corrupt matter, coupled with its objectionable habit of sampling everything on the breakfast table, rather discounted the claims put forward on its behalf in other respects."[63] This stigmatization of the fly as an unsanitary little menace indicated a modern hygienic discourse that was at odds with the juggling fly films' aesthetic of astonishment.

Kleine released *The Fly Pest* on April 6, 1910; he imported seventy-three prints, some of which went directly to such public health authorities as the state boards of health in Michigan, Virginia, New Jersey, Indiana, Louisiana, and Florida; various city boards of health; and the University of Wisconsin.

FIG. 4.3 Advertisement for *The Fly Pest*. Library of Congress, George Kleine papers.

Fifty-two prints were delivered to film exchanges for rental to thousands of individual theaters. The film's final audience was sizeable; Kleine claimed that "The lesson of cleanliness taught by this film was seen by not fewer than five million people."[64] In a letter to Urban, Kleine stated, "The 'Fly Pest' film has received more advertising than any other subject ever issued in this country."[65] The likelihood of self-serving hyperbole here is high, but *The Fly Pest* was remarkable for both the amount and the type of publicity it generated. The film was able to tap into the publicity mechanisms not only of the motion picture industry but also of other constituencies, in particular Progressive uplifters and public-health workers. The amount of publicity for *The Fly Pest* is even more notable considering that most films of this era played in a given cinema for considerably less than a week and received little if any advance publicity or discussion[66] (Fig. 4.3). In an era when most films had a lifespan shorter than that of a fly, *The Fly Pest* was sharply distinguished from the ephemeral nickelodeon program.

This distinction in terms of publicity and longevity was indicative of a larger change in the American cinema landscape at the turn of the 1910s. *The Fly Pest* served as one answer to the increasingly prominent chorus of voices calling for the transformation of cinema, which reformers characterized widely as a "school of crime." These reformers envisioned the cinema as a place where cinema's impressionable audiences could learn about useful things, like science, history, and civics.[67] *The Fly Pest* heralded a different approach to cinema as an institution; it was both a film about hygiene and itself a form of inoculation against what reformers tended to characterize as the filthy mass of films that constituted the average nickelodeon screening.[68]

More specifically, *The Fly Pest* was the product of the "new public health" movement that emerged in the United States between 1890 and 1910.[69] The fly had emerged as one of the prime targets of this movement; numerous public-health campaigns sprang up with an aim to eradicate the fly danger. The anti-fly campaign that generated *The Fly Pest* had begun in 1908 under the auspices of the New York Merchants' Association, which commissioned *The Fly Pest* from Urban.[70] H. V. Andrews "suggested" the film to Urban when he went to England in the summer of 1909 "on a special mission to obtain material" for Edward Hatch Jr., chairman of the New York Merchants' Association's Water Pollution Committee.[71] Hatch would later be chairman of a different committee with similar goals, the "Fly-Fighting Committee" of the American Civic Association, which was formed in February 1910.[72]

Urban, who was in the United States to demonstrate the Kinemacolour process with his collaborator Albert Smith, presented *The Fly Pest* to its sponsors at an initial screening that took place at the office of the Kleine Optical Company, 19 East Twenty-First Street, Manhattan, on December 12, 1909. In attendance were Hatch and Jackson, as well as "thirty" "physicians, sociologists, settlement workers, three reporters and one dramatic critic."[73] At that screening, Hatch was quoted as saying, "in that twelve minutes the average man, woman, or child learns more of the dangers arising from the fly pest than could be imparted by twelve months of lectures or twelve volumes of literature on the subject. These pictures will be the most important features of the anti-fly campaign of 1910, and will be shown in thousands of moving pictures theatres throughout the country as well as before schools and scientific societies."[74] These accounts illustrate the different audience to which reformers sought to reorient the cinema: the average man, woman, and child addressed by films brought to them via professionals—physicians, sociologists, or settlement workers.

A number of other screenings for specialist audiences soon followed. Dr. Daniel D. Jackson, the laboratory director of the New York Water Supply, gave a lecture to the Duchess County Medical Association at Vassar Institute about the fly's role in spreading disease, "illustrated by moving pictures, enlarging the fly until the size of a dog and in some cases larger."[75] Jackson also spoke with the films at the New York Academy of Medicine.[76] Richard B.

Watrous, secretary of the American Civic Association, mentioned screening the film seven times in a single day when it was first released.[77]

The film both took advantage of new methods of publicity and distribution as well as its striking visual qualities that in part were drawn from preexisting methods of visualizing public-health problems. Previous anti-fly campaigns had emphasized the adult fly as a mechanical vector for such diseases as tuberculosis and typhoid, even though targeting fly larvae and their breeding grounds was a more effective control method.[78] (Fig. 4.4). Originally, the organizers of the anti-fly campaign wanted to use a large-scale model: "Our first idea was to construct a huge model of the housefly, showing its physical structure on a highly magnified scale, like the model of the mosquito in the American Museum of Natural History. We decided, however, that this would not answer our purpose so well as moving pictures of the insect. The model would take a long time to construct and could appeal to only comparatively limited numbers, while the motion pictures could be shown to millions of persons at once."[79] With *The Fly Pest*, nineteenth-century visualization techniques, epitomized by the model of the mosquito in the American Museum of Natural History, gave way to a medium that could incorporate these appeals while also taking advantage of the emerging mass medium's abilities to circulate on an international scale.[80]

A number of references to censorship indicate that the film's emphasis on striking visuals tested the limits of public decency. At least one screening of the film in Indianapolis was stopped by the police.[81] Other statements indicated similar responses that stopped short of prohibiting the film. The Bulletin of the Municipal Commission on Tuberculosis of St. Louis contained the following assessment:

> The film, by George Kleine, of Chicago, has received great praise from many leading sanitarians, and has been pronounced by them a powerful aid in educational work. To be sure, it has been described by some theatres as 'too disgusting' for exhibition; but is it as disgusting as the reality? The justification for representing vice upon the stage is to condemn it; there is physical as well as moral vice that wants condemning also. We hope that these pictures will be allowed to teach their lesson far and wide in the moving picture shows—the lesson whose moral is, "*Kill the fly!*"[82]

A similar sentiment appeared in the account of *The Fly Pest* screening by Frank Altman, manager of the Theatre Voyons in Lowell, Massachusetts: "We gave a special showing of *The Fly Pest* recently to the members of the Board of Health, School Officials, Police officials, representatives of women's clubs and public officials generally. It was given with the understanding that possibly part of the film would be withdrawn from general showing because of its disagreeable features but as we expected practically every one of the officials who attended personally asked us to show every bit of the film."[83] A Portland

FIG. 4.4 Magnification and monsters. Library of Congress, George Kleine papers.

newspaper put it succinctly: "'The Fly Pest' is the most educational as well as most revolting motion picture film that has ever been exhibited anywhere."[84] These reactions acknowledged the possibility of objections but insisted on the overall necessity of such images, an attitude that indicated the film's inscription into a Progressive ethos challenging certain aspects of genteel society in the name of (scientific) advancements. Indeed, inciting anxiety was part of the repertoire of hygiene campaigns, and Kleine incorporated the story about the film being censored in Indiana as part of his own publicity.[85]

As disconcerting as *The Fly Pest* could be, however, it was also capable of evoking reactions of fascination and wonder. *Technical World Magazine*'s description of the film evinced a dual reaction to the film that endorsed its ostensible message while also registering an appreciation for a countervailing aesthetic dimension. The writer noted that "These pictures will tell more vividly, perhaps, than anything else could, what a vile and altogether dangerous little beast the fly is. In the pictures, however, the flies are not so small. They appear as marvelous creatures, with transparent wings, great hairy legs and strange eyes with wonderful range of vision."[86] This alternation between the "dangerous little beast" and the "marvelous creature" encapsulates the palimpsestic relationship between the sober discourse of hygiene and an aesthetic of wonder.

The shot most likely responsible for this reaction occurs approximately two-thirds of the way into the film, when the fly is fed honey from the tip of a needle (Fig. 4.5). Many descriptions of the film take note of its

FIG. 4.5 Fly eating from the tip of a needle, video still from *The Fly Pest*. BFI.

multipart structure: The first two-thirds introduces the fly via the standard popular-science narrative of the life cycle, while the last third makes the argument about how the fly is a carrier of disease.[87] The shot of the fly eating honey from the tip of the needle serves as a hinge between the two parts of the film, properly belonging to neither.

This shot is unusual for a number of reasons. It is exceptionally long; at fifty seconds it represents almost twenty percent of the film's total run time, and it is five times longer than the next-longest shot in the film (Fig. 4.6). Not only is this shot much longer than any other shot, but the film's style also changes in it. The mise-en-scène is different; instead of a view taken from above, the camera films from the side, which alters both the view of the fly and the appearance of the background. In the rest of the film, flies frequently are seen against recognizable backgrounds, as when they walk on either putrid meat or human food, which emphasizes how flies contaminate the environment. In this shot the background is indistinct, which focuses attention on the particularities of the insect (the effect is similar to the camera placement in *The Acrobatic Fly*).

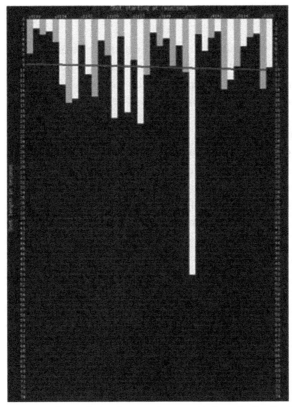

FIG. 4.6 Cinemetric analysis of *The Fly Pest*, showing the length of individual shots as separate bars. Cinemetrics.lv

The framing is also different. In this shot the fly is framed much more closely than in any other shot in the film. Usually there are at least a few and usually many flies in the frame at once, a compositional choice that supports a view of flies as creatures that exist in swarming, threatening overabundance. The closer framing allows for a more individualized view of the fly that leads to an appreciation of its particularity. This kind of contemplation has the opposite effect of the swarming/hygienic view; instead of seeing the fly as part of a menacing mass, it appears as a fascinating individual.

A possible source of this anomaly is an earlier film by F. Martin Duncan entitled *Head of House Fly*, which first appears in the Urban catalogue in 1905. The catalogue description of this film reads as follows:

> This is probably the first time that a fly has ever sat for its portrait to the bioscope, and a most strange looking face and head it has. To keep him in a good temper a needle point coated with honey is placed within reach of his tongue. The tongue of the fly is a most extraordinary piece of apparatus. Although it can tuck away into a small space, when expanded it appears to be as large as the insect's head. It is expanded in a fan-like manner, and consists of hollow tubes through which the sustenance is sucked into the mouth. 75 ft.[88]

Based solely on the description of the fly being fed from the tip of a needle, it seems likely that the shot in *The Fly Pest* is taken from this film. Urban's tendency toward reusing footage makes this scenario more likely. In addition, the length of the Duncan film accords closely with the length of the shot in *The Fly Pest*.[89]

This shot represents an attitude toward the fly that is markedly different from the rest of the film, portraying the insect as an "extraordinary" creature. The use of the pin to feed the fly also contains the suggestion that a fly can be "trained," thus bringing it into proximity with the world of the circus or of pets. It is not surprising that the catalogue blurb for Duncan's film contains a number of anthropomorphic moves: The fly "sat for its portrait," has a "face," and must be kept in a "good temper." This different view of the fly offers pleasures absent from the rest of the film. Providing by far the closest views of the fly, this sequence provides the wonder of watching a single animal in motion.

The two microcinematographic shots that follow the shot of the fly eating from the tip of the needle extend the ambiguity of this sequence. These shots are filmed lantern slides, which is evident both from the telltale curve of the circular mask, so distinctive of lantern-slide framing, in the first shot of the fly's tongue, and in the characteristic stillness of the image for the duration of the shot[90] (Fig. 4.7). These shots are a good example of the ambiguous status of visual evidence in the popular-science film. A talking point for the

FIG. 4.7 A filmed lantern slide of fly tongue, from *The Fly Pest*. BFI.

anti-fly users of the film was that the mechanisms for the transmission of bacteria were the fly's tongue and its feet.[91] These shots ostensibly provide the visual basis for these arguments, but nothing about them inherently shows infection. Indeed, the abstract beauty of fly body parts seen greatly magnified could more easily underscore the sense of wonder at the fly's amazing physiology.

The shot of the fly eating from the tip of a needle exemplifies *The Fly Pest*'s deployment of specifically cinematic appeals. Beyond the use of magnification, which links it to a long tradition of viewing insects through the microscope, it highlights the inherent fascination of the moving image, particularly when it shows the unusual movement of the fly's tongue as it expands to suck the honey from the point of the needle.[92] In terms of film history, this shot exemplifies the cinema of attractions, with its explicit solicitation of the viewer's curious gaze.

By contrast, the film's final sequences, where it makes the argument for how flies spread disease, demonstrate an affinity with the cinema of narrative integration, and particularly the codes of classical editing. In this section Urban, who edited the majority of the films produced by his company, twice uses a similar editing pattern. In the first instance, a five-shot sequence demonstrates how flies can spread contagion. An intertitle introduces the scene's argument ("How the fly spreads decay."); it is followed by two shots of flies on decomposing fish; these shots are followed by three shots of flies on sugar cubes (Fig. 4.8).

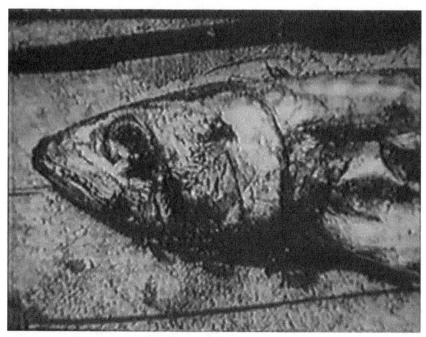

FIG. 4.8 Two instances of cutting in from *The Fly Pest*. BFI.

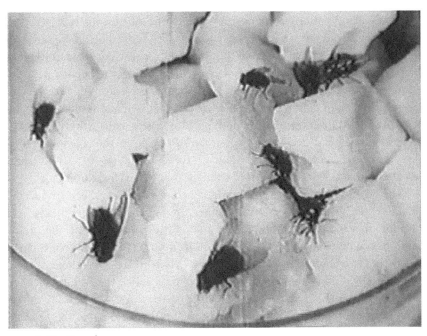

FIG. 4.8 Continued.

FIG. 4.8 Continued.

This editing pattern was novel for this period of film history. Barry Salt writes that "from 1907 to 1909, cuts within a scene continued to be rare," and he does not see cutting in as something that becomes widespread until 1912 in fiction films.[93] This sequence also obeys a rule of editing associated with classical Hollywood cinema that stipulates that longer framings receive more screen time than closer framings, a pattern that is made visible in Fig. 4.6. Urban cuts to closer framings in both parts of this sequence; this technique is typical of classical decoupage, where an establishing shot is generally followed by closer views, and in particular it typifies what would become a prevalent popular-science film editing strategy, that of looking closer.[94]

The second instance of this pattern concludes the film; it is introduced by an intertitle, "How the fly transmits tuberculosis." Here a shot of flies walking around on a spittoon is followed by a shot of flies on a baby's pacifier, and finally a shot of a baby with the pacifier in its mouth (Fig. 4.9). What is particularly notable about this sequence is how Urban creates a synthetic space by the juxtaposition of shots, what will come to be called the Kuhleshov effect. The final three-shot sequence does not display the same adherence to the rule that correlates shot scale to length, although it is possible that the final shot was originally longer than in the currently existing print (here a comparison among existing prints might provide further insight). Nevertheless, the use of the Kuhleshov effect is remarkable, and the effect would have been even more alarming in an era of significantly higher infant mortality.[95]

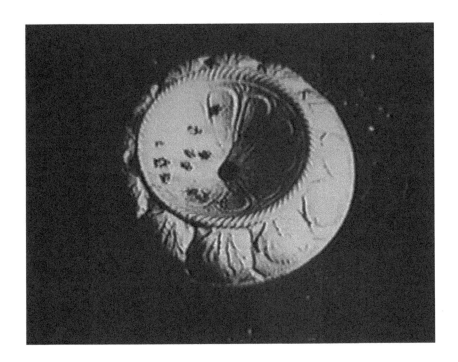

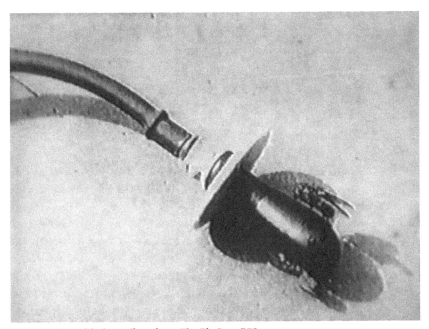

FIG. 4.9 The Kuhleshov effect; from *The Fly Pest*. BFI.

FIG. 4.9 Continued.

The imperiled infant was an established image in the anti-fly propaganda campaigns. Samuel J. Crumbine in Kansas put together a Sanitation Parade in 1915 that featured a fly float pulling thirteen empty baby carriages.[96] In particular the baby's pacifier (or in some cases the bottle nipple) recurred as an image of something that flies could easily contaminate (Fig. 4.10). The concluding sequence to *The Fly Pest* is thus not a novelty in terms of content, but it does constitute an excellent example of how cinema could infuse established images with a new energy, modernizing the appeals of the cabinet of curiosity.[97]

The catalogue can be seen as a modern cabinet in part because of its mixture of the appeals to curiosity with modern discourses. *The Fly Pest* provides an instance where the microscopic mirrors the macroscopic. This mixture recurs in the films themselves, which display a similar mixture of old appeals and modern discourses. By combining a discourse of public health that sought to identify the fly as a carrier of disease with a discourse of wonder that saw the magnified fly as an instance of the marvelous, *The Fly Pest* encapsulates the mixed appeal of the Kleine catalogue, combining the discourses of sobriety and the marvelous, even within the film itself at the level of individual shots.[98]

This mixture of venerable and contemporary, of dry and vivid characterizes Kleine's catalogue, and it is due to a conception of how popular-science

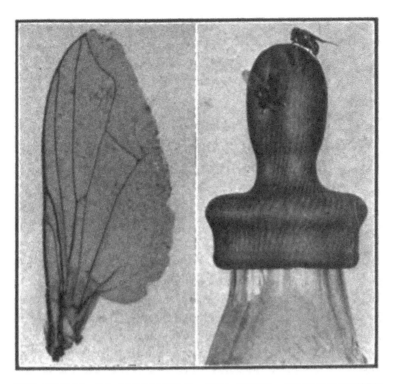

MODERN SLAUGHTER OF THE INNOCENTS

A MAGNIFIED WING SHOWING SPECKS OF DIRT WHICH THE FLY SHEDS OVER THE NIPPLE OF THE BABY'S BOTTLE

FIG. 4.10 From Frank Parker Stockbridge, "How to Get Rid of Flies: The Way They 'Swat' Them in Topeka and Order Out the Boy Scouts to Slaughter Them—How They Trap Them in Wilmington."

films constitute living facts. What allowed Kleine to combine films from a wide range of producers about an even wider range of subjects was an understanding of the films as containing knowledge that was not subject to the same kind of obsolescence as commercial fiction films. Kleine's attempt to lay the foundation for a cinema of the future is also a monument to the circulation of factual cinema.

{ Chapter 5 }

Popular Science and Crime Melodrama: Louis Feuillade and the Serial

The serial, which occupies an important place in the commercial end
of the industry, does not concern us. The episodes which run week
after week in the cheaper neighborhood theatres are always sensational
and often utterly preposterous. But they are seldom really harmful,
and although they do not tend to elevate the standard of taste, they
often develop the motion picture in a technical way, and fulfill the
cravings of the less sophisticated for adventure. Thrills, suspense, and
lightning action are demanded of serials. Each episode must leave the
audience gasping as the hero is left suspended over a lofty cliff with the
villain about to cut the rope. At this moment the episode ends, and the
audience must return next week to continue the story. A touch of
erudition is often attempted by the advertisement that such a serial is a
powerful study of hypnotism, a marvel of engineering, or of physical
prowess, and while it may be, it will not be exactly educational,
nevertheless![1]

These remarks contain a familiar view of the serial's relationship to the field of
nonfiction. The initial assertion—that the serial "does not concern us"—
places the serial at the "commercial end of the industry," far removed from the
goals of "educational" films. A primary way this opposition appears is the reliance on a common understanding of sensationalism that sees it closely tied to
bodily desires. Rendered here as the "cravings of the less sophisticated for adventure" who must be left "gasping," this understanding of the serial accords
with a reception of it as a mass-cultural form, in the tradition of nineteenth-
century melodrama, both in its theatrical and serialized-fiction incarnations.
This quotation sees the serial, then, as a body genre, having little to do with
the life of the mind. To the extent that the serial had been singled out as instructive at all, it was by those who regarded it as a "school of crime."[2]

The quotation also contains ambivalence, however. Not only is the serial "seldom really harmful," but it also "often develops the motion picture in a technical way."[3] The serial often attempts to display "a touch of erudition."[4] This phrase implies a limited educational value, and it is part of a series of backhanded compliments culminating with the judgment that the serial is "not . . . exactly educational." The serial has its place and may even be something other than directly pernicious, the authors imply, but it cannot capture the attention of people interested in the cinema as an educative force. This inexactitude, the "not . . . exactly," is a good indication of popular science's transitional position, its tendency to travel among cultural spaces and contexts, and the alternation of respect and contempt for the serial is congruent with the ambivalent reception of popular science.

This chapter will consider how the French crime melodrama of the mid-1910s portrayed scientific progress, especially as incarnated in technological devices. The serial, for all its intemperance, its indulgence in thrills, suspense, and lightning action, nonetheless maintains close contact with what Bill Nichols has called "the discourses of sobriety."[5] Whereas scholarship on the serial has often adopted an attitude similar to the epigraph's, sometimes noticing the serial's involvement with science and technology only to dismiss or trivialize the importance of those links, this chapter will put pressure on the serial's "touch of erudition," considering how it involves an incorporation and transformation of popular-science filmmaking. The French crime series *Zigomar* (Victorin Jasset, Éclair, 1911–1912) and *Fantômas* (Louis Feuillade, Gaumont, 1913–1914) and the serial *Les Vampires* (Louis Feuillade, Gaumont, 1915–1916) will provide the primary instances of the incorporation and modification of the popular-science film.

The Serial Tradition: The Detective Story, Popular Science, Melodrama

The serial form as it developed over the course of the nineteenth century, especially in print media, served as a crucial intertext for the cinema serial, with popular serialized fiction as the most direct influence. Zigomar first appeared in Léon Sazie's serial novels, beginning with *Zigomar, le maître invisible*, which was a weekly *feuilleton* in *Le Matin* from December 7, 1909, to June 22, 1910.[6] Fantômas made his debut in the novels of Pierre Allain and Marcel Souvestre in September 1911; Allain and Souvestre produced thirty-two Fantômas novels over the course of two years for publisher Arthème Fayard. Both the Zigomar *feuilleton* and some of the Fantômas novels were adapted for the screen in short order. Victorin Jasset directed three Zigomar films for Éclair beginning in 1911, and Louis Feuillade directed five films based on the Fantômas novels for Gaumont from 1913 to 1914. The flow of adaptation also could be reversed; *Les Vampires* (and Feuillade's subsequent serials) appeared in print editions called *"films racontés"* that coincided with the release of the films and supplemented the cinema experience.[7]

These films fall into two closely related categories: series films, like *Zigomar* and *Fantômas*, where individual episodes formed self-contained stories with recurring characters; and serials, like *Les Vampires*, where a running narrative bridged episodes, and the narrative action at the end of an episode often was left unconcluded, stopping at a point of maximum narrative suspense, the so-called cliffhanger. The series began with single-reel films (i.e., roughly ten minutes) that were released at irregular intervals; the Nick Carter series at Éclair, which starred the American detective and was based on a well-known series of dime novels, typified the series.

These distinctions are not always clear-cut, however. Both the cliffhanger ending and the recapitulative intertitle, characteristics of the serial, also appeared in the series film. For instance, the second episode of the Fantômas series, *Juve contre Fantômas*, ends with Fantômas detonating an explosive device that demolishes the villa containing Juve, Fandor, and the police. The episode ends with an intertitle that poses the question of whether Juve and Fandor have survived the blast; the next film in the series, *Le Mort qui tue*, begins with an explanatory intertitle that recapitulates events from the previous episode. With the extension to multiple-reel films, the series format reestablished itself at the new, longer length (as in the *Fantômas* series) and gradually gave way to the serial format. The distinction between series and serial has as much to do with the logics of marketing and distribution as it has to do with significant differences in visual or narrative style. Especially in the early 1910s, when the serial format was supplanting the series format, the differences were often minimal. Many of the serial episodes in *Les Vampires* form self-contained units. The distinction also relates to the history of print marketing. Some of the covers of the Fantômas books carried the phrase "each book contains a complete story" as a way to differentiate their product from the *feuilleton*, with its endless episodes.

In any case, the differences between the series and the serial are not nearly as important as the similarities between the two modes, which involve their common heritage in the tradition of crime melodrama.[8] The French crime melodramas responded to preexisting desires for and familiarity with serialized narratives; they also picked up on the fascination with science and technology that featured prominently in sensational serial fiction. Such celebrated examples of detective fiction as Sir Arthur Conan Doyle's Sherlock Holmes stories contained a sustained reflection on the importance of science and technology. Holmes, like Doyle, is a student of science, albeit an eclectic one. Myriad details attest to Holmes's allegiance to scientific ideals of analytic reason, from the name of the profession Holmes has invented for himself, "consulting detective," formed by analogy to the "consulting physician," to Holmes's frequent laboratory work.[9] Holmes's methods of deduction, his "passion for definite and exact knowledge," have become synonymous with scientific reason.[10] But as with most instances of popular science, the allegiance to scientific thought constitutes only one side of the equation. The detective story engages with science, after all, not to produce data for a research agenda but to present a struggle between the forces of order and crime, staging "a dramatization of the ambiguities of vision in a new age of flexible identities and technological vision."[11]

In Peter Brooks's influential study, melodrama arises out of a post-Revolutionary need to negotiate a postsacral world, where the prior guarantors of meaning, such as the church, no longer wield absolute authority.[12] Unsurprisingly, science and technology, arguably the most prominent emblems of the modern age, play important roles in the melodrama's search for meaning. The recurring situation in these films of a criminal battling the forces of order is characteristic of melodrama's requirements for a clear, absolute opposition between good and evil. But in addition to the basic melodramatic structure, there is a relationship to the time in which the melodrama appears: "Melodrama is best understood as a combination of archetypal, mythic [elements] and time-specific responses to particular cultural and historical conditions."[13]

While many aspects of the serial's production history and cultural context have been described with increasing precision, the importance of popular science as an intertext for the French crime melodrama remains unaddressed. Ben Singer does note, "sensational melodrama was tied to modernity in other respects, as well. To begin with, technology was at its core, both on stage and behind the scenes." Indeed, his study is punctuated with insights about the importance of science and technology for melodrama. He writes that "the new dangers of the technologized urban environment" provided a major source of hyperstimulus, of which melodrama was both an instigator and a result, and that the pervasive sense of unease in the modern metropolis was due to "modern technology as a monstrous assault on life and limb," also noting that "[m]elodrama's action-adventure stories were designed to showcase the wonders of modern technology."[14] His study, however, does not explore the possibility of the serial as a popular interpretation of science and technology. If, as Singer points out, "[s]erial melodrama fixated on and magnified crucial aspects of the emergence of advanced capitalism and urban modernity," then surely science and technology are central aspects of advanced capitalism and urban modernity that feature prominently in serial melodrama.[15]

Fantastic Realism

"Fantastic realism" has become a staple of descriptions of the French crime serial, and is linked to a reading of Feuillade that originates with the Surrealists. It was passed along to current cinema historians via Georges Sadoul, who writes of Feuillade, "He who had once transposed the most extravagant *trucs* of Méliès into the street, filmed [*mit en scène*] the fantastic adventures of *Fantômas* in the décor of real Paris or its suburbs, and in reconstructions of furnished studios by the Dufayel department store. A strange poetry was born out of this opposition between a minute naturalism and extraordinary adventures."[16] This characterization of the films' "strange poetry" as a mixture of the fantastic and the realistic has carried over into contemporary scholarship. Richard Abel invokes this reading and lays out its basic premise when he writes, "The first episode [of *Fantômas*] . . . skillfully establishes the 'fantastic realism' that so characterizes the series—in which the mundane, reassuringly sober façade of daily life masks incredible, sometimes bloody exploits."[17] Abel reiterates his definition in slightly different terms later in his book, expanding the films to which it applies: "In the *Zigomar, Main de fer,* and *Fantômas* films, the three filmmakers [Jasset, Perret, and Feuillade] also developed a particular aesthetic—then, as now, labeled 'fantastic realism'—that explored the fantastic, diabolical powers surging beneath the surface and charging the most ordinary objects of everyday life."[18] These "diabolical powers" that fantastic realism seeks to describe include the myriad sudden ambushes perpetrated by the villains in the serial film, the way the seemingly placid bourgeois exteriors of *belle époque* Paris conceal elaborate criminal conspiracies, and how everyday objects—a fountain pen, for example—can in fact be implements of death.[19]

A question that emerges from these descriptions is: Where, exactly, does the fantastic come from? What are some of the sources of these extraordinary, incredible incidents? It is useful to turn to some of the earliest Feuillade criticism written by the Surrealists, in this case the poet Robert Desnos, who wrote about *Fantômas*:

> the whole period that precedes the war is described there with exactly the kind of precision that aspires to the phenomenon of lyricism. International intrigues, the lives of ordinary people, views of great cities and Paris in particular, society life as it really is . . . the ways of the police, and for the first time the presence of the fantastic [*merveilleux*] in a fitting form for the twentieth century, the natural use of machines and recent inventions, the mystery of things, of mankind and of destiny.[20]

Here the basic outline of fantastic realism becomes apparent—a lyricism that emerges from precise description of "life as it really is." The fantastic is tied to the twentieth century, to "the natural use of machines and recent inventions." This linkage to modern mechanism is a crucial aspect of Feuillade's fantastic realism.

Some critics have suggested the technological horrors of World War I as a source for this atmosphere of peril in *Les Vampires*.[21] To read the menace of everyday objects and places as emanating from the war makes sense, especially when confronted with things like the portable artillery gun used by Satanas in episode eight of *Les Vampires*. The war is not the sole source of this sense of threat, however, nor is it available as an explanation for the presence of this aesthetic in the prewar films; rather, the war forms but a part of a larger technological ensemble that threatens bourgeois normality even as it underwrites it. A crucial aspect of the "diabolical powers surging beneath the surface" stems from the ambivalent popular reception of scientific and technological advances.[22]

A scene that can serve as an example of fantastic realism occurs in the second film in the Fantômas series, *Juve contre Fantômas*. Having learned of Fantômas's plans to murder Juve, Juve and his loyal companion, the newspaper reporter Jerome Fandor, are waiting in Juve's apartment for the fulfillment of a threat, namely that of one of Fantômas's helpers, the so-called silent executioner, will pay Juve a visit. The silent executioner is already known to have caused one death in which the victim was crushed almost beyond recognition. As a precautionary measure, Fandor helps Juve don three leather belts studded with metal spikes, one around each arm and one around his chest. Juve then extinguishes the lights, and Fandor hides in a trunk at the foot of the bed. The executioner turns out to be a giant boa constrictor, and Juve's spiked bands allow him to avoid being crushed (Fig. 5.1). The combination of seemingly bizarre elements in this scene—the boa constrictor and the spiked belts—makes it a prime candidate for the epithet "fantastic realism." These elements are not as bizarre as they may at first seem, however.

On January 8, 1910, Jean Jacques Liabeuf, a young cobbler, killed a member of the vice squad, gravely wounded his partner, and injured six other officers

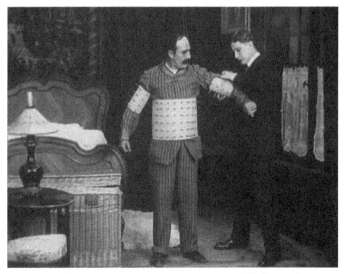

FIG. 5.1 Video stills from *Juve contre Fantômas* (Louis Feuillade, 1913).

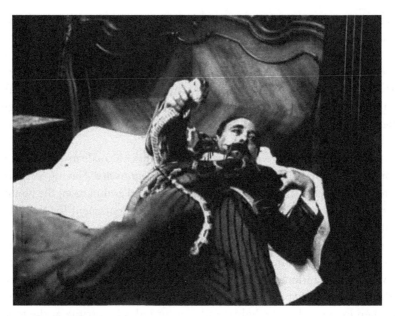

FIG. 5.1 Continued.

before finally being subdued and arrested. Liabeuf had just spent three months in prison on false charges of pimping; after his release he hunted down the policemen who framed him. Liabeuf became an important figure for the anarchist movement. Gustave Hervé, an anarchist journalist, defended Liabeuf in his newspaper *La Guerre Sociale*, which earned him a four-year prison term. On July 2, 1910, Liabeuf was guillotined in Paris; the execution set off large-scale riots. This story is related to the boa constrictor sequence in *Juve contre Fantômas* by a detail of the mise-en-scène usually attributed to the excesses of "fantastic realism." A manual of police science from 1911 described how Liabeuf "wore leather armbands spiked with numerous steel points (fig. 13). On each arm he had two, one for the upper arm and another for the lower arm. He concealed his arms, which were protected in this fashion, under a roomy cape"[23] (Fig. 5.2).

The novel confirms that Juve's costume is an allusion to the famous anarchist: "'It's not a new device,' said Juve. 'Liabeuf wore arm guards like these under his jacket, and when the officers wanted to seize him they tore their hands.'"[24] This anarchist device that Juve wears is a good example of how those elements of the films that have been singled out as "fantastic" often can be revealed as embedded in contemporary contexts. What has been taken for the fantastic reveals itself instead as realism. Indeed, many moments of "fantastic realism" can be repositioned such that their fantastic elements emerge not as mysterious in the sense of being unexplainable, but as mysterious and bizarre like so many other things embedded in the fabric of everyday modern life.[25]

FIG. 5.2 Liabeuf's spiked armbands. Image from R. A. Reiss, *Manuel de police scientifique* (1911).

Read in the context of Tzevtan Todorov's definition of the fantastic, "fantastic realism" can take on a different meaning, rooted less in the mysterious or the unknowable, but rather, as in Todorov's sense of the term, coming about as a result of a moment of hesitation and uncertainty. Todorov defines the fantastic in the following terms:

> In a world which is indeed our world, the one we know . . . there occurs an event which cannot be explained by the laws of this same familiar world. The person who experiences the event must opt for one of two possible solutions: either he is the victim of an illusion of the senses, of a product of the imagination—and the laws of the world then remain what they are; or else the event has indeed taken place, it is an integral part of reality—but then this reality is controlled by laws unknown to us. . . . The fantastic occupies the duration of this uncertainty. . . . The fantastic is that hesitation experienced by a person who knows only the laws of nature, confronting an apparently supernatural event.[26]

Other categories occupy the space on either side of the fantastic's razor-thin profile; if the surprising event can be accounted for according to natural laws, it becomes attributable to "the uncanny," but should the event flout the laws of nature, it becomes assigned to the realm of "the marvelous." Since the fantastic moments in Feuillade ultimately receive some form of natural explanation, Todorov's category of the uncanny is perhaps the best term, but the fantastic is a useful conceptual tool to describe certain effects that have become a fixture of Feuillade's critical reception, especially the general sense of uncertainty about what lurks beneath the surface of modern life.

Zigomar

The aesthetic of fantastic realism did not originate with Feuillade, although it did reach a zenith in his work. Criminals appeared in the French cinema with increasing frequency after 1911.[27] The Zigomar series of films at Éclair starred the red-hooded supercriminal already famous from Sazie's popular *feutillion*. The film adaptations began in 1911 with *Zigomar*, continued with *Zigomar contre Nick Carter* (1912), and concluded with *Zigomar, peau d'anguille* (1913). They signaled a twofold shift in filmmaking practice: the introduction of the multiple-reel format and the emphasis on the criminal as opposed to the detective. In addition, the series demonstrated "a sharp increase in the level of thrills and sensational violence, so that the genre almost became a specialized form of grand guignol."[28] The Zigomar films are immediate precursors to Feuillade's multiple-reel crime melodramas and offer an initial example of how the crime melodrama registered an uneasy reaction to technological modernity.

The following quotation appeared in a March 1912 synopsis of *Zigomar contre Nick Carter* in *Ciné Journal*, one of the major French film-industry publications: "Marvelously adept of using the resources of modern science, he [Zigomar] can 'trick out' [*truquer*] everything he touches. One could say that his diabolical imagination gives him the talent for perpetual transformation and a disconcerting ubiquity."[29] The oscillation here between the marvelous and the disconcerting, between exhilaration and apprehension, is indicative of how the crime melodrama figures the anxieties and fantasies about modern scientific discoveries in the figure of the supercriminal. The word "*truquer*" succinctly raises a number of issues. The very fact that things can be "tricked out" indicates the extent to which science and technology have penetrated everyday life and rendered it mysterious, both by revealing hitherto unimagined realms (the microscopic, the electromagnetic spectrum, etc.) and by introducing such an abundance of new devices that are as ubiquitous as they are baffling. *Truquer* also contains an etymological link to the genre of the trick film, which in French is called the *scène à trucs*, a connection that can lead to the question of the affiliations among the trick film, popular science, and the serial.

The crime melodrama flourished during a transitional time in the development of narrative cinema, at the cusp of the widespread acceptance of the feature-film format. The serial came in the wake of the transition from the cinema of attractions, a mode marked by an aesthetic of spectacular display, to the cinema of narrative integration, which involved a move toward more "classical" modes of absorbed spectatorship. The shift to feature-length, narrative cinema entailed a number of things: a reformist desire on the part of the film industry to attract a new, more upscale audience; the utilization of a more subtle, "naturalistic" performance style; and a move away from the physicality/acrobatics that were characteristic of performances in early cinema. In the crime melodrama of the 1910s, however, this transition, which has never been fully completed, is notably unfinished. Tom Gunning writes about the Zigomar series, "This series of detective thrillers provides a compilation of genres of early film while reworking the lessons of these earlier forms into a new more modern pattern, the prototype of the later detective genre," and posits a "volatile mutability of this new transitional stage in film stylistics."[30] Abel refers to "something like a bricolage model of film construction, in which heterogeneous genre elements could be cobbled together into feature-length format."[31]

An idea common to both analyses is that the multireel crime melodrama consists of what Gunning alternately calls "component parts" or the "dramatic unit," which derive from previous genres.[32] While Gunning and Abel take the chase film and the trick film as their examples of this process of adaptation, popular-science films are also a component part of the crime melodrama. The popular-science moments in serial films partook of both aspects of popular-science films. On the one hand, they participated in the sober mode of seeing something explained, a mode of demystification, the visual correlative to rational argument. On the other hand, these moments also often had recourse to the tradition of the scientist as modern magician, as the revealer of unseen worlds and, in some cases, the possessor of a demiurgic power. If Zigomar "absorbs the delirious energy of the trick film, its ability to transform objects, identities and locales without cease," then these delirious energies reside, at least in part, in the tradition of the scientist as illusionist.[33] Abel writes, "The film's [*Zigomar contre Nick Carter*] principal interest, however, lies in its unique blend of the realistic, the fantastic, and the melodramatic—in what *Bioscope* described as an 'orgy of sensationalism.' . . . Along with this strong sense of verisimilitude comes an unexpected array of *truc* effects taken over wholesale from Méliès and Pathé's earlier trick films and *féeries*. Not only are disguises rampant throughout . . . but Zigomar's power literally becomes magical."[34] The array of *truc* effects can appear less unexpected if these moments are seen not from the standpoint of the development of classical narrative but rather from a standpoint that sees the trick film as not necessarily opposed to realism in a manner similar to that of popular-science films.[35] A way to link trick films and popular-science films, in other words, is to see them both as instances of fantastic realism.

Popular-science films and the crime melodrama also share a type of subject matter. Éclair's emphasis on violence, a tendency that the Zigomar series inaugurated, finds an echo in popular-science films that often foregrounded violence as well, with animals' predatory behavior receiving detailed attention. *Un bandit des grands chemins, la larve de fourmi-lion* (Pathé, May 1912), exemplifies this fascination with violence.[36] The film begins with a typical anatomization of the insect and a description of its behavior. The anthropomorphization of the ant-lion effected by the film's title, which is typical of the genre, continues near the end when the film stages an encounter between the ant-lion and its prey, depicting the insect's unique trap in action. As the ant falls into the trap and disappears under the sand, a single-word intertitle—"E r f a s s t [Caught]"—underscores the drama of the events. The following intertitle, "Ein anderes Schauspiel [A different drama]," precedes a scene in which an ant struggles to escape from the bottom of the pit. The film's final intertitle, "Sehr wenige entkommen [Very few escape]," and the final image, in which carcasses litter the rim of the funnel, illustrate the rapacious appetite of the film's star. Both films depict the behavior of violent predators, and both exhibit a fascination with how tricks and traps are set up and sprung.

Popular-science films include both a didactic mode, aligned with the "view aesthetic," and a mode of spectacular display; they partake of a dialectic between what Walter Benjamin characterized as the hands of the surgeon and hands of the magician.[37] The attractions of the popular-science moment become increasingly transformed into special effects—that is, moments of (sometimes fantastic) display that have been harnessed toward a narrative end. Abel encapsulates these commonalities between popular-science films and the serial when he writes about Zigomar that the films present us with "'the strange and the fantastic within the very real fabric of everyday life.' . . . a fascinatingly schizoid vision of the world as simultaneously normal and abnormal, as marvelous as it is disorienting."[38] The Zigomar series contains a number of scenes that illustrate these claims—the mechanized cage that traps Broquet in the first film, the automated casino/recital hall and the photographic safe of the second film, and the elephant and hydroplane in the third film. These scenes are examples of how popular science becomes an intertext for the French serial crime melodrama, and the interpenetration of popular science and crime melodrama present in the Zigomar series reaches a pinnacle with the films of Feuillade.

Fantômas: The Enigma of Modern Identity

"Fantômas.
"What did you say?
"I said: Fantômas.
"And what does that mean?
"Nothing . . . . Everything!
"But what is it?
"Nobody . . . . and yet, yes, it is somebody!
"And what does the somebody do?
"Spreads terror!"[39]

This dialogue, which takes place at the beginning of the first Fantômas novel, functions like an epigraph for the entire series, crucially foregrounding the protean identity of its central figure. In both the thirty-two books that Pierre Allain and Marcel Souvestre dictated at the pace of one per month from 1911 to 1913, and in the five films that Feuillade would make based on the first, second, third, sixth, and twelfth books of the series, Fantômas emerges as a specter haunting the technological ensembles that define the modern individual, an exposure of their limits, their worst-case scenario—someone who leaves no traces, or, even worse, leaves counterfeit fingerprints, a nobody who is yet somebody who could be anybody.[40] Fantômas appears only as a name in the first novel; someone Inspector Juve, detective of the Sureté, *son semblable, son frère*, can only suspect is behind numerous disguises. Later in the series Juve will liken Fantômas to a puppetmaster—the unseen force behind the scenes that puts the spectacle in motion. Fantômas's signature spectacles are violent crimes, which were rendered all the more memorable by their realizations in Gino Starace's lurid cover illustrations.[41]

Fantômas displays an uncanny ability to slip through the grids of modern identity, stymieing the techniques that were invented to track the masses of people in the modern metropolis's bewildering flux. These systems of identification had just taken a quantum leap forward in the early 1880s with Alphonse Bertillon's science of anthropometry. The significant difference of Bertillon's system from previous methods of criminal identification was that it no longer relied on the analogic similitude of the verbal description or the detective's so-called photographic memory. Instead it depended on methods that reduced people to unique sets of data that were stored in rationalized retrieval systems[42] (Fig. 5.3).

While differentiation is the goal of these systems, they also require a particular kind of abstraction; in a certain sense, the person's individuality must be effaced, the individual must be made absolutely comparable to all other individuals, one card like all the others. It is an operation not unlike the transformation of the thing into the commodity that Marx describes in *Capital* 1.1, which results in the creation of exchange value. And as the transformation into the commodity results in a ghostly residue (*gespenstische Gegenstänlichkeit*) that is, precisely, equality, Fantômas, too, is a kind of everyman, a skeleton key, equivalent to everything, a figure for the pleasures and the horrors of modern systems of identity, providing an image of what the terrible freedom that they can grant might look like.[43]

Fantômas will doubtlessly remain, as one of his epithets has it, *l'Insaissable* (the uncatchable). But the figure of the supercriminal as it emerges in Feuillade's serial films does emerge in sharper relief by emphasizing how it is indebted to popular science. Fantômas and *Les Vampires* allegorize the ambivalent reception of scientific knowledge with a particular emphasis on the anxieties

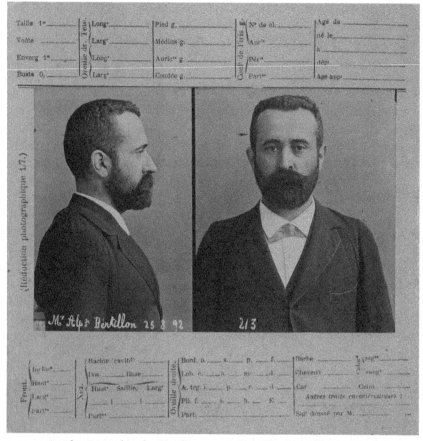

FIG. 5.3 An identity card in the Bertillon system (Bertillon himself is pictured). UCL, The Grant Museum of Zoology.

surrounding modern identity. The proliferation of scientific innovations is inseparable from the processes of modernization that transformed life and culture in the West over the course of the nineteenth and twentieth centuries. From rapid advances in medicine and the physical sciences to the steady increase in communication technologies that bridged vast distances to the multitude of devices that enabled the creation of a mass-cultural marketplace, the accelerated pace of scientific discovery made the inexplicable omnipresent. Barely understood scientific advances became integral parts of the fabric of everyday life in the form of steam and combustion engines, electricity, telegraphy, telephony, the cinema, radio, and myriad other technologies. The discovery of unseen worlds that had begun with the invention of the telescope and the microscope accelerated, revealing all manner of fascinating and disquieting invisible worlds. One way modern society dealt with the increase in scientific discovery was through an increased production of popular-science products, including books, magazines, lantern slides, and public lectures. These instructive entertainments made sense of scientific advances for the public. In their emphasis on the fantastic and the wondrous aspects of modern science, these aids to understanding constructed their own forms of knowledge.

As exhilarating as the rapid developments in modern technology could be, the onslaught of new devices also generated a considerable amount of apprehension. The cinema, itself a part of the panoply of technical advancement, certainly supplied a steady stream of images of scientific progress, but it also offered a rogue's gallery of criminals who availed themselves of the latest advances in science and technology to facilitate their nefarious enterprises. Another passage near the beginning of the first Fantômas novel indicates how this tension figured prominently in the novel, which the films develope as well. President Bonnet, a minor character, is discussing Fantômas, whom he has placed in a tradition of "enigmatical beings who are difficult to trace" such as Cagliostro, Vidocq, and Rocambole. "Now why should we suppose that in our time no one exists who emulates the deeds of those mighty criminals?" he asks. Another guest remarks that "The police do their work better in our time than ever before," to which he responds:

> That is perfectly true, [. . .] but their work is also more difficult than ever before. Criminals who operate in the grand manner have all sorts of things at their disposal nowadays. Science has done much for modern progress, but unfortunately it can be of invaluable assistance to criminals as well; the hosts of evil have the telegraph and the motorcar at their disposal just as authority has, and some day they will make use of the airplane.[44]

This passage highlights, on the one hand, how the crime melodrama takes as its central conflict what has been termed the "dialectical drama of modernity," in which the criminal attempts to take advantage of the complexity of the systems of circulation and the detective uses his critical intelligence to see through the criminal's dissimulations and restore order.[45] On the other hand, as the references to the telegraph, the motorcar, and the airplane make clear, Bonnet's observation indicates that this drama revolves around the control of technoscientific knowledge.

The first film in the Fantômas series premiered at the Gaumont-Palace in Paris on May 9, 1913. Fantômas, the dandified assassin, possessed an even more lethal command of the most modern technologies than Zigomar. In the opening sequence of the first Fantômas film, *In the Shadow of the Guillotine*, he lies in wait in Princess Sonia Danidoff's hotel room. When she returns, he emerges from behind a curtain and robs her of jewels and 120,000FF. Before he leaves the hotel room, he hands her a carte-de-visite. A close-up on the card in the princess's hands reveals that it is blank. Later the name of the card's owner appears in a close-up dissolve that shows the name Fantômas slowly fading into visibility (Fig. 5.4).

FIG. 5.4 Video stills from *Fantômas* (Louis Feuillade, 1913).

It is difficult to imagine a more apt object for introducing Fantômas: The black ink materializing out of the "nothing" of the white card mimics how Fantômas himself appears from the deep, dark backgrounds or curtains that hide him.[46] In this sense, the card functions as a metaphor, simulating Fantômas's spectral qualities; however, the basis for this metaphor, invisible ink, comes from the area of contemporary scientific technology. For, as the film reveals in a later scene when Juve finds a cache of blank cartes-de-visite in the office of Gurn (one of Fantômas's identities), the ink's mysterious appearing act is triggered by heat, a chemical reaction that Juve precipitates by breathing on one of the cards. In other words, Fantômas's cards achieve their effect via a sophisticated chemical trick. A manual of police science from 1911 contains an entire section devoted to a discussion of *"encres sympathiques"* or invisible inks, which reveals that Feuillade's visual metaphor to introduce Fantômas comes from the realm of popular science.[47]

Feuillade's crime melodramas are filled with objects of this kind, which at first may seem ridiculous or quaint but which can be revealed as popularizations of scientific advances. The central-heating system in Lady Bentham's villa in the third episode of *In the Shadow of the Guillotine*, can serve as a case in point of how the presence of science and technology literally underpins the diegesis. The villa's central-heating system receives a significant, and perhaps unexpected, amount of narrative exposition. The attention to this now-mundane detail of modern climate-control systems begins when the caretaker of the house explains its workings in detail. An intertitle reads, "That's the central heating. It is connected with the furnace in the basement." Following this information, a close-up of the heating duct demonstrates the difference between the grate's open and closed positions. The caretaker then takes Juve and Fandor to the basement to see the furnace.

Central heating in homes was unusual until after World War I, so the technology's novelty can account in part for Feuillade's care in explaining the system's workings. Primarily, however, the central heating serves crucial plot functions: It allows Juve and Fandor to eavesdrop on the secret meetings between Fantômas and Lady Bentham, and it provides the setting for one of the serial's most memorable moments when Juve, Fandor, and the police fish Fantômas's "silent executioner," a giant boa constrictor, out from behind the grate and blow its head off. Read from this perspective, the film's narrative subordinates the educative element of seeing how the central-heating system works. One might argue that the central heating serves primarily as a narrative device, but this type of argument ignores the register of meaning that comes from Feuillade's attention to the details of contemporary life.

The film devotes so much attention to the central-heating system not only because it furthers the narrative or because it is a new technology but also because it is emblematic of a disquieting aspect of modern technology, namely its penetration into the most ordinary aspects of everyday life. Behind the facades of modern homes lurk support systems that can be used against their original purposes, conduits that undermine the integrity and security of the home even as they supposedly serve it (the frequency of gas heating or lighting systems being used as a weapon, while, again, in *Les Vampires* perhaps related in some fashion to the War, is relevant here as well).

A further example of how devices both underpin and undermine safety in the modern metropolis occurs in the aforementioned sequence at the beginning of the first Fantômas film where Fantômas robs Princess Sonia Danidoff. A prominent feature of this sequence is the hotel's guest elevator. Feuillade takes a minor detail from the novel and makes it into a central component of his cinematic version of the robbery. When the princess returns to the hotel, the elevator takes her to her rooms, which are on the fourth floor. Feuillade includes separate shots as the elevator passes each floor, a repetition that from the perspective of narrative economy is excessive. When Fantômas leaves the princess's suite and reenters the elevator to make his escape, Feuillade again includes a shot that shows the elevator passing each floor.

There are a number of reasons that might account for this floor-by-floor depiction of the elevator's transit. Tracking the elevator's progress builds suspense, especially when Fantômas is making his escape during the elevator's descent. The real-time effect of watching the elevator descend underscores Fantômas's abilities as a quick-change artist, since in the relatively brief period of the elevator ride he overpowers a hotel bellhop and appropriates his uniform. One might also connect the inclusion of each floor to Feuillade's stylistic preference for long takes, although Feuillade clearly had no qualms about cutting to a noncontiguous floor, as he does when the bellhop, roused by the princess's call to the front desk, ascends to her floor, where he is ambushed by Fantômas. In addition, since Feuillade does not represent the elevator's ascent in a single tracking shot but rather cuts each time when the elevator moves on to the next floor, as dictated by the constraints of the set, the decision to include a shot of each floor actually deviates from an uninterrupted style.

The elevator sequence also, however, is related to the tendency for the crime melodrama to engage with what Gunning has called the "effective but enigmatic internal structures" that underpin the modern city.[48] The possibility of what is usually described as "the underworld" here takes on a more disturbing dimension, as Fantômas repurposes an elevator, making this novel mode of transport into his quick-change booth. Fantômas makes this amenity, a marker of luxury and technological progress, his helper, underscoring the vulnerability of all modern systems to criminal ingenuity.

Realizing how these scenes in *Fantômas* contain an ambivalent reaction to modern science and technology facilitates a better understanding of these films' vaunted attention to the texture of their time, locating it in specific strategies and relating it to prior aesthetic modes. To the extent that, as John Ashbery writes, "in Fantômas what we savor most are the details and décor," we should acknowledge that the source of this flavor of the real is rooted in a nonfiction aesthetic, a realization that can lead us to speak of Feuillade's indebtedness to the *documentaire* tradition.[49] Feuillade's biographer, Francis

Lacassin, writes about how one of his favorite moments is when a policeman unscrews the grate to the central-heating shaft:

> Perhaps the most beautiful scene in *Fantômas* isn't the struggle with the boa constrictor and the latter's death-pangs, nor the gunfight among the wine-barrels nor the masked criminal slipping into a cistern, but simply that in which a policeman is expertly unscrewing the grill of a ventilating duct, holding on to the fastened side of the plaque and experiencing from time to time the resistance of the screws, then carefully placing them beside the piece of metal once it has finally been removed. In this marvelous poetic anthology, each of us has at our disposal beforehand an image that is destined to thrill us. And for each of us it will never be the same one.[50]

The poetic thrill that this shot gives Lacassin stems from a moment where the film documents a process, where it adopts an instructional mode whose charm Lacassin mystifies in a way analogous to how fantastic realism mystifies its sources. The pleasure that Lacassin takes in this shot derives from the same type of pleasure that spectators took in watching films about the production of artificial flowers or the workings of the gyroscope.

Another aspect of the shot that Lacassin singles out for comment deserves to be highlighted—namely, that it is one of the many closer views in these films. As Abel has noticed:

> inserted throughout these scenes of combat between Juve and Fantômas . . . are an unusual number of close shots. Although serving a narrative function . . . these close shots give added weight and significance to the ordinary objects of everyday life. They, too, are circumscribed by Fantômas's power, symptoms not of the moral truth that Pathé's earlier melodramas sought to reveal through intensification but its grand guignol opposite—the criminal, the mad, and the perverse.[51]

These moments must not necessarily be seen as symptoms of criminality, madness, or perversion, however. They also can be read as a stylistic link to popular-science films' reliance on closer framings. Indeed, close-ups provide the strongest stylistic link between popular-science films and the crime melodrama. David Bordwell contends, "Feuillade stubbornly adheres to a precept that he will provide a close-up only if something is not fully visible in the long shot because it is tiny (printed matter, a cameo), peripheral (a hand under a bed), or blocked from view."[52] While not disagreeing with this claim, it is worth adding that many of Feuillade's close-ups are not of "tiny" objects so much as they are of scientific or technical objects for which Feuillade provides a close-up in order to show their workings in detail.[53]

In the climactic scene of *Juve contre Fantômas*, for instance, Feuillade cuts to a closer shot of a wine bottle that Fantômas uses to breathe while submerged in a cistern.[54] In a typical long shot, Feuillade shows how Navarre, dressed *en cagoule*, breaks out the bottom of the bottle on the tines of the bottle rack; then he cuts to a close-up on the bottom of the bottle (Fig. 5.5). The closer shot allows the viewer to see clearly the result of the action in the previous shot. Details of the acting in the close shot, such as how Navarre's finger clears away shards from the inside of the bottle, attempt to mitigate the jarring effect of this closer view by incorporating it into the narrative action. Nevertheless, the shot is not integrated smoothly into the flow of the diegesis as would be the case in later narrative films from the 1910s. The frontality of the framing relies on the monstrative aesthetic strategies that Feuillade shares with popular-science films.[55]

*   *   *

The question opening this section persists: Who is Fantômas? Is he the dapper figure who looms over the rooftops of Paris? This image began as a cast-off publicity image for a patent medicine—Fantômas initially hawked "pink pills for pale persons"—and became, with the subtraction of a dagger, less menacing as the poster illustration for the first Fantômas film, which also refined his physiognomy[56] (Fig. 5.6). This images would serve as a lodestone for the avant-garde reception of *Fantômas*, figuring in paintings by Juan Gris and René Magritte.

Fantômas as the dandified assassin has become synonymous with the character, although an equally important image is that of Fantômas *en cagoule*, as the hooded man in black, which provides the strongest iconographic

FIG. 5.5 Fantômas fashioning a breathing device from a bottle. Video stills from *Fantômas* (Louis Feuillade, 1913).

FIG. 5.5 Continued.

FIG. 5.6A Original cover for Pierre
Souvestre and Marcel Allain, *Fantômas*
(Paris: Fayard, 1911).

FIG. 5.6B Original poster for *Fantômas*
(Louis Feuillade, 1913).

ties between *Fantômas* and *Les Vampires* (Fig. 5.7). This image has many antecedents, from the executioner's hood to the garb of secret societies to the magical theater, and it appears as an aspect of Zigomar's costume as well, although there the hood is red.

Another figure in black that deserves consideration as an antecedent of Fantômas and the Vampires, however, is the man in the black bodysuit from Etienne-Jules Marey's chronophotographic experiments (Fig. 5.8). For Marey, the black bodysuit solved the problem of blur that had arisen as a result of photography's surfeit of detail. The black bodysuit reduced the figure in motion to an outline of underlying structures (Fig. 5.9). Bertillon's criminal identification system solved a similar problem: For the modern individual to emerge, the person in all his or her particularity first must be erased in order to appear again more clearly in the analytic systems designed to capture him or her.

M. NAVARRE

DANS LE ROLE DE L'HOMME NOIR

FIG. 5.7 Publicity photo for *Fantômas*.

FIG. 5.8 Georges Demenÿ in the black bodysuit.

Chronophotographie sur plaque de verre : Morin, course de vitesse, 18 juillet 1886.

FIG. 5.9A A chronophotograph with the black bodysuit.

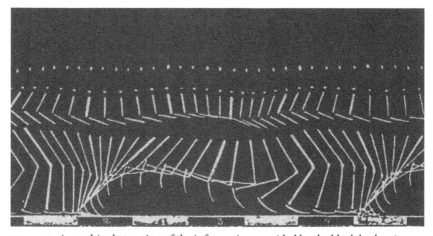

FIG. 5.9B A graphic abstraction of the information provided by the black bodysuit.

In addition to the clearly organized collection of data that emerges from these systems, however, another image arises, the phantom image of the blacked-out body that serves as the backdrop for modern identity, the blank card upon which the individual is written. The paradox that occurs at the establishment of modern identity is that it suddenly becomes conceivable that there is someone, or something, a phantom, that can assume any identity, or none at all. Like Edgar Allen Poe's man of the crowd, Fantômas is the type and genius of deep crime. Profoundly inscrutable, like the German book that Poe references, *er lässt sich nicht lesen*, he does not permit himself to be read. The most modern thing about Fantômas might be that there is no real unmasking him, that there is nothing behind the mask. Or rather, instead of a complete identity, there is an inexhaustible collection of trifles, all those little bits that, when pieced together, constitute yet another alias.

Les Vampires and the Cipher of Identity

Les Vampires, the ten-part serial that appeared from 1915 to 1916, is often seen as Feuillade's masterpiece. As in the Fantômas series, *Les Vampires* teems with technological gadgets that range from myriad forms of poison and poison-delivery devices (a ring, a pen, an atomizer, wine, etc.), more invisible ink, various cryptograms, a portable artillery gun with explosive shells, a lesson about how to duplicate keys, knockout potions, and so on.[57] These devices appear in the hands of the Vampires but also in the hands of the forces of law and order—Philippe Guérande, reporter for a major Parisian newspaper, and Mazamette St. Cloud, a onetime Vampire but now Philippe's trusted ally.

Secret writing features prominently in *Les Vampires*. The third episode, *The Red Codebook*, features a lengthy sequence in which Philippe deciphers the notebook he has taken from the Vampires' Grand Inquisitor (who, it is revealed in one of the many moments that demonstrate how the Vampires have infiltrated civic institutions, is the Chief Justice of the Supreme Court). In a lengthy close-up, the film treats the spectator to a detailed account of the process of decipherment, much in the way the spectator of a popular-science film would witness a process in its entirety. In the previously cited scientific police manual, the chapter devoted to the varieties of criminal ciphers (*ecriture en colonne, ecriture en diagonale, ecriture à l'envers*) contains a number of examples of codes that are very similar to the codes in *Les Vampires*. Indeed, the sequence where Philippe cracks the red codebook could serve as an illustration for this book[58] (Fig. 5.10).

Another remarkable instance of decryption in *Les Vampires* occurs when Philippe deciphers Irma Vep's name as an anagram for Vampire. Philippe, thanks to his decryption of the Vampire codebook, has found the locale where Irma Vep performs. Disguised as an *apache*, he scrutinizes the poster advertising Irma Vep in front of the "Rowdy Cat." After a cut to a closer view that isolates the name "Irma Vep," the letters that compose the name rearrange themselves to spell "Vampire" (Fig. 5.11). The stop-motion rearrangement of the letters can be read as a representation of Philippe's mental activity,

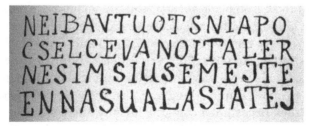

FIG. 5.10A An example of a criminal cipher. From R. A. Reiss, *Manuel de police scientifique* (1911).

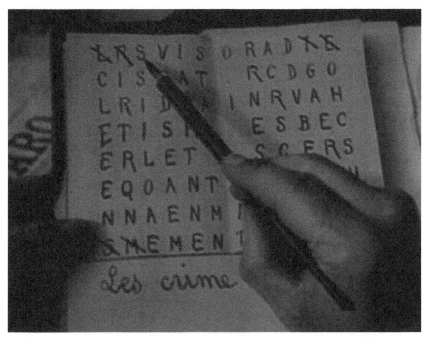

FIG. 5.10B Video still from *Les Vampires* (Louis Feuillade, 1915); episode 3, *The Red Codebook*.

a display of his thoughts as he realizes that Irma Vep is a member of the Vampire gang, and an efficient and clever way to convey this information. It is also something that could be found in an instructional film on verbal puzzles.[59] Not only is secret writing itself a popular-scientific object on display, but the way the film decrypts the information for the viewer is a popular-science moment.

This instance of stop-motion animation provides both narrative information and a lesson about the deceitfulness of appearances, of how names can conceal secret messages. As Gunning writes about Zigomar, "The spectator is not only amazed and amused, but becomes aware that everything s/he is seeing may have a hidden purpose, a concealed motive."[60] By revealing the deceitfulness of appearances, the film puts the spectator on her guard, providing an example of how the crime melodrama can perform a pedagogic function, how the school of crime can be a guide to modernity.

Feuillade thematizes the issue of identity in two instances of identity theft, one in the third Fantômas film and one in the eighth episode of *Les Vampires*. The greatest impact of forensic science and technology on the crime melodrama can be located among the technologies of identity, whose redefinition of the nature of the individual forms a logical target for anxieties about modernization. The systems of organization and control that came into increasing

FIG. 5.11 Phillipe deciphers Irma Vep. Video stills from *Les Vampires* (Louis Feuillade, 1915); episode 3, *The Red Codebook*.

FIG. 5.11 Continued.

use at the end of the nineteenth century, such as anthropometrics, an umbrella term that included Bertillon's system as well as the nascent science of fingerprinting, functioned by fostering a form of internalized surveillance. These technologies, developed to keep track of individuals within the flux of urban modernity, fostered a self-image that was based on certain statistical collections of data, increasingly turning the individual into a cipher.

A phrase for this branch of inquiry supplied by the films themselves is suggestive; an intertitle in *Fantômas* refers to the "*police scientifique*." The aforementioned manual on this subject contains a preface written by Louis Lépine, the *préfet* of the Paris police, that pragmatically explains the reasons behind the police's adoption of scientific methods: "The increase in public wealth tempts the audacity of criminals all the more since the prey is easier and the gains more profitable: modern discoveries have permitted them in many cases to perfect their tools by utilizing scientific processes. The police would be beneath its task if it did not also call science to its aid. Methods of identification and photography applied to judicial recording have become, thanks to Mr. Bertillon, a valuable assistant to the police."[61] The book's author, R.-A. Reiss, held the chair of *police scientifique* at the University of Lausanne; created in 1906, it was the first of its kind in Europe (Reiss notes that the subject had been taught at the university since 1902). In his prefatory remarks, Reiss makes a point of distinguishing his book from other accounts of police science: "The present work is made by a practitioner for the use of practitioners. I allow myself to insist on this point because it has appeared, several times, in the domain of the scientific police works that were nothing by simple compilations of popularizers never having gained in their lives the least expertise."[62] Reiss no doubt would have been irked by Feuillade's use of police science, although, as Lépine goes on to remark in terms that admit the difficulty of any rigorous separation of science from forms of entertainment, "As it stands, Mr. Reiss's book is an accomplished manual of practical policing, interesting like a novel, rigorous like a work of science."[63]

The incident of identity theft in *Fantômas* occupies the entire third episode, *Le Mort qui tue*. Fantômas frames Jacques Dollon, a young painter, for a murder and then has him murdered in prison. The film spends a significant amount of time showing the various stages of Dollon's visit to the anthropometry station (in the novel, Bertillon is named as a character). There he is photographed, his measurements are taken, and he is fingerprinted; this results in an identity card (Fig. 5.12). This sequence constitutes an instructional film within the film.

After Dollon's murder, Fantômas has his body spirited out of the prison, at which point he removes the skin from Dollon's hands. He wears this skin as gloves, which allow him to perpetrate crimes using Dollon's identity. The gloves of human skin demonstrate the subversion of the disciplinary sciences, how, when identity becomes statistical, or digital, so to speak, according to the Bertillon method of anthropometrics (whose residue is the practice of fingerprinting), identity becomes fluid and can be usurped.[64] The criminal appropriation of the technologies of identity results in an animation of the dead; when identity becomes impersonal, a card in a filing system, people in general are spectralized and a dead man can kill. While the film ends with a nominal restoration of order as Juve strips the glove of skin from the hand of

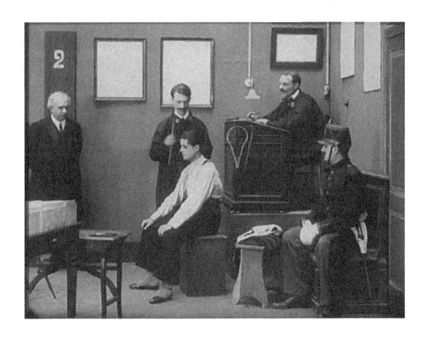

FIG. 5.12 Police scientifique. Video stills from *Le Mort qui tue* (Louis Feuillade, 1913).

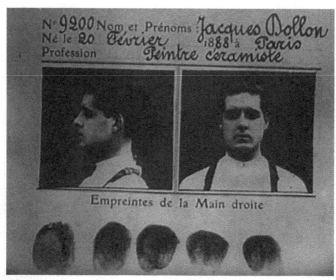

N° 9200 Nom et Prénoms : *Jacques Dollon*
Né le 20 *Février* 1888 à *Paris*
Profession *Peintre céramiste*

Empreintes de la Main droite

FIG. 5.12 Continued.

one of Fantômas's aliases, the banker Nanteuil, Fantômas immediately escapes again, having sown the seeds of doubt about systems of positivist
identity.

The second instance of identity theft occurs with the graphological and
phonographic impersonation of the American millionaire George Baldwin in
the *Satanas* episode of *Les Vampires*. The second Grand Vampire, Satanas,
plans to steal both Baldwin's signature and voice, which will allow him to
impersonate the millionaire at the bank. Lily Flower, a Vampire agent, arrives
at Baldwin's office posing as Henriette de Granville, a representative of
Modern Woman magazine.[65] She prevails upon Baldwin to sign a book so that
the magazine can feature him in its section of celebrity autographs. Of course,
the book he signs is *truqué*, utilizing a number of sheets that, when unfolded,
leave his signature isolated on a blank sheet of paper. The second component
of the scam involves Irma Vep posing as one Marie Boissier, an emissary of La
Compagnie Universelle des Phonographes. She asks Baldwin to record something that the company can offer its subscribers, who presumably pay to hear
the voices of visiting notables. Conveniently, Baldwin only knows one phrase
of French, *"Les Parisiennes sont les plus charmantes femmes,"* and he repeats it
all the time, to the point that it has become a unique and singular token of his
identity, something like an auditory signature. To use these two items in
tandem, Irma Vep must assume the role of a hotel telephone operator, playing
Baldwin's voice over the telephone to convince the bank agent that the with-
drawal slip Lily has brought is legitimate. The Vampires succeed in defraud-
ing Baldwin, at least temporarily, of $100,000 (Fig. 5.13).

FIG. 5.13 Identity theft. Video stills from *Les Vampires* (Louis Feuillade, 1915); episode 7, *Satanas*.

In both cases, the criminals (and the cinema) reveal how the technical prostheses of physical presence—fingerprints, the signature, the voice as heard through a telephone—are capable of being tricked out via modern technologies. Scientific knowledge leads to the permeability of class boundaries, which is another reason the supercriminal can move so easily from position to position. In modernity, having the right knowledge, being a polymath, a sharp operator, bestows a protean power.[66] Popular science dramatizes technical progress, providing a space for imagining its dark side, the dystopian imaginary, modern life's haunting double, the "terrors of technology."[67]

Fantômas and *Les Vampires* contain marked similarities to popular-science films, both stylistically and in terms of their obsession with registering the impact of science and technology on modern life. Stylistically, the serial and popular-science films share a tendency to utilize far more close-ups than was typical for fiction films of the time. For both types of film, the close-ups often function to demonstrate the workings of a technological device, indicating a common investment in an operational aesthetic. This link between popular-science films and the serial helps to modify the invocation of the term "fantastic realism" to characterize the aesthetic particularity of the French crime melodrama. When considered from the vantage point of popular-science films, episodes of "fantastic realism" can seem less mysterious (if no less fantastic), since their effects tend to come from the domain of popular-science imagery.

The figure of the scientific supercriminal registers fears about the potential dangers of an increasingly technologized world. Competing with these fears, however, is the figure of the scientific detective, who is locked in a Manichean struggle with the supercriminals in his attempt to provide an antidote to the terrors of technology. This classically melodramatic struggle tends to take place on the field of individual identity, with a proliferation of deceptions, disguises, and identity thefts that dramatize the ambiguities of personhood in an era that saw the rise of technologies of positive identification. The serial thus becomes itself a type of popular-science film, providing its audience with examples of the pleasures and the pitfalls of scientific advances.

Conclusion

Round and Round: From the Somersaulting Monkey
to "Bug Workout"

The scorpions from *L'Âge d'or* with which this book began, I suggest, mark a wider ambit for popular-science films, providing an example of how these images circulated. Two further instances of animals on film can serve as a concluding gesture to complement Buñuel's scorpions. While the scorpions demonstrated Surrealism's interest in popular science, *The Daily Dozen at the Zoo* (British Instructional Films, 1930) provides an instance of how a mainstream popular-science film can itself harbor a Surrealist dimension. "Bug Workout," a digital video posted to YouTube in 2014, recapitulates Percy Smith's juggling fly films, attesting both to continuities and transformations of popular-science films. Taken together, these two popular-science films gesture toward the mode's enduring relevance over the course of the twentieth century and up to the present day. These readings are not meant as a representative sampling of the vast domain of popular-science films after World War I. Rather, they function as emblems and extensions of the history that this book has established.

Animals are notoriously difficult to film, from F. Martin Duncan's denizens of the deep who had to be shot into a tank to provide moments of interesting incident, to the Éclair company's staging of the "fight" between the scorpion and the rat, to Feuillade's awkward handling of the boa constrictor in *Fantômas*. Whether disturbed by the simple proximity of humans, startled by the noise of the apparatus, overly attentive to the camera, or, as in the cases of certain microorganisms, morbidly photosensitive, animals present difficulties that are of another order when compared to even the fussiest of human actors. A short sequence near the conclusion of *The Daily Dozen* supplies an emblematic instance of an animal on film. In *The Secrets of Nature*, the 1934 companion book to the film series of which *The Daily Dozen* was a part, Mary Field wrote about the filming of this sequence: "We were trying to get a series of pictures of that monkey, so well known to Zoo visitors, who turns back somersaults continuously against the side of his cage until you feel dizzy with watching."[1] The film's central conceit is to anthropomorphize zoo animals so that they appear to be doing their daily exercises, their "daily dozen." It prompts us to read the monkey's somersaulting, then, as a workout. This tactic does not exhaust the meaning of this sequence, however. The soundtrack's use of a snare-drum roll and the climactic clash of the cymbals to punctuate the somersaults links the monkey's actions with the domain of circus performance, and, indeed, this sequence occurs almost at the end of the film, providing its big finale.

The sequence also can be seen as an allegory of mimetic innervation, however. Innervation here refers specifically to Walter Benjamin's idiosyncratic appropriation of a term that originated during the second half of the nineteenth century in the psycho-physiological laboratory. Miriam Hansen glosses the concept as follows: "What seems important to me regarding Benjamin's concept of innervation and its implications for film theory is the notion of a physiologically 'contagious' or 'infectious' movement that would trigger emotional effects in the viewer, a form of mimetic identification based on the phenomenon known as the Carpenter Effect."[2] That the somersaulting monkey makes sense as an image of innervation finds support in a detail of Field's previously quoted description of the monkey, who "turns back somersaults against the side of his cage until you feel dizzy with watching."

There are two components to mimetic innervation. The first involves a decentering, a movement beyond the limits of the individual body, a type of perception where the perceiver "gets lost" in something or someone else. Benjamin gives the example of the lover's accepting gaze at the wrinkles on the beloved's face for this type of perception; here the sensation of dizziness caused by looking at the monkey is a similar type of perception. The second dynamic has to do with incorporation, with a type of introjection—some of Benjamin's examples of this aspect are the cannibal or a man who remains seated even when the chair he is sitting on has been pulled away. In this second example, we can note that an apparatus external to the body has, via a corporeal performance, become a part of the body.

Benjamin calls the figure who unites these "opposite but complementary" elements of mimetic innervation the "excentric," whom he identifies in both the figures of Charlie Chaplin and Mickey Mouse. The excentric, as Hansen explains, gives "the encounter with technology an expression in the 'image world.'"[3] The somersaulting monkey provides an example of an excentric in Benjamin's sense. Indeed, *The Daily Dozen* was one of the first "Secrets of Nature" films to be made with a synchronized soundtrack, and the production crew described their aim as "to reproduce the Walt Disney technique with real animals instead of cartoons."[4]

A series of figural readings of the incessant somersaulting can follow, seeing in the repetitive, circular movement representations of the daily grind;

of the body adapted to modern, serial time; or of the extent to which precise iteration, without which modern mechanism would be unthinkable, has become a generalized characteristic of contemporary daily life. This type of argument spins off into other areas, including the avant-garde's engagement with the machine aesthetic in general and its fascination with spinning disks, such as the Duchamp's rotoreliefs, in particular. At some point this trajectory also involves a discussion of what is perhaps the preeminent collection of machines that spin, cinematic technology itself.

More immediately relevant for the current argument is that the monkey going round and round can provoke laughter. Humor, or more precisely the audience's collective laughter in the movie theater, is a crucial dimension for Benjamin's valorization of mimetic innervation as a mode of film practice, since it provides what he terms "a psychic inoculation" against mass psychoses, sadistic fantasies, and masochistic delusions.[5] Theodor Adorno argued against Benjamin's more optimistic stance toward collective laughter directed at Mickey, stressing Disney's sadomasochistic character (albeit in part via a redirection of his criticism toward Donald Duck). Of course, Benjamin's position is itself significantly ambivalent—as Hansen notes, "The dream memory Mickey innervates . . . is inseparable from that of nightmares, in particular modern nightmares induced by industrial and military technology."[6] It is worth mentioning in this context that the monkey's behavior in this sequence contains a darker dimension, since the somersaulting is the manifestation of a stress disorder that wild animals occasionally exhibit in zoo settings, especially when their enclosures are too small. The monkey's actions, when viewed from this perspective, are akin to the involuntary, repetitive motor disorders that afflicted shell-shocked soldiers in the wake of World War I.

There is another dimension to this sequence, something that the film tries to hide and as a result encrypts. What appears in the sequence is not exactly a somersaulting monkey, not just. Instead the film presents a monkey who has been made to somersault incessantly primarily by film editing. The reason for this artifice emerges from the filmmakers' account of the filming:

> You might easily think that the battery of lights, from which human film actors always declare they wince, might prove upsetting to the animals in the Zoo; but, on the contrary, I believe that the visits of our unit with its lamps mark high spots of enjoyment in the lives of the Zoo inmates. . . . But the pleasure the inmates of the Monkey House took in this artificial summer led to a good deal of trouble. We were trying to get a series of pictures of that monkey, so well known to Zoo visitors, who turns back somersaults continuously against the side of his cage until you feel dizzy with watching. When we arrived and set up the cameras and lamps he came, full of curiosity, to the front of the cage, until, finding that there was nothing to watch while we were waiting for the current to be switched on, he went

back to his exercises. But once the electrical connection was made and the lamps had been switched on one by one as the cameraman lit the cage, there was no more somersaulting. He swung on to the wire netting and, clinging on with all four paws, proceeded to toast his tummy. To get him back to the somersaulting we turned off the lights, but the moment we turned them on again he sprang into position on the wire. A tedious hour went past—we could have a first-class performance and no lights, or the lamps and an immobile monkey, but never lights and somersaults together. We tried to trick him by turning on the lamps quickly and filming him as he turned over, before he realized that the warmth was switched on again, but you need to be very quick to be quicker than a monkey, and we were a poor second. Worse still, after two hours he had learned that the call to the head electrician, 'Switch 'em on, Charlie!' always preceded the lovely flood of warmth, and after that he was always in position and ready for his sun-bathing seconds before the men had had time to turn the switches. We outwitted him at last by leaving him in the usual temperature of the Monkey House for a quarter of an hour until he began to somersault furi-ously. Then the camera was started and was running before, at a prear-ranged and silent signal, the lamps were switched on with a sudden glare and his own impetus carried him through a couple more revolutions before he could stop. In this way we 'stole' a number of somersaults which, when put together, made a long continuous series in the film. One morning, and an untold length of film gone for one sequence of less than one hundred feet, or about one minute's picture on the screen.[7]

This production story underscores the difficulty of filming animals, or, rather, the difficulty of having animals conform to the filmic convention of ignoring the cinematic apparatus. In this sense, animals differ fundamen-tally from most adult human actors. Benjamin writes about the film actor: "To act in the stream of klieg lights and simultaneously meet the require-ments of sound recording is a highly demanding test. Passing this test means to maintain one's humanity in the fact of the apparatus."[8] This sen-tence is unthinkable for animals, since it is paradoxical to speak of an animal actor. Animals lack the understanding of the camera's relation to memory; they do not have a sense of the audience that the camera repre-sents that at some point in the future will see them on film. The bright lights are not a glare that makes them wince; rather, the lights are an "artificial summer."

This aspect of the animal on film does not invalidate the figural reading, but it does point toward the incompleteness of such an approach. The film-makers likely would have preferred one, perhaps two long takes of the mon-key's somersaulting, which the monkey's unexpected reaction to their lights, however, made impossible. In reconstructing the absent profilmic event, the filmmakers followed conventions that Benjamin describes in a crucial passage:

> In the theater one is well aware of the place from which events on stage cannot immediately be detected as illusionary. There is no such place for the movie scene that is being shot. Its illusionary nature is a nature of a second degree, the result of editing. That is to say, in the studio the mechanical equipment has penetrated so deeply into reality that its pure aspect freed from the foreign substance of equipment is the result of a special procedure, namely, shooting from a particular camera set-up and linking the shot with other similar ones. The equipment-free aspect of reality here has become the height of artifice; the sight of immediate reality has become the "blue flower" in the land of technology.[9]

The unscreened images, those discarded shots of the monkey sunning itself in the lights, remain attached to the film in a certain sense. In the final frames of the slow-motion sequence, there is a brief glimpse of the blue flower, that sight of immediate reality, when the monkey turns to look at the camera (Fig. 6.1).

For Benjamin the goal of a cinema redeemed as a medium of experience was "making second nature return the look," and he warned against a redemptive reading of the direct address of the camera, which is not "a question of the photographed animals, people or babies 'looking at *you*' which implicates the viewer in such an unsavory manner."[10] This moment of direct address, however, is different when read in conjunction with the production history, since encrypted in these frames is the story that does not make it onto the screen, the story of the monkey engaged in a type of game with the camera crew, the interplay between nature and humanity that innervation regulates.

FIG. 6.1 Video still from *The Daily Dozen at the Zoo* (1930). British Pathé.

Immediately after this glance, the monkey raun toward the camera, leapt onto the wire mesh of its cage, and sunned its tummy. The humor of this moment is quite different from the kinds of laughs that the film's anthropomorphism elicits; here the joke is on the filmmakers. The humor of this moment is reflexive and based in a different kind of world, "a world," to quote Benjamin again, "in which the true surrealist face of existence breaks through."[11]

The second example I would like to turn to by way of conclusion raises the issue of repetition. In April 2014, "Zain the pain" posted "Bug Workout" to YouTube. The video consists of a single shot, a medium-close framing of a stinkbug as it "juggles" a piece of Styrofoam (Fig.6.2). In a little over a month, "Bug Workout" received over 500,000 views along with attention in traditional and online media.[12]

"Bug Workout" recalls Percy Smith's juggling fly films in its depiction of the same behavior, in its anthropomorphization, and in its popularity. Instead of the circus as invoked by Smith's notion of the "juggling" or "acrobatic" fly, however, this video conceives of the movements of the insect against the backdrop of the gym. The comments section of the video's YouTube page contains hundreds of reactions that both recapitulate and extend the reception of Smith's fly films.[13] Many comments refer to the "workout" context—marveling at the bug's stamina, wondering whether it will skip legs tomorrow, and so forth. Predictably, there are meme references; more than one poster asks "Do you even work out, bro?" or some other variation. Other comments echo the question of animal cruelty, wondering whether the bug had been glued down, and speculating about its need for food (the poster mentioned that he observed the bug performing this activity for over three hours).

Almost entirely missing from the comments on "Bug Workout," however, is the framework of popular science. There is no presentation before a learned

FIG. 6.2 Video still from "Bug Workout" (2014).

society, no discussion of the entomological knowledge that underlies the striking image. Instead, the video is presented more in the spirit of a decontextualized curiosity. The music, Wagner's "Ride of the Valkyries," provides an ironic gloss, probably also informed by its use in *Apocalypse Now* (Francis Ford Coppola, 1979). (Several commentators called for substituting "Eye of the Tiger.") The metaphorical connotations are especially prominent. Numerous comments refer to the bug as Atlas, seeing it as carrying the world on its back, or juggling the world, or both. The other classical allusion that receives mention is Sisyphus. And then there are combinations: "Gregor Samsa + Sisyphus + aerobics."

Another intriguing variation in reception involves the reflexive technological reading. Smith's fly films caused some viewers to question whether the film was a cinematic trick (and we can recall here as well *The Unclean World*'s recasting of *Cheese Mites*' spectacle as a technological illusion). The variant that occurs repeatedly in responses to "Bug Workout" is to interpret the insect as malfunctioning software, as in "buggy bug," "error 404, insect not found," or "stack overflow." Given the repetitive nature of the action, some commenters wondered whether the action was looped, and calls for an animated gif were quickly answered. Although the video is only two minutes and twenty-nine seconds long, the fact that it consists of a single, uninterrupted shot raises the issue of duration in a manner different from Smith's fly films.

As this book's penultimate image, "Bug Workout" points to the long afterlife of early popular-science films. With the closing of the circle, however, it should be clear that it is not a matter of a closed loop but rather of spiraling, of repetition as a form of change. The somersaulting monkey was part of the expansion of popular-science filmmaking in the 1930s, and popular-science films continued to proliferate over the course of the twentieth century. A tendency of this history is repetition—already in the first decade of popular-science filmmaking, Percy Smith was reusing F. Martin Duncan's work, either literally or approximately, and the catalogues of the French popular-science filmmakers were replete with titles from their British predecessors, whose topics in turn were taken from the lantern shows of the latter half of the nineteenth century. The phenomenon of remaking is of course far from limited to nonfiction filmmaking, although the different conception of what factual films represent did make them subject to different types of recycling, as in Charles Urban's inveterate repackaging of his archival footage.[14]

Enduring Curiosity: The Raised Curtain

I dream of a new age of curiosity. We have the technical means for it; the desire is there; the things to be known are infinite; the people who can employ themselves at this task exist. Why do we suffer? From too little: from channels that are too narrow, skimpy, quasi-monopolistic, insufficient. There is no point in adopting a protectionist attitude, to prevent "bad" information from invading and suffocating the "good." Rather, we must multiply the paths and the possibility of comings and goings.[15]

This book has aimed not only to bring early popular-science films out of obscurity but also to insist on their multiplicity, both their location within a long history of scientific display and their irreducible circulation beyond what might be thought of as their proper boundaries. As a keyword, "curiosity" indicates a venerable tradition for popular-science films, and it is a concept that has become more prominent in the last few decades, as evidenced by PBS's "Stay Curious" campaign from 2000, with spots directed by Errol Morris; the Discovery Channel's nonfiction series, "Curiosity," and its educational website curiosity.com; and the naming contest for the Mars rover, where an essay proposing the name "Curiosity" was the winner.[16] Indeed, the cultures of art and science, which never were entirely separate, seem increasingly entwined.

FIG. 6.3 *The Artist in His Museum* (Charles Wilson Peale, 1822).

The image of a raised curtain, a well-known example of which is *The Artist in His Museum* (1822), can serve as a final emblem of the tradition of curiosity of which popular-science films are a part (Fig. 6.3). A raised curtain appears in several of the images related to popular-science films already discussed—in Charles Urban's promotional slide for *The Unseen World* as well as in the cover image of George Kleine's educational film catalogue.[17] The motif of the raised curtain signals an apt encapsulation of core qualities of popular-science films, particularly the centrality of the process of "unveiling" or "revealing." The moment of unveiling is temporally ambivalent; half-raised, the curtain could be opening or closing. As a gesture, it is an epistemological incitement, informed by the showman's flair for drama and the dramaturgy of knowledge. Popular-science films, too, are devices of revelation, lifting the curtain on images that fascinate, educate, and circulate in ways that are simultaneously venerable and novel, familiar and strange.

{ NOTES }

Epigraph

1. Hollis Frampton, "Digressions on the Photographic Agony," in *Circles of Confusion: Film-Photography-Video: Texts 1968–1980* (New York: Visual Studies Workshop Press, 1983), 180. Thanks to Ken Eisenstein for sharing the quotation with me.

Introduction

1. See John Hammond, *L'Âge d'or* (London: BFI, 1997), 7.

2. For more detailed accounts of *Le Scorpion Languedocien*, see my "Ethologie and *L'Âge d'or*," *Montage A/V* 14 (November 2005): 44–51; and Chapter Three of this book. For an account of Surrealism's embrace of the science film, see my "'Beauty of Chance': *Film ist.*" *Journal of Visual Culture* 11, no. 3 (2012): 307–327.

3. James Secord, "Knowledge in Transit," *Isis* 95, no. 4 (December 2004): 654–672.

4. Méliès, quoted in Maurice Bessy and Lo Duca, *Georges Méliès: Mage* (Paris: Prisma, 1945), 43; quoted in Laurent Mannoni, *The Great Art of Light and Shadow*, 462.

5. In the extensive bibliography on the founders of cinema, the works that have contributed the most to my understanding of the role of science in cinema's emergence are Charles Musser, *The Emergence of Cinema: The American Screen to 1907* (Los Angeles: University of California Press, 1990); Marta Braun, *Picturing Time: The Work of Etienne-Jules Marey, 1830–1904* (Chicago: University of Chicago Press, 1992); Laurent Mannoni, *The Great Art of Light and Shadow: Archaeology of the Cinema*, trans. Richard Crangle (1994; Exeter: University of Exeter Press, 2000); Phillip Prodger, *Time Stands Still: Muybridge and the Instantaneous Photography Movement* (New York: Oxford University Press, 2003); and Virgilio Tosi, *Cinema before Cinema: The Origins of Scientific Cinematography*, trans. Sergio Angelini (London: British Universities Film and Video Council, 2005).

6. Lisa Cartwright, *Screening the Body: Tracing Medicine's Visual Culture* (Minneapolis: University of Minnesota Press, 1995), 3. Cartwright draws heavily on Michel Foucault's concept of the "medical gaze," for which see Michel Foucault, *The Birth of the Clinic: An Archeology of Medical Perception*, trans. A. M. Sheridan Smith (New York: Vintage Books, 1975).

7. See Laura Mulvey, *Fetishism and Curiosity* (London: BFI Publishing, 1996), esp. ch. 4, "Pandora's Box: Topographies of Curiosity." See also Victoria Reid, *André Gide and Curiosity* (Amsterdam: Rodopi, 2009), for an investigation that makes use of a different psychoanalytic framework, that of Kleinian epistemophilia.

8. On the historical changes in the concept of curiosity, see Lorraine Daston and Katherine Park, *Wonders and the Order of Nature, 1150–1750* (New York: Zone Books, 2001).

9. My choice of this understanding of curiosity as a structuring concept is indebted to Tom Gunning, who explains how curiosity is related to what he terms the cinema's "gnostic mission" in the following way: "It is as though the two aspects of Augustine's *curiositas*, the investigation of nature and the fascination with novelties, has been rejoined in a peculiarly modern Gnostic impulse" (Tom Gunning, "In Your Face: Physiognomy, Photography, and the Gnostic Mission of Early Film," in *The Mind of Modernism*, ed. Mark S. Micale [Stanford, CA: Stanford University Press, 2004], 141–171, at 167).

10. Hans Blumenberg, *The Legitimacy of the Modern Age*, trans. Robert M. Wallace (1966: Cambridge, MA: MIT Press, 1985).

11. Lorraine Daston and Peter Galison, *Objectivity* (New York: Zone Books, 2010), 18.

12. For an account of the science film as a stimulus to desire, see James Leo Cahill, "Hors d'oeuvre: Science, the Short Film, and *The Perception of Life*," *Framework: The Journal of Cinema and Media* 52, no. 1 (spring 2011): 66–82.

13. [Michel Foucault], "The Masked Philosopher: Interview with Christian Delacampagne for *La Monde*, April 1980," in *Foucault Live (Interviews, 1966–84)*, trans. John Johnston, ed. Sylvère Lotringer (New York: Semiotext[e], 1989), 198–199. I first encountered this quotation as the epigraph to Park and Daston, *Wonders and the Order of Nature*, 9.

14. For the literary genre of the journey through the microscope, see Bernard Lightman, "The Microscopic World," *Victorian Review* 36, no. 2 (fall 2010): 46–49; and Melanie Keene, "Object Lessons: Sensory Science Education, 1830–1870," Ph.D. dissertation, University of Cambridge, 2008, esp. the sections "Drops of Water, or Object Lesson as Instrument," 55–60; and "Enchanted Horses and Drops of Water, or Object Lessons as Fact and Fancy," 74–86. For the nineteenth-century microscope show, see Richard D. Altick, *The Shows of London* (Cambridge, MA: Belknap, 1978); and Iwan Rhys Morus, "'More the Aspect of Magic than Anything Natural': The Philosophy of Demonstration," in *Science in the Marketplace: Nineteenth-Century Sites and Experiences*, ed. Aileen Fyfe and Bernard Lightman (Chicago: University of Chicago Press, 2007), 336–370, esp. 344–50; see also Hannah Landecker, "Creeping, Drinking, Dying: The Cinematic Portal and the Microscopic World of the Twentieth Century Cell," *Science in Context* 24, no. 3 (2011): 381–416.

15. The essays collected in *Early Cinema: Space, Frame, Narrative*, ed. Thomas Elsaesser (London: BFI, 1990), provide a useful point of entry into the scholarship on this period. For a more recent survey of the field, see *The Encyclopedia of Early Cinema*, ed. Richard Abel (New York: Routledge, 2005); and *The Cinema of Attractions Reloaded*, ed. Wanda Strauven (Amsterdam: Amsterdam University Press, 2006).

16. Grierson's definition is imprecise, however. In the essay that most clearly sets out a definition, the "formal limits of the species" are not categorical but rather a matter of a passage from one kind to another. "This is indeed a particularly important limit to record, for beyond the newsmen and the magazine men and the lecturers . . . one begins to wander into the world of documentary proper. Here we pass from the plain (or fancy) descriptions of natural material, to arrangements, rearrangements, and creative shapings of it" (John Grierson, "First Principles of Documentary," in *Grierson on Documentary*, ed. Forsyth Hardy [1946: New York, Praeger Publishers, 1971], 146). What precisely separates the one kind from the other is not spelled out. And not only is the question of what constitutes documentary proper largely a matter of opinion, but Grierson's own first use of the term "documentary," an anonymous review of Flaherty's *Moana*, also is

unorthodox—antithetical, in fact, to its later meaning: "Of course, *Moana* being a visual account of events in the daily life of a Polynesian youth and his family, has documentary value. But that, I believe, is secondary to its value as a soft breath from a sunlit island washed by a marvelous sea as warm as the balmy air" ([John Grierson], "Poetic Moana," in *The Documentary Tradition*, ed. Jacobs, 25–26). These brief examples are meant to serve as representative placeholders for the general point that Grierson's separation of early nonfiction from "documentary proper" was more arbitrary and unsustainable than its canonization would admit.

17. Grierson, "First Principles," 146.

18. The phrase "uninterpreted fact" was used in the title of a film program at the Museum of Modern Art in 1939; the full title was "The Nonfiction Film: From Uninterpreted Fact to Documentary." See Tino Balio, *Grand Design: Hollywood as a Modern Business Enterprise, 1930–1939* (Los Angeles: University of California Press, 1996), 353.

19. Tom Gunning, "Before Documentary: Early Nonfiction Films and the 'View' Aesthetic," in *Uncharted Territory: Essays on Early Nonfiction*, ed. Daan Hertogs and Nico DeKlerk (Amsterdam: Stichting Nederlands Filmmusuem, 1997), 12.

20. Lewis Jacobs, ed. *The Documentary Tradition: From* Nanook *to* Woodstock (New York: Hopkinson and Blake, 1971). For a thorough, insightful discussion of Grierson's (and Rotha's) appropriation of "documentary" and the repercussions for other forms of nonfiction filmmaking, particularly the popular-science film, see James Leo Cahill, "Jean Painlevé's Cinematic Wildlife," Ph.D. dissertation, University of Southern California (2010): 30–50.

21. See Bill Nichols, "Documentary Film and the Modernist Avant Garde," *Critical Inquiry* 27 (summer 2001): 580–610. See also Bill Nichols, *Introduction to Documentary*, 2nd ed. (Bloomington and Indianapolis: University of Indiana Press, 2010), esp. ch. 5, "How Did Documentary Filmmaking Get Started?"

This neglect has occurred in spite of the fact that the term "documentary" frequently was used before Grierson to describe nonfiction cinema. Roland Cosandey provides numerous instances of the prevalence of the category *documentaire*, and Luke McKernan notes that Charles Urban used the term in 1907. See Roland Cosandey, "Some Thoughts on 'Early Documentary,'" in *Uncharted Territory*, 49. The English usage occurs in a translation from a lecture in French given by Dr. Eugène-Louis Doyen at the International Congress of Medicine in Madrid in 1903; for extracts from Urban's text, including the citation of Doyen, see http://www.charlesurban.com/documents_cinematograph.html [accessed November 6, 2013]. A catalogue from 1912 uses *"documentaire"* as an overarching category, and the subtitle of George Maurice's first article calling for popular-science cinema is entitled "Chronique Documentaire." The catalogue is *Liste complete des Principaux Films Instructifs, Éducatifs, Scientifiques, Documentaires, et de Voyages parus en 1912 avec le nom de l'Editeur, le métrage et tous reseignments utiles*. This text was published by the Charles Mendel periodical *Cinéma-Revue* and is from the collection of the Nederlands Filmmuseum; my thanks to Jennifer Peterson for making it available to me. Many more examples could be adduced here, but the point is to indicate how easy it is to forget, especially from an Anglo-American point of view, the widespread use of "documentary" pre-Grierson.

22. The essays in *Uncharted Territory* were instigated by a conference on early nonfiction hosted by the Filmmuseum, the transcript of which was published as *Nonfiction from the Teens: The 1994 Amsterdam Workshop*, ed. Daan Hertogs and Nico DeKlerk

(Amsterdam: Stichting Nederlands Filmmuseum, 1994). A number of special journal issues dedicated to this area also appeared: *Images du réel: La non-fiction en France (1890–1930)* ed. Thierry Lefebvre *1895* no. 18 (summer 1995); *Griffithiana* 66–70 (1999–2000) on "The Wonders of the Biograph," ed. Luke McKernan and Mark van den Tempel; *Film History* 13, no. 2 (2001) "Non-Fiction Film," ed. Stephen Bottomore; and *Historical Journal of Film Radio and Television* 22, no. 3, ed. Frank Kessler (2002). Important exhibition events in this context include the retrospectives in 1995 at the Bologna and Pordenone film festivals as well as a program at the Haus des Dokumentarfilms in Stuttgart. For a critique of the programming logic of these "revivals," in particular the Pordenone program, see Stephen Bottomore, "Rediscovering Early Non-Fiction Film," *Film History* 13, no. 2 (2001): 160–173.

23. See Dan Streible, Marsha Orgeron, and Devin Orgeron, eds., *Learning with the Lights Off: Educational Cinema in the United States* (New York: Oxford University Press, 2010); Charles Acland and Haidee Wasson, eds., *Useful Cinema* (Durham, NC: Duke University Press, 2011); Vinzenz Hediger and Patrick Vonderau, eds., *Films that Work: Industrial Film and the Productivity of Media* (Amsterdam: Amsterdam University Press, 2009); Paula Amad, *Counter-Archive: Film, the Everyday, and Albert Kahn's Archives de la Planète* (New York: Columbia University Press, 2010); Scott Curtis, *Managing Modernity: Art, Science, and Early Cinema in Germany* (New York: Columbia University Press, 2015); Lee Grieveson, *Policing Cinema: Movies and Censorship in Early-Twentieth-Century America* (Los Angeles: University of California Press, 2005); Luke McKernan, *Charles Urban: Pioneering the Non-Fiction Film in Britain and America, 1897–1925* (Exeter: University of Exeter Press, 2013); Kirsten Ostherr, *Medical Visions: Producing the Patient through Film, Television and Imaging Technologies* (New York: Oxford University Press, 2012); Jennifer Peterson, *Education in the School of Dreams: Travelogues and Early Nonfiction Film* (Durham, NC: Duke University Press, 2013); Matthew Solomon, *Disappearing Tricks: Silent Film, Houdini, and the New Magic of the Twentieth Century* (Champaign: University of Illinois Press, 2010); Dan Streible, *Fight Pictures: A History of Boxing and Early Cinema* (Los Angeles: University of California Press, 2008); Nana Verhoeff, *The West in Early Cinema: After the Beginning* (Amsterdam: University of Amsterdam Press, 2006); Valérie Vignaux, *Jean-Benoit-Lévy ou le corps comme utopie. Une histoire du cinema éducateur dans l'entre-deux-guerres en France* (Paris: AFRHC, 2007); and Kristin Whissel, *Picturing American Modernity: Traffic, Technology, and Silent Cinema* (Durham, NC: Duke University Press, 2010).

24. For a consideration of the different perspectives that cinema history and the history of science can provide to a study of the moving image, see Scott Curtis, "Science Lessons," *Film History* 25, no. 1–2 (2012): 45–54.

25. For an overview of scholarship on science's visual dimension, see Daston and Galison, *Objectivity*, 420, fn. 2.

26. See Sidney Perkowitz, *Hollywood Science: Movies, Science, and the End of the World* (New York: Columbia University Press, 2010).

27. See the introduction to a special section on the history of science in film, Rima D. Apple and Michael W. Apple, "Screening Science," *Isis* 84, no. 4 (December 1993): 750–754; and "Special Forum: Films Every Environmental Historian Should See," *Environmental History* 12, no. 2 (2007): 280–293.

28. See Hannah Landecker, *Culturing Life: How Cells Became Technologies* (Cambridge, MA: Harvard University Press, 2010); David Kirby, *Lab Coats in Hollywood:*

Science, Scientists, and Cinema (Cambridge, MA: MIT University Press, 2011); Jimena Canales, *A Tenth of a Second: A History* (Chicago: University of Chicago Press, 2011); Hanna Rose Shell, *Hide and Seek: Camouflage, Photography, and the Media of Reconnaissance* (New York: Zone Books, 2012); and Tania Munz, *The Dance of the Bees* (Chicago: University of Chicago Press, forthcoming).

29. See Martin Pernick, *The Black Stork: Eugenics and the Death of "Defective" Babies in American Medicine and Motion Pictures Since 1915* (New York: Oxford University Press, 1999); and Nancy Anderson and Michael R. Dietrich, eds., *The Educated Eye: Visual Pedagogy in the Life Sciences* (Hanover, NH: Dartmouth University Press, 2012).

30. The book that most directly overlaps with this study is Timothy Boon, *Films of Fact: A History of Science in Documentary Films and Television* (New York: Wallflower Press, 2008). On the "natural history" genre, see Gregg Mitman, *Reel Nature: America's Romance with Wildlife on Film* (Cambridge, MA: Harvard University Press, 1999); Derek Bousé, *Wildlife Films* (Philadelphia: University of Pennsylvania Press, 2000); Palle B. Petterson, *Cameras into the Wild: A History of Early Wildlife and Expedition Filmmaking, 1895–1928* (Jefferson, NC: McFarland & Company, 2011); Jean-Baptiste Gouyon, "The BBC Natural History Unit: Instituting Natural History Film-Making in Britain," *History of Science* 49, no. 4 (2011): 425–451; and Jean-Baptiste Gouyon, "From Kearton to Attenborough— Fashioning the Telenaturalist's Identity," *History of Science* 49, no. 1 (2011): 25–60.

Another area that could be included in the domain of popular-science cinema is anthropology, for which see Fatimah Tobing Rony, *The Third Eye: Race, Cinema, and Ethnographic Spectacle* (Durham, NC: Duke University Press, 1997); and Alison Griffiths, *Wondrous Difference: Cinema, Anthropology, and Turn-of-the-Century Visual Culture* (New York: Columbia University Press, 2003).

31. Roger Cooter and Stephen Pumfrey, "Separate Spheres and Public Places: Reflections on the History of Science Popularization and Science in Popular Culture," *History of Science* 32 (1994): 237–267.

32. Jonathan R. Topham, "Rethinking the History of Science Popularization/Popular Science," in *Popularizing Science and Technology in the European Periphery, 1800–2000*, ed. Faidra Papanelopoulou, Agustí Nieto-Galan, and Enrique Perdiguero (London: Ashgate, 2009), 1–20, at 2.

33. Secord, "Knowledge in Transit," 661. See also Ludwig Fleck, *Genesis and Development of a Scientific Fact*, ed. Thaddeus J. Trenn and Robert K. Merton (1935; Chicago: University of Chicago Press, 1979).

34. See Katherine Pandora, "Knowledge Held in Common: Tales of Luther Burbank and Science in the American Vernacular," *Isis* 92(2001): 484–516; Pamela Smith, *The Body of the Artisan: Art and Experience in the Scientific Revolution* (Chicago: University of Chicago Press, 2006); Peter Broks, *Media Science before the Great War* (New York: St. Martin's Press, 1996); and Rae Beth Gordon, *Dances with Darwin, 1875–1910: Vernacular Modernity in France* (London: Ashgate, 2009). See also, on "vernacular globalization," Arjun Appadurai, *Modernity at Large: Cultural Dimensions of Globalization* (Minneapolis: Minnesota University Press, 1996); and Stuart Hall's invocation of the notion of "vernacular modernity" in "A Conversation with Stuart Hall," *Journal of the International Institute* (fall 1999): 15.

35. Miriam Bratu Hansen, "The Mass Production of the Senses: Classical Cinema as Vernacular Modernism," *Modernism/modernity* 6 (April 1999): 60. For my own use of "vernacular" to discuss these films, see my "'A Drama Unites Them in a Fight to the

Death': Some Remarks on the Flourishing of a Cinema of Scientific Vernacularization in France, 1909–1914," *Historical Journal of Film, Radio, and Television* 22, no. 3 (2002): 353–374.

36. As Peter Bowler has pointed out, the diffusionist model of popularization, for all its limitations, was operative, especially in the early twentieth century; see Peter Bowler, *Science for All: The Popularization of Science in Early Twentieth-Century Britain* (Chicago: University of Chicago Press, 2009).

37. Topham, "Introduction," 312.

38. Ralph O'Connor, "Reflections on Popular Science in Britain: Genres, Categories, and Historians," *Isis* 100, no. 2(2009): 333–345, at 344.

39. Bernard Lightman, *Victorian Popularizers of Science: Designing Nature for New Audiences* (Chicago: University of Chicago Press, 2007), 495.

40. For the creation of the identity of the scientist, see Sydney Ross, "*Scientist:* The Story of a Word," *Annals of Science*, 18, no. 2 (June 1962): 65–85; and on the formation of scientific disciplines, see Timothy Lenoir, *Instituting Science: The Cultural Production of Scientific Disciplines* (Palo Alto, CA: Stanford University Press, 1997); and David Cahan, ed., *From Natural History to the Sciences: Writing the History of Nineteenth-Century Science* (Chicago: University of Chicago Press, 2003).

41. Lightman, *Victorian Popularizers*, 494.

42. Secord, *Victorian Sensation*, 2; cited in Lightman, *Victorian Popularizers*, 31.

43. Lightman, *Victorian Popularizers*, 37. Other historians of science who have paid particular attention to the importance of the visual in the nineteenth-century scientific culture include Iwan Rhys Morus, Anne Secord, Jennifer Tucker, and Kelley Wilder.

44. See *Science in the Marketplace: Nineteenth-Century Sites and Experiences*, ed. Bernard Lightman and Aileen Fyfe (Chicago: University of Chicago Press, 2007).

45. More work remains to be done on this front, on popular-science films produced during this period in Italy, Germany, and Russia, as well as the use of popular-science films in colonial settings.

46. F. Martin Duncan, *Cassell's Natural History* (London: Cassell and Company, 1913), viii.

Chapter 1

1. See Tom Gunning, "1902–1903: Movies, Stories, and Attractions," in *American Cinema, 1890–1909: Themes and Variations*, ed. André Gaudreault (New Brunswick, NJ: Rutgers University Press, 2009), 112–132. See also Charles Musser, *The Emergence of Cinema: The American Screen to 1907* (Los Angeles: University of California Press, 1994), where he argues for 1903 as the year when story films began to predominate.

2. The story of how Urban sold a deluxe edition of the final title to Marshall Field became part of his persona; see Charles Urban, *A Yank in Britain: The Lost Memoirs of Charles Urban, Film Pioneer*, ed. Luke McKernan (London: The Projection Box, 1999), 23–26. As McKernan notes, the Marshall Field anecdote also appears in Terry Ramsaye, *A Million and One Nights: A History of the Motion Picture* (New York: Simon and Schuster, 1926), 358–360. In a particularly memorable example of the culture-as-commodity dynamic, Urban relates an anecdote about selling "books by the yard" to an illiterate wholesale hardware merchant: "So long as the backs of the books were bound in red, green or

brown leather with famous authors' names stamped in gold lettering he was satisfied to buy dozens of sets of Dickens, Thackeray, Longfellow, Mark Twain, etc. etc." (*A Yank in Britain*, 20).

3. Luke McKernan, *Charles Urban: Pioneering the Nonfiction Film in Britain and America, 1897–1925* (Exeter: University of Exeter Press, 2012), 7–8. McKernan's monograph is a comprehensive and thoughtful account of Urban's work to which I am greatly indebted. My synopsis of Urban's early career also draws on the elaborate website on Urban that McKernan maintains, http://www.charlesurban.com

4. It may be that Urban already had met and engaged Duncan before the establishment of the CUTC. "Previous to 1903, Mr. Charles Urban joined issue with Mr. Martin Duncan in the production of micro-kinematographic films" (Thomas Clegg, "Hyper-micro-kinematography," *The Kinematograph and Lantern Weekly*, 11 November 1909; Charles Urban Papers, National Media Museum, Bradford, UK; URB 8/2, 2).

5. See T. G. Bonney, "Duncan, Peter Martin (1824–1891)," rev. Yolanda Foote, *Oxford Dictionary of National Biography*, Oxford University Press, 2004 [http://www.oxforddnb.com/view/article/8228, accessed November 4, 2013].

6. This book was number 23 in "The Amateur Photographer's Library," a series that also contained Cecil Hepworth's *Animated Photography: The A B C of the Cinematograph* (1897). Duncan makes a distinction here, as will Percy Smith, between photomicrography and microphotography, the latter being the field pertaining to microscopic photographs, such as were used during the German siege of Paris in 1870 to transmit secret messages via pigeons. By extension, the term "cinemicrography" could be regarded as the more correct term as opposed to "microcinematography," but both terms were used during the 1910s to refer to motion pictures obtained through a microscope, and since "microcinematography" is currently in more widespread use, I have opted for its use.

7. Tim Boon, *Films of Fact: A History of Science in Documentary Film and Television* (New York: Wallflower Press, 2008), 12.

8. These articles are reprinted in the booklet "Reprints of Press Articles Re: The Urban-Duncan Micro-Bioscope: Series of Animated Pictures of Nature's Closest Secrets . . ." n.d. [September 1903], 3–8; Charles Urban Papers, URB-10; hereafter cited as "Reprints."

9. "New Camera Wonders," *Daily Mail*, 10 July 1903; quoted in "Reprints," 3.

10. *The Amateur Photographer*, 16 July 1903; quoted in "Reprints," 7.

11. *Focus*, 2 July 1903; quoted in "Reprints," 8.

12. "New Camera Wonders," quoted in "Reprints," 3–4.

13. For an account of Percy Smith's work for Urban, see Chapter Two.

14. See Yuri Tsivian, *Early Cinema in Russia and Its Cultural Reception*, trans. Alan Bodger (Chicago, IL: University of Chicago Press, 1998).

15. E. P. S., "Pictures of the Unseen," *Daily Express*, 15 July 1903; quoted in "Reprints," 4.

16. Daily Mail, quoted in "Reprints," 3.

17. *Daily Express*, quoted in "Reprints," 4.

18. For more on the relations of microscopic scale and magnified time, see Chapter Two's discussion of time-lapse plant growth films.

19. *Focus*; quoted in "Reprints," 8.

20. "Considering the time of year, the enormous business done at the Alhambra last week was truly remarkable" (*The Referee*, 23 August 1903; quoted in *List of Urban Film Subjects* (London: Charles Urban Trading Company, 1903), 91; Charles Urban Papers, National

Media Museum, Bradford, UK; URB 10-1; hereafter abbreviated *List*. This catalogue is also available on *Early Rare Filmmakers' Catalogues: 1896-1913*, collected by the British Film Institute [London: World Microfilms Publications, 1983], reel 6).

21. *Daily Express*, quoted in "Reprints," 4.

22. Quoted in *List*, 66. The mention of the bee series forming the second part of the program is from *The Era*'s review (quoted in *List*, 89–90). The catalogue supplements that contain the first announcements of *The Unseen World* shows note, "This striking series of pictures were procured through the courtesy of Mr. C. T. Overton, Bee Expert, Crawley" (*Early Rare Filmmakers' Catalogues: 1896-1913*, collected by the British Film Institute [London: World Microfilms Publications, 1983], reel 7).

23. *List*, 89.

24. McKernan, *Charles Urban*, 43.

25. *List*, 64.

26. *Daily Express*, quoted in "Reprints," 4. For more on the importance of the movement/stillness dichotomy for an understanding of science and film, see Scott Curtis, "Still/Moving: Digital Imaging and Medical Hermeneutics," in *Memory Bytes: History, Technology, and Culture*, ed. Lauren Rabinovitz and Abraham Geil (Durham, NC: Duke University Press, 2004), 218–254; and Hannah Landecker, "Cellular Features: Microcinematography and Film Theory," *Critical Inquiry* 31, no. 4 (2005): 903–937.

27. *Free Lance*, 21 August 1903; quoted in *List*, 91.

28. *Weekly Dispatch*, 23 August 1903; quoted in *List*, 92.

29. See Richard D. Altick, *The Shows of London* (Cambridge, MA: Harvard University Press, 1978), 386. See also 363–389, where, among many other facts, Altick mentions that John Henry Pepper lectured on a number of subjects at the Polytechnic, such as the purity of Burton's ale. There were numerous optical entertainments at the Polytechnic, from life-sized models, most famously the diving bell, to regular lantern shows, to Pepper's ghost show. For more on Pepper's scientific showmanship, see James Secord, "Quick and Magical Shaper of Science," *Science*, New Series, 297, no. 5587 (6 Sept. 2002): 1648–1649; and Bernard Lightman, "The Showmen of Science: Wood, Pepper, and Visual Spectacle," Chapter Four in *Victorian Popularizers of Science: Designing Nature for New Audiences* (Chicago, IL: University of Chicago Press, 2007), 167–218. For more on nineteenth-century scientific showmanship, see also Iwan Rhys Morus, "More the Aspect of Magic than Anything Natural: The Philosophy of Demonstration in Victorian Popular Science," in *Science in the Marketplace: Nineteenth-Century Sites and Experiences*, ed. Bernard Lightman and Aileen Fyfe (Chicago, IL: University of Chicago Press, 2007), 336–370.

30. *The Referee*, quoted in *List*, 91. The reference is to Thomas Day, *The History of Sandford and Merton* (1783), a children's book that espoused Rousseauian ideas.

31. *The People*, 23 August 1903; quoted in *List*, 92.

32. *Nature*, 27 August 1903; quoted in *List*, 93.

33. *Morning Post*, quoted in *List*, 89.

34. "Popular Science at the Alhambra," *Court Circular*, 29 August 1903; quoted in *List*, 94.

35. *The Morning Advertiser*, quoted in *List*, 92. See also *Science in the Marketplace: Nineteenth Century Sites and Experiences*, ed. Aileen Fyfe & Bernard Lightman (Chicago, IL: University of Chicago Press, 2007).

36. Titles cited are from the Magic Lantern Society Library, whose titles are consultable at www.magiclantern.org.uk. The human physiology lecture is W. Furneaux, "The Human Body; or, the House We Live in" (Magic Lantern Society collection, 90,608.htm). See also Terry Borton, "238 Eminent American 'Magic-Lantern' Showmen: The Chautauqua Lecturers," *The Magic Lantern Gazette* 25, no. 1 (spring 2013): 3–34, for an overview of a late-nineteenth- and early-twentieth-century U.S. practice that has many similarities to Duncan's cultural milieu.

37. "Nature on the Stage," *Daily Telegraph*, 21 October 1903; quoted in *List*, 79.

38. "Popular Science at the Alhambra," *The Court Circular*, 29 August 1903; quoted in *List*, 94.

39. "New Alhambra Wonders," *The Court Circular*, 24 October 1903; quoted in *List*, 81.

40. In 1905, Urban also began to advertise "The 'Nature' series of permanent photographic enlargement," images that were described as "suitable for hanging in class and lecture rooms, school rooms, play rooms, etc., etc." (*Revised List of High-Class Original Copyrighted Bioscope Films* [London: The Charles Urban Trading Company, 1905], 64; Charles Urban Papers, National Media Museum, Bradford, UK; URB 10-2; hereafter abbreviated *Revised List*. This catalogue is also available on *Early Rare Filmmakers' Catalogues: 1896–1913*, collected by the British Film Institute (London: World Microfilms Publications, 1983), reel 7).

41. *Revised List*, 8.

42. "University and Educational Intelligence," *Nature* 68, no. 1774, (29 October 1903), 638. On the rise of nature study, see Sally Kohlstedt, "Nature, Not Books : Scientists and the Origins of the Nature-Study Movement in the 1890s," *Isis* 96 (2005): 324–352; and Kevin C. Armitage, *The Nature Study Movement: The Forgotten Popularizer of America's Conservation Ethic*(Lawrence: University of Kansas Press, 2009).

43. "The Nature-Study Exhibition," *Nature* 69, no. 1775 (5 November 1903): 18. See also David Allen, *The Naturalist in Britain: A Social History* (Princeton, NJ: Princeton University Press, 1994), who mentions Duncan in connection with birdwatching.

44. *List*, 66. This film is partially preserved at the NFTVA under the title *[Reptilen und Amphybien]*. It has been identified by the archive as an Edison film because it begins with an Edison logo. Either an exhibitor edited together footage from various sources, or Edison duped Urban's footage. The latter possibility seems likely, since there are a number of titles in early Edison catalogues that match Urban's films exactly (a fifteen-part film about bees, for instance). More elements of Duncan's films may therefore exist than previously thought.

45. Jean Painlevé uses a human skull to similar effect in *The Octopus* (1928).

46. *Revised List*, 149.

47. *Manchester Evening Chronicle*, 18 August 1903; quoted in *List*, 91.

48. *Morning Post*, 18 August 1903; quoted in "Reprints," 9–10.

49. *Sunday Special*, 23 August 1903; quoted in *List*, 92.

50. Bernard Lightman, "The Microscopic World," *Victorian Review* 36, no. 2 (fall 2010): 46–49; and Melanie Keene, "Object Lessons: Sensory Science Education, 1830–1870," PhD dissertation, University of Cambridge, 2008.

51. *Morning Leader*, 24 August 1903; quoted in *List*, 92. Luigi Cornaro, an Italian nobleman and author of *Discorsi della Vitta sobria* (Discourses on the sober life), radically changed his diet and lifestyle at the age of forty from indulgence to abstemiousness. He lived to be 102 (b. 1464, d. 1566).

52. *Topical Times*, 29 August 1903; quoted in *List*, 94.

53. *News of the World*, 23 August 1903, quoted in *List*, 92.

54. "Microbic Monsters," *Daily Express*, 31 August 1903; quoted in *List*, 93.

55. See Tom Dewe Mathews, *Censored* (London: Chatto and Windus, 1994), 3–4, where he states that *Cheese Mites* was the first instance of film censorship.

56. See "Cheese Mites and Other Wonders," a BBC news article about the 2008 exhibition at the Science Museum in London: http://news.bbc.co.uk/2/hi/uk_news/magazine/7423847.stm [accessed November 4, 2013].

57. Jutta Schickore, *The Microscope and the Eye: A History of Reflections, 1740–1870* (Chicago, IL: University of Chicago Press, 2007), 117–118.

58. "Science in a Music Hall," *The Tatler* Aug. 26/Sept. 2, 1903; quoted in *List*, 94. My first evaluation of Urban's science films, "The Sources of 'The Secrets of Nature': The Popular Science Film at Urban, 1903–1911," in *Scene Stealing: Sources for British Cinema before 1930*, ed. Alan Burton and Laraine Porter (Trowbridge: Flicks Books, 2003), 36–42, mistakenly claimed that the original version of *Cheese Mites* in *The Unseen World* contained two shots. I thank Luke McKernan for pointing out the mistake to me.

59. *List*, 84.

60. For an account of how this film was found, see my contribution to the "Primal Screen: The World of Silent Cinema," column, *Sight & Sound* (February 2015): 59.

61. The latter description comes from an Edison catalogue: "A gentleman is here shown partaking of a little lunch of bread and cheese, and occasionally is seen to glance at his morning paper through a reading glass. He suddenly notices that the cheese is a little out of the ordinary, and examines it with his glass. To his horror, he finds it to be alive with mites, and, in disgust, leaves the table. Hundreds of mites resembling crabs are seen scurrying in all directions. A wonderful picture and a subject hitherto unthought of in animated photography" (*No. 200, Edison Films, Supplement* [January 1904], 16; consulted at http://hdl.rutgers.edu/1782.2/rucoreo0000001079.Book.16864; accessed July 8, 2013).

62. The stated length of the film in the catalogue of 150ft would mean a print length of 2,400 frames; the existing print contains 2,250 frames (140.6ft). If the current print of the film is missing 150 frames, which represent approximately ten seconds of action at 16fps, a brief final shot that returned to the initial framing showing the gentleman throwing away the cheese is possible.

63. See Tom Gunning, "An Aesthetic of Astonishment: Early Film and the (In)Credulous Spectator," *Art & Text* 34 (1989): 31–45; and Stephen Bottomore, "The Panicking Audience?: Early Cinema and the 'Train Effect,'" *Historical Journal of Film, Radio, and Television* 19, no. 2 (1999): 177–216.

64. In a later edition of the catalogue, the mites are described as a "large and happy family," presumably because there are different sizes of mites (parent mite, baby mite). In this version, the description of the shot where the investigator looks at the piece of cheese, entitled "The Naturalist at Lunch," has changed as well; here he places the cheese under his magnifying glass because he is "prompted by curiosity" (the films are part of the series "Through the Microscope" (560ft) in *Catalogue: Scientific and Educational Subjects: Urbanora, the World's Educator, 2nd and Enlarged Edition* [London: 1909], 59). This catalogue is available on *Early Rare Filmmakers' Catalogues: 1896–1913*, collected by the British Film Institute (London: World Microfilms Publications, 1983), reel 7.

65. The most famous example is Maxim Gorky, "The Lumière Cinematograph" (1896), reprinted in *In the Kingdom of Shadows: A Companion to Early Cinema*, ed. Colin Harding and Simon Popple (Madison & Teaneck, NJ: Fairleigh Dickinson University Press, 1996), 5–6; see also Tom Gunning, "Intermediality and Modes of Reception," in *Encyclopedia of Early Cinema*, ed. Richard Abel (New York: Routledge, 2010), 324–325.

66. *Le Déjeuner du savant* (Pathé, 1905) is similar to *Cheese Mites* as well. See Emily Godbey, "The Cinema of (Un)attractions: The Microscopic On Screen," in *Allegories of Communication: Intermedial Concerns from Cinema to the Digital*, ed. Jan Olsson and John Fullerton (Rome: John Libbey, 2004), 277–298.

67. *Third Supplementary Catalogue of the Latest Hepwix Films* (London: Hepworth & Co., June 1904), 19.

68. Iwan Rhys Morus has noted, "Historians of science should be interested in the history of illusions. . . . They provide us with a way of probing the relationship between seeing and believing science" ("Seeing and Believing Science," *Isis* 97, no. 1 [2006]: 102). The issue of fakery is a prominent offshoot of this nexus of science–demonstration–illusion.

69. See Tom Gunning, "What I Saw from the Rear Window of the Folies-Dramatiques, or, the Story Point-of-View Films Told," in *Ce que je vois de mon ciné*, ed André Gaudreault (Paris: Méridiens Klincksieck, 1988), 33–43.

70. Laurent Le Forestier, "Une Disparition ins*tru*ctive: Quelques hypotheses sur l'évolution des 'scènes à trucs' chez Pathé," *1895* 27, "Pour une histoire des trucages," ed., Thierry Lefebvre (September 1999): 68.

71. Tom Gunning, "'Those Drawn with a Very Fine Camel's Hair Brush': The Origins of Film Genres," *Iris* 19 (1995): 58.

72. *The Court Circular*, quoted in *List*, 94.

73. Clegg, "Hyper-micro-kinematography." The argument that cinema could serve as an alternative to the saloon later would become a mainstay of the uplift approach to reforming film culture; see Lee Grieveson, *Policing Cinema: Movies and Censorship in Early-Twentieth-Century-America* (Los Angeles: University of California Press, 2004).

74. For more on the importance of programming for early cinema, see Nico de Klerk, "Program Formats," in *Encyclopedia of Early Cinema*, ed. Richard Abel (New York: Routledge, 2005), 533–535.

75. Urban himself contributed to this impression; the section in the *Revised List* entitled "The Unseen World" consisted solely of microcinematographic films, although in previous version of the catalogue, the microscopic and macroscopic subjects are interspersed.

76. McKernan, *Charles Urban*, 43.

77. *The Era*, quoted in *List*, 89–90.

78. *Revised List*, 41.

79. "Nature on the Stage," *Daily Telegraph*, 21 October 1903; quoted in *List*, 80.

80. For an account of cinema's role in promoting closeness to nature, see Gregg Mitman, *Reel Nature: America's Romance with Wildlife on Film* (Cambridge, MA: Harvard University Press, 1999), esp. Chapter 3, "Zooming in on Animals' Private Lives," 59–84.

81. *Daily Telegraph*, 18 August 1903; quoted in *List*, 89.

82. Nico de Klerk mentions that by 1897, the British Mutoscope and Biograph show at the Palace Theatre was thirty minutes long ("Program Formats," *Encyclopedia of Early Cinema*, 533); see also Musser, *The Emergence of Cinema*, 38–42 and 193–223; and Dan

Streible, *Fight Pictures: A History of Boxing and Early Cinema* (Los Angeles: University of California Press, 2008).

83. "Sugar-Coated Science," *Manchester Chronicle*, n.d. [Dec. 1904]; quoted in *Revised List*, 118.

84. "'Urbanora.' Amusement Combined with Instruction. Novel Matinees." *Daily Express*, n.d.; quoted in *Revised List*, 120.

85. *The Referee*, n.d. [January 1905]; quoted in *Revised List*, 121.

86. Rosenthal, Lomas, and Avery all were active for Urban in other areas; see McKernan, *Charles Urban*; and Stephen Bottomore, "Joseph Rosenthal: The Most Glorious Profession," *Sight & Sound* 52, no. 4 (autumn 1983): 261.

87. Program for Alhambra Theatre, n.d. [1905?]; Charles Urban Papers, National Media Museum, Bradford, UK, URB 3/2, 68.

88. See Daston and Galison, *Objectivity*, 55–114.

89. *The Sunday Times*, n.d. [January 1905]; quoted in *Revised List*, 119.

90. *Westminster Gazette*, n.d. [January 1905]; quoted in *Revised List*, 119.

91. *Revised List*, 139.

92. Ibid., 143. The description of "wooden animals . . . descending the gangway in pairs" suggests that this prologue was a trick film.

93. *List*, 68. By 1904 450ft was not an unprecedented length for a single title. The titles of the individual parts were *Capturing a Swarm of Bees, The Old-Fashioned Straw Skep, The Platform in Front of the Hive after a Spell of Wet Weather, Bees Carrying Away Flowers Which Have Dropped in Front of the Hive, Skep Showing Comb and Bees, Smoking out the Bees from Skep into Basket, Inside View of Basket Containing Bees, Placing Bees in Front of Hive, General View of a Modern Bee Farm, Bee Farmer Examining Hive, Foundation Ready To Be Placed into Hive, Foundation Worked by Bees, Brood Comb with Queen and Workers, Comb with Cells Capped,* and *Magnified View of Comb.*

94. The description for *The Primrose and the Bee* noted, "This subject added to No. 2020 [i.e., *The Busy Bee*] enhances the interest of both," so it was likely additional material. The total footage of these individual films is 675ft, so they either included some footage not present in *The Busy Bee* or footage was repeated among the films.

95. *List*, 86.

96. On Urban's prominence in the formation of nontheatrical cinema, see McKernan, *Charles Urban*, 125–198.

97. See McKernan, *Charles Urban*, 31–33.

98. F. Martin Duncan, *Daily Mail*, n.d.; quoted in "Reprints," 3.

99. *Revised List*, 6.

100. See Thierry Lefebvre, "Charles Urban et le film d'éducation: Brèves réflexions sur quelques documents des Archives Will Day," *1895*, "The Will Day Historical Collection of Cinematography and Moving Picture Equipment," Hors-série (October 1997): 129–135.

101. Charles Urban, *The Cinematograph in Education, Science, and Matters of State* (London: Charles Urban Trading Company, 1907), 7.

102. Urban, *Cinematograph*, 15, 10. For an analysis of the rhetoric of education employed by early producers, see my "The Cinema of the Future: Visions of the Medium as Modern Educator," in *Learning with the Lights Off: Educational Film in the United States*, ed. Dan Streible, Marsha Orgeron, and Devin Orgeron (New York: Oxford University Press, 2011), 67–89.

103. On Doyen, see Thierry Lefebvre, *Le Chair et le celluloïd: Le cinema chirurgical du docteur Doyen* (Bar-le-Duc: Jean Doyen, 2004).

104. Urban, *Cinematograph*, 40.

105. "Ants and Their Ways," in *Readings for Lantern Slides: Tenth Series* (London: Walter Tyler, c. 1893), 44; from the Magic Lantern Society Slide Reading Library, no. 90,816. My thanks to Vanessa Toulmin for making this material available to me. For a thorough and fascinating account of ants in nineteenth- and twentieth-century science, see Charlotte Sleigh, *Six Legs Better: A Cultural History of Myrmecology* (Baltimore, MD: The Johns Hopkins University Press, 2007).

106. *Revised List*, 121.

107. *Uncle Tom's Cabin* (Edwin S. Porter, 1903) is one of the first films to use intertitles.

108. Thanks to Luke McKernan for sharing this cartoon with me. The contextual information about Urban and his attempts to stamp out dupers is also from McKernan (personal communication, October 28, 2002). The cartoon seems to be by Theodore Brown, the journal's editor.

109. "Chats with Trade Leaders: No. 1—Mr. Charles Urban," *The Optical Lantern and Cinematograph Journal* 1 (Nov. 1904–Oct. 1905): 15; consulted through the Media History Digital Library.

110. *The Optical Lantern and Cinematograph Journal* 1 (Nov. 1904–Oct. 1905): 69; consulted through the Media History Digital Library.

111. The dates for the various foundings and changes in ownership come from McKernan's detailed account of Urban's business history, 103–105 for Eclipse and Kineto, and 135 for the Natural Color Kinematograph Co., Ltd. For more on Kinemacolor and popular science, see Chapter Two.

112. Duncan gave a presentation to the Essex Field Club on Saturday, November 25, 1905, on "The Romance of Plant Life" (*Nature*, no. 1882, vol. 73 [23 Nov. 1905]: 96). On Wednesday, November 22, 1905, Duncan lectured on "The Cinematograph and Its Applications" at the Society of Arts (*Nature* 1881, vol. 73 [16 November 1905]: 72). On January 1 and 8 Duncan was back at the Society of Arts with a similar lecture, "The Scientific Applications of the Kinematograph," which was advertised as "suitable for a juvenile audience" (*Nature* 1990, vol. 77 [19 December 1907]: 154). Further research into the daily and periodical press may very well turn up further speaking engagements.

113. *Nature,* no. 1996, vol. 77, 30 January 1908: 312.

114. *Nature,* no. 2013, vol. 78, 28 May 1908: 94.

115. *Nature,* no. 2011, vol. 78, 14 May 1908, 48; *Nature,* no. 2137, vol. 84, 13 October 1910: 468; *Nature,* no. 2211, vol. 89, 14 March 1912: 54. Urban's publicity never mentions this organization, but the frontispiece of the 1913 edition of *Cassell's Natural History* identifies Duncan as "member of the Marine Biological Association of the United Kingdom." The Association was founded in 1884 by E. Ray Lankester, and its research profile concerned "the advancement of our knowledge of the life and habits of the marketable marine fishes, the organisms upon which they feed at various stages of their life, their migrations, rate of growth, and the effects which modern trawling is having upon their numbers" (*Cassell's Natural History* [1913], 202).

116. The photograph of the boa constrictor is opposite 256 in *Cassell's* and on 69 of the *List*; the infusorian is after 16 in *Cassell's* and on 86 of the *List*; the fresh-water hydra

photograph is after 40 in *Cassell's* and on 84 in the *List*; and the photograph of the porcupine is after 388 in *Cassell's* and on 25 of *Revised List*.

117. See Caroline Fuchs, "Das Autochrom als Medium der Wissenschaft," Chapter Two of "Farbwerte - Das Autochrom und der Stellenwert der Farbe in der Fotografie in Großbritannien," Ph.D. dissertation, University of Vienna (2013). See also the website "Exhibitions of the Royal Photographic Society, 1870–1915," http://erps.dmu.ac.uk/ [accessed July 3, 2014], which contains records of Duncan's involvement as an exhibitor beginning in 1904, lists him as a Fellow of the Society beginning in 1907, and lists him as a judge beginning in 1909.

118. See J. A. Arkwright, A. Bacot, and F. Martin Duncan, "The Association of *Rickettsia* with Trench Fever," *Journal of Hygiene* 18, no. 1 (1918): 76–94.

119. See *Golden Days: Historic Photography of the London Zoo* (London: Duckworth, 1976).

120. F. Martin Duncan to Messrs. W. Butcher & Sons, Ltd., Cinematograph Department, Camera House, Farringdon Avenue, R. C. 4; 16 May 1922 (Library out-letter book, 1921–1924, Zoological Society of London, 134). My thanks to Michael Palmer, Archivist of the Zoological Society of London, for making this letter available to me.

121. For more on the cultures of nineteenth-century popularization in England, see Lightman, *Victorian Popularizers of Science.*

122. McKernan, *Charles Urban*, 58.

Chapter 2

1. F. A. Talbot, *Moving Pictures: How They Are Made and Worked* (1912; New York: Arno Press, 1970), 190.

2. [Anonymous], "A Kinematographic Wizard," *Daily News and Leader*, n.d.; clipping in Charles Urban Papers, National Media Museum, Bradford, UK, URB 8–1, 33.

3. Undated MS. note by Percy Smith; Charles Urban Papers, URB 8–7.

4. For more on the Quekett Club and Duncan's and Smith's involvement in it, see Boon, *Films of Fact*, 19–22.

5. See Lynn K. Nyhart, "Natural History and the 'New Biology,'" in *Cultures of Natural History*, ed. N. Jardine, J. A. Secord, and E. C. Spary (New York: Cambridge University Press, 1996), 426–443.

6. Boon, *Films of Fact*, 16. See also Jean-Marc Drouin and Bernadette Bensaude-Vincent, "Nature for the People," in *Cultures of Natural History*, ed. N. Jardine, J. A. Secord, and E. C. Spary (New York: Cambridge University Press, 1996), 408–425.

7. Boon, *Films of Fact*, 28. J. V. Pickstone, *Ways of Knowing* (Manchester: Manchester University Press, 2000), 76; quoted in Boon, *Films of Fact*, 16.

8. On the continuing viability of popularization in the early twentieth century, see Peter Bowler, *Science for All: The Popularization of Science in Early Twentieth-Century Britain* (Chicago: University of Chicago Press, 2009). For an admirably thorough account of Smith's career that demonstrates his increasing visibility over the course of his career, see the series of articles by Mark Burgess, "F. P. Smith and the Secrets of Nature," *Quekett Journal of Microscopy* (1993–94): 146–160; 234–250; 326–340.

9. For descriptions of the Keartons' films for Urban, see "Marvellous Pictures of Bird Life," Urban catalogue supplement no. 204; *Early Rare British Film Catalogues* microfilm, reel 7. The Keartons wrote the first natural history book illustrated with photographs,

British Bird Nests (1895), and were also responsible for expedition films, notably *With Roosevelt in Africa* (1910); see also, for instance, Richard Kearton, *With Nature and a Camera: Being the Adventures and Observations of a Field Naturalist and an Animal Photographer* (London: Cassell and Company, 1898); Cherry Kearton, *Photographing Animal Life across the World* (1913; London: Arrowsmith Ltd., 1923). Mavroyani made *The Story of the Mantis: Bloodthirsty Insects of the Locust Order* (1911) and the travel films *A Trip Through Asia Minor* (1911) and *Scenes around Smyrna* (1911). He also is most likely responsible for *The Naturalist in Asia Minor* (1912?).

10. For more on Pike, see his *Nature and My Cine Camera: Story and Lessons of Making Eighty Nature Films* (London: Focal Press, 1946). F. Martin Duncan made a long film also entitled *In Birdland* for Urban in 1907—versions of this material were part of Urban's catalogues for years (see "Marvellous Pictures of Bird Life," Urban catalogue supplement no. 204; Early Rare British Film Catalogues microfilm, reel 7).

11. Bee-Mason, who changed his name to include his favorite insect, made a number of films about bees, two of which survive at the BFI, *The Bee's Eviction* (Warwick 1909) and *The Life of the Honey Bee* (Tyler 1911); see http://www.screenonline.org.uk/people/id/1266258/index.html. Spitta was a microscopist, a member of the Royal College of Surgeons, and a president of the Quekett Microscopical Club. Examples of Spitta's photomicrographs can be seen in George Newman, *Bacteria: Especially as They Are Related to the Economy of Nature, to Industrial Processes, and to the Public Health* (London: John Murray, 1900). See also Spitta, *Microscopy: The Construction, Theory, and Use of the Microscope*, 3rd ed. (1907; London: John Murray, 1920), and idem., *Photo-Micrography* (London: Scientific Press, 1898). See http://www.screenonline.org.uk/film/id/1354036/index.html for a description of his film *Nature's Hidden Beauties: Pond Life* (Williamson 1908). Williamson also produced *The History of a Butterfly—A Romance of Insect Life* (1910), which is preserved at the BFI and is available for viewing at http://www.wildfilmhistory.org/film/28/The+History+of+a+Butterfly+-+A+Romance+of+Insect+Life.html. The film is notable as a very early example of time-lapse photography, which it employs in sequences of butterflies emerging from the pupa stage.

12. This chapter does not present a complete account of Smith's early career. A next step would be to construct a complete filmography of Smith's films at Urban as well as Smith's scientific publications.

13. "Experiences of Mr. Percy Smith. His Scientific Work on Behalf of Kinemacolor and Kineto, Ltd.," *The Kinematograph and Lantern Weekly* (30 March 1911): 74.

14. F. J. Mortimer, "The Topic of the Week," *The Amateur Photographer and Photographic News* 48, no. 1260 (24 November 1908): 487. The main point of this editorial was to promote the Kinora, a home film-viewing machine.

15. Percy Smith, "Cinematograph work 1908 May 22 to 1910 Jun. and 1930 Sep," URB 8/6–3, 1.

16. Blowfly (also carrion fly or bluebottle) is the common term for the *Calliphoridae* family of flies, which is distinct from the housefly (*Musca domestica*).

17. F. Martin Duncan was also a member of Quekett, a connection that may have led to Smith's contact with Urban.

18. The most elaborate version of the story is in Irene Wilson, "His Name Was Smith," *Cine-Technician* 54 (May/June 1945): 56, 62–63.

19. Smith, "Cinematographic work," 2.

20. "New Urban Films," Supplement no. 234, n.d. [1908]; *Early Rare British Film Catalogues*, reel 7. Since the supplements are not dated, there is no precise date of release.

21. The Urbanora show had been transferred to the Palace Theatre from the Alhambra August 3, 1908 (McKernan, *Charles Urban*, 86).

22. Interview with Percy Smith, *The Kinematograph and Lantern Weekly*, 30 March 1911.

23. Anonymous, "New Friends," *St. James's Gazette*, 12 November 1908; URB 8/1, 55.

24. Interview with Smith, *Kinematograph and Lantern Weekly*.

25. The figure of 150 press notices appears in George L. Clue, "Our Interviews. No. 6—Mr. F. Percy Smith," *Civil Service Observer* 17, no. 6 (June 1911): 103. A transcript of the lecture suggests that the films were added to Smith's lecture as an afterthought: "Hearing he [Smith] was lecturing that evening, Mr. Charles Urban had kindly sent down a cinematograph apparatus, the records for which had been prepared from his (Mr. Smith's) negatives" (Frank P. Smith, "Flies and Their Foes, through Microscope and Camera," *The Photographic Journal* [December 1908]: n.p.; clipping in URB 8/1, 49). The transcript also recorded the discussion after the lecture, where F. Martin Duncan praised Smith's work.

26. Interview with Smith, *Kinematograph and Lantern Weekly*.

27. Percy Smith, "The True Story of the Juggling Fly," *Civil Service Observer* 15, no. 1 (January 1909): 13. In addition to the aforementioned transcript of Smith's presentation at the Royal Photographical Society, which was published in *The Photographic Journal*, Smith provided the following accounts of the juggling fly films: "The Evolution of the Juggling Fly," *Pearsons Magazine* (1909) [URB 8/2, 43–7]; "The Physical Energy of the Blue-Bottle," *Chambers's Journal*, undated clipping, URB 8–1, n.p.; "Experiences of Mr. Percy Smith: His Scientific Work on Behalf of Kinemacolor and Kineto, Ltd.," *Kinematograph and Lantern Weekly* (30 March 1911): 74; "Our Interviews: No. 6—Mr. F. Percy Smith," *Civil Service Observer* 17 no. 6 (June 1911): 103–105.

28. "Our Interviews," 103.

29. "Evolution of the Juggling Fly," first page.

30. Smith, "True Story of the Juggling Fly," 13.

31. Ibid., 13–14.

32. Smith describes this device in the *Pearsons* and the *Chambers's Journal* articles. For a later instance of "educated insects," perhaps influenced by Smith's films, see Yuri Tsivian, "The Case of the Bioscope Beetle: Starewicz's Answer to Genetics," *Discourse: Journal for Theoretical Studies in Media and Culture* 17 (spring 1995): 119–125. The anthropomorphic dimension is even more prominent in Starewicz's films.

33. "Our Interviews," 103.

34. "Fly Actors Big as Dogs in Moving Pictures," *New York Herald*, December 18, 1909; "Fly Pest" folder, George Kleine Papers, Manuscripts Division, Library of Congress.

35. W. M., "What to Teach Flies," *Daily Mirror*, 14 November 1908; clipping in URB 8–1, n.p.

36. This film no longer exists, although images from it do survive. Additionally, some shots from it seem to have been reused in *The Fly Pest*, for which see the discussion in Chapter Four.

37. "Latest Urban Films," Supplement no. 249, n.d. [1908]; *Early Rare British Film Catalogues*, reel 7. Length 135ft. *Blue-Bottle Flies Feeding* contains a mixture of the "fly as menace" approach (as in the shots of flies on putrid meat and flies swarming) and the "fly

as fascinating individual" approach (as in the shot of a fly eating from the point of a needle). The fly eating from a needle shot was most likely reused in *The Fly Pest*. For more on this mixture of views of the fly, see the discussion of *The Fly Pest* in Chapter Four.

38. Smith, "Evolution," 4.

39. "Novelty" in "Evolution," 4; Smith, "True Story," 13.

40. Smith, "Evolution."

41. Interview with Smith in *The Kinematograph and Lantern Weekly*.

42. Smith, "Evolution."

43. See Altick, *The Shows of London*, 306, for more on educated insect shows. The only surviving version of the juggling fly films is *The Acrobatic Fly*, a reissue of *The Balancing Blue-Bottle*. The film can been viewed on the BFI's YouTube channel: https://www.youtube.com/watch?v=8hlocZhNcoM [accessed August 10, 2012].

44. Description quoted from George Kleine, *Catalogue of Educational Motion Picture Films* (1910), 256. *The Acrobatic Fly* was released in the United States on Feb. 16, 1910. Listed at 200ft, it was released on a split reel with *The Blue Swan Inn* (770ft). See *MPN*, 19 Feb. 1910, 15 (title list); *MPW*, 19 Feb. 1910, 271 (title list), 274 (title list); *MPW*, 26 Feb. 1910, 293 (mentioned in an article), 299 (review). Another Smith film that contains similar material, *The Strength and Agility of Insects* (191?), is included on the BFI's Jean Painlevé set. See also the other fly films mentioned in Chapter Four, especially the Pathé film that also contains "acrobatic" footage.

45. *MPW*, 26 Feb. 1910, 299.

46. Mary Field and Percy Smith, *Secrets of Nature* (London: Scientific Book Club, 1939), 138.

47. For an account of Smith's predecessors in the field of time-lapse plant-growth records, who included Charles Darwin, Ludwig Pfeffer, and investigators at the Institute Marey, see my "The Secret Life of Plants: Visualizing Vegetative Movement, 1880–1903," *Early Popular Visual Culture* 10, no. 1 (February 2012): 51–69.

48. [Anonymous,] "A Kinematographic Wizard," *Daily News and Leader*, n.d.; clipping in URB 8/1, 33. In *The Secrets of Nature*, Smith writes about "the year or two" that it takes for a time-lapse study of any given plant (147).

49. "Our Interviews," 104.

50. See *Secrets of Nature* for a more complete description of the machine; see also "Our Interviews," where he goes into more detail about the necessity for daylight when making Kinemacolor films and mentions having created "artificial daylight."

51. Smith, *Secrets*, 139. Smith refers to the earlier films as "films in monochrome," although monochrome is a somewhat misleading term since even the non-Kinemacolor version of the film featured tinted release prints.

52. For a detailed account of Kinemacolor, see McKernan, Chapter 3, "The Eighth Wonder of the World," in *Charles Urban*, 75–124.

53. *Kinemacolor versus "Colour" Cinematography* [1911], Barnes collection, Hove Museum; quoted in McKernan, *Charles Urban*, 98.

54. Palace Theatre Programme, Special Invitation Matinee, The First Presentation of Kinemacolor, 26 February 1909; available at http://www.charlesurban.com/images/paleprogrammelarge.jpg (emphasis in original)

55. *Kinemacolor versus "Colour" Photography* [1911], Barnes collection, Hove Museum; quoted in McKernan, *Charles Urban*, 98.

56. Scala program, n.d., included in *Early Rare British Film Catalogues*, reel 8.

57. See, for instance, "Science and Natural History," *Illustrated London News*, 6 March 1909; F. Martin Duncan, "The Progress of Cinematography in Colours," *The Bioscope*, 9 June 1910; URB 2, 235–6; J. Q. Roberts, "How the Colors of Nature Are Reproduced in Moving Pictures," *Popular Mechanics* (June 1911): 806–808; "What Puts the Color in Kinemacolor," *Popular Electricity and the World's Advance* (September 1913). URB 2 and URB 3/1 contain a sampling of these articles.

58. "Programme," URB 3/1, 22. Dick, Mark & Brock were the Canadian rightsholders to Kinemacolor; "see the world from an opera chair" was their motto.

59. "Kinemacolor as an Educational Medium (Reprinted from a Special Programme of Educational Subjects Presented to Members of the Education Committee of the London City Council at the Scala Theatre, London, on Nov. 12, 1912)," *Kinemacolor Supplement to the Kinematograph & Lantern Weekly* (21 November 1912), URB 3/1, 11.

60. [Anonymous,] "A Kinematographic Wizard," *Daily News and Leader*, n.d.; clipping in URB 8/2, 16.

61. Tom Gunning, "Colorful Metaphors: The Attraction of Color in Early Silent Cinema," *Fotogenia I: Il Colore nel Cinema/Color in Cinema*, ed. Richard Abel (Bologna: Editrice Clueb, 1995), 249. For an example of a natural-history, stencil-colored film, see *Glimpses of Bird Life* (Oliver Pike/Pathé 1910), which is preserved at the BFI as a stencil-colored print (http://www.screenonline.org.uk/film/id/1271010/index.html). Pike includes an account of his visit to the Pathé factory to watch the stencil-coloring process in *Nature and My Cine Camera* (1946).

62. For an extended discussion of color in early cinema, see Joshua Yumibe, *Moving Color: Early Film, Mass Culture, Modernism* (New Brunswick, NJ: Rutgers University Press, 2012).

63. "Methods of Kinemacolor Presentation," *Kinemacolor Supplement to the Kinematograph & Lantern Weekly* (21 November 1912); URB 3/1, 11.

64. Scala program, URB 3/1.

65. "Our Interviews," 103.

66. *Catalogue of Kinemacolor Film Subjects*, (1912), 64; on *Early Rare British Filmmakers' Catalogues*, reel 8.

67. Kinemacolor program, Sandringham, July 29, 1911; URB 3/1, 18; *Detroit Free Press*, n.d.; quotation reproduced in *Catalogue of Kinemacolor Film Subjects* (1912), 67; on *Early Rare British Film Catalogues*, reel 8.

68. *The Birth of the Flower* is also the film that is currently easily accessible, especially since its inclusion on the BFI's "Jean Painlevé" DVD set. Kinemacolor prints are rare both because they were run through the projector at double speed, which resulted in greater wear and tear, and because they were popular. There is, however, an existing print of *From Bud to Blossom* at the Cineteca di Bologna, which, unfortunately, came to my attention too late to consult for this book.

69. *The Birth of a Flower* was released on March 16, 1911, so the date of 1910, which is currently in use, could be adjusted to reflect the release date, although it is clear from Smith's notebooks that the filming took place in 1910 (Smith, *Secrets of Nature*, 139). The announcement of the release is in URB 8/1, 3.

70. *Catalogue of Film Subjects* (London: Kineto Ltd., 1912), 7; URB 10/13a.

71. Fritz W. Wolters to A. R. St. Joux, 29 March 1911; quoted in *Catalogue of Film Subjects* (London: Kineto Ltd., 1912), 6.

72. Ibid.

73. *Bulletin du Photo-Club de Paris*, April 1895, 125; quoted in Laurent Mannoni, *The Great Art of Light and Shadow*, 425.

74. *New York Mail and Express*, October 13, 1896, 5; quoted in Charles Musser, *The Emergence of the American Screen*, 152. Thanks to Tom Gunning for these references.

75. McKernan, *Charles Urban*, 43. It is possible that another reason why audiences wanted to see *The Birth of a Flower* again was because it recalled the conventions of stage magic, particularly the prevalence of the time-lapse effects of plant growth by nineteenth-century magicians, especially Robert Houdin's blooming orange tree illusion. See *Memoirs of Robert-Houdin, Ambassador, Author, and Conjuror. Written by Himself* (London: Chapman and Hall, 1860), 184; see also Colin Williamson, "Obscured Histories of Modern Magic in the Cinema: Science, Animation, and Wonder from the Enlightenment to Digital Effects," Ph.D. dissertation, University of Chicago, 2013.

76. [Anonymous], "Botany by Bioscope: Birth of a Flower Depicted on Screen," *The Evening Standard* (11 March 1911): n.p.; clipping in URB 8/1, 35.

77. *Catalogue of Kinemacolor Film Subjects*, 66; *Early Rare British Film Catalogues*, reel 8.

78. *The Yorkshire Observer*, 13 March 1911; quoted in *Catalogue of Film Subjects* (London: Kineto Ltd., 1912), 7. This thread of reception is picked up in the Moody Institute of Science's first popular-science film, *God of Creation* (1946), which featured time-lapse footage of flowers blooming that provided "evidence of a Divine plan in the universe" (quoted in Gregg Mitman, *Reel Nature*, 128). As Mitman details, this argument for design using time-lapse footage as evidence also took root in a number of the Disney True-Life Adventure films, particularly *Nature's Half-Acre* (1951). For more on the Moody Institute of Science's films, see Marsha Orgeron and Skip Elsheimer, "Something Different in Science Films: The Moody Institute of Science and the Canned Missionary Movement," *The Moving Image* 7, no. 1 (spring 2007): 1–26; James Gilbert, *Redeeming Culture: American Religion in an Age of Science* (Chicago: University of Chicago Press, 1998); and Heather Hendershot, *Shaking the World for Jesus: Media and Conservative Evangelical Culture* (Chicago: University of Chicago Press, 2004).

79. [Anonymous], "Botany by Bioscope."

80. *Catalogue of Kinemacolor Subjects*, 64–5; *Early Rare British Film Catalogues*, reel 8.

81. "The Birth of a Flower," *Kine Weekly* (2 March 1911): n.p.; URB 8–1, 34.

82. *Truth* (London), n.p.; quoted in *Catalogue of Kinemacolor Subjects*, 66; *Early Rare British Film Catalogues*, reel 8.

83. *Catalogue of Kinemacolor Subjects*, 66; *Early Rare British Film Catalogues*, reel 8. This scene also displays an internal dramatic structure, since two buds bloom immediately, which leads to a period of suspense until the third blossom finally opens as well.

84. Released March 30, 1911, as noted in *Picture Theater News* (22 Feb. 1911); clipping in URB 8–1, 32.

85. *Catalogue of Film Subjects* (London: Kineto Ltd., 1912), 8.

86. Ibid.

87. *Picture Theater News* (22 Feb. 1911); clipping in URB 8–1, 32. "Botany by Bioscope."

88. "A New Urban Science Series. Popular Releases by Kineto, Ltd." *The Kinematograph* (16 Feb. 1911); clipping in URB 8–1, 34.

89. Percy Smith continued to make time-lapse, plant-growth films for most of his career; for a sampling, see the "Secrets of Nature" DVD set from the BFI. Jean Comandon also made a number of time-lapse, plant-growth films. For a rich and sensitive reading of how these films figured in the discourse of the French avant-garde of the 1920s, see Paula Amad, "'These Spectacles Are Never Forgotten': Memory and Reception in Colette's Film Criticism," *Camera Obscura* 59, no. 2 (2005): 119–163. J. C. Mol was another prominent time-lapse filmmaker of the interwar period; see Malin Wahlberg, "Wonders of Cinematic Abstraction: J. C. Mol and the Aesthetic Experience of Science Film," *Screen* 47, no. 3 (autumn 2006): 273–89. McKernan claims that Smith made over fifty films while at Urban (McKernan, *Charles Urban*, 62). A complete filmography of the popular-science films Smith made for Urban would be a welcome resource.

90. Smith was married in June 1907. Allegedly, he took along camera equipment with instructions from Urban to "shoot anything that bites, scratches, or moves," so his filmmaking work must have commenced before what is recorded in his notebook, which begins in mid-1908.

91. The secret of the pseudonym is revealed in an interview with Smith (conducted by an improbably named Mr. Clue) that also was published in the *Civil Service Observer*: "Mr. Smith is known to *Observer* readers—but under another name—the familiar one of 'Maxwell Pyx,' as being the writer of the interesting detective stories entitled 'The Adventures of Percival Browne.' Mr. Smith gave me permission to divulge this secret." (George L. Clue, "Our Interviews. No. 6—Mr. F. Percy Smith," *Civil Service Observer* 17, no. 6 [June 1911]: 104–105).

92. Maxwell Pyx [Percy Smith], "The Adventure of the Stepney Doctor (conclusion)," *Civil Service Observer* 17, no. 5 (May 1911): 93.

93. Doyle describes Holmes as "an enthusiast in some branches of science." (Arthur Conan Doyle, *A Study in Scarlet* [1887: Project Gutenberg, 2008], https://www.gutenberg. org/ebooks/244, accessed 31 October 2014). Holmes first appeared in 1887, and, except for the hiatus in publication from 1893 to 1901, Doyle continued to write Holmes stories into the 1920s, with the last "canonical" story appearing in 1927.

94. Maxwell Pyx [Percy Smith], "The Adventure of the Missing Shadow," *Civil Service Observer* 15, no. 5 (May 1909): 93.

95. Arthur Conan Doyle, "The Musgrave Ritual," in *The Memoirs of Sherlock Holmes* (1893: Project Gutenberg, 1997), https://www.gutenberg.org/ebooks/834, accessed 31 October 2014.

96. Pyx, "The Missing Shadow," 95; Arthur Conan Doyle, *The Sign of Four* (1890: Project Gutenberg, 2000), https://www.gutenberg.org/ebooks/2097, accessed 31 October 2014.

97. Doyle, "The Musgrave Ritual"; Pyx, "The Adventure of the Missing Shadow, continued," *Civil Service Observer* 15, no. 6 (June 1909): 113. This detail recalls Smith's story of his own "nervous breakdown" in the wake of the press attention to the acrobatic fly films. Also like his protagonist, Smith's mind is in chronic need of occupation.

98. See Andrea Goulet, "Curiosity's Killer Instinct: Bibliophilia and the Myth of the Rational Detective," *Yale French Studies* 108 (2005): 48–59.

99. Doyle, *Sign of Four*.

100. Doyle, "The Man with the Twisted Lip," in *The Adventures of Sherlock Holmes* (1891: Project Gutenberg, 2011), https://www.gutenberg.org/ebooks/1661, accessed 31 October 2014.

101. Maxwell Pyx [Percy Smith], "The Adventure of the Grey Lady," *Civil Service Observer* 15, no. 9 (September 1909): 177–179; continued in 15, no. 10 (October 1909): 200–201, at 177. As Pyx further explains, "A slight temporary weakness of the eyes, which precluded any hard work with the microscope, had brought several scientific problems to a standstill, and he was obviously fretting under the enforced idleness" (177).

102. Doyle, *Sign of Four*; Pyx, "Missing Shadow," 95.

103. See Ely Liebow, *Dr. Joe Bell: Model for Sherlock Holmes* (Bowling Green, OH: Bowling Green University Popular Press, 1982).

104. Laura J. Snyder, "Sherlock Holmes: Scientific Detective," *Endeavour* 28, no. 3 (September 2004): 104–108.

105. Carlo Ginzberg, "Clues: Roots of an Evidential Paradigm," in *Clues, Myths, and the Historical Method*, trans. John and Anne C. Tedeschi Baltimore, MD: (Johns Hopkins UP, 1989), 96–125, at 117. For Ginzberg, the detective story is both "very ancient and very modern," an argument that resonates with my claims in Chapter Four.

106. Doyle, "A Scandal in Bohemia," in *Adventures of Sherlock Holmes*.

107. Pyx, "The Missing Shadow," 113; Pyx, "The Adventure of the Mysterious Incendiary," *Civil Service Observer* 16, no. 3 (March 1910): 47–48; continued in 16, no. 4 (April 1910): 67–68; concluded in 16, no. 5 (May 1910): 87–88, at 67.

108. Maxwell Pyx [Percy Smith], "The Adventure of the Namarobi Extension," *Civil Service Observer* 16, no. 1 (January 1910): 8–9, at 9.

109. The story contains a wonderful reference to Smith's understanding of cinema. Pyx describes his reaction to the screening thusly: "In less than half-an-hour we were all rushing in imagination through some of the most wonderful tropical scenery in the manner familiar to patrons of that most entrancing of educators, the cinematograph" (9).

110. "The Adventure of the Missing Shadow" also hinges on Browne's skill at reading a photographic clue. Here Browne interprets a photograph differently from other "photographic experts" by considering a constellation of meteorological and photographic knowledge that allows him to determine that the "missing shadow" in a photograph judged a fake by experts is in fact not missing at all, since the supposed shadow of the gate is in fact unevaporated water. This observation allows him to exonerate a falsely accused man. An irony here is that Pyx, a supposed "photographic expert," is unable to solve the mystery; Browne notes trenchantly with regard to Pyx's "expertise": "ah yes, I'd forgotten that you had a Kodak."

111. Pyx, "The Adventure of the Black Crag," *Civil Service Observer* 16, no. 8 (August 1910): 168–170; continued in 16, no. 9 (September 1910): 187–188, at 168. This detail of going on vacation with camera equipment recalls the story of Smith's honeymoon excursion.

112. See Derek Bousé, *Wildlife Films* (Philadelphia: University of Pennsylvania Press, 2000), 43.

113. For more information about Oliver Pike, see Bousé, *Wildlife Films*, 45. Both films are available on screenonline.org.uk.

114. Maxwell Pyx [Percy Smith], "The Adventure of the Crack-Shot Colonel," *Civil Service Observer* 16, no. 12 (December 1910): 251–252. The technical explanation is as follows: "double electric bell wire, the free ends, where it 'cuts,' being connected by means of a tiny piece of platinum. The smaller portion of the cord is hung on the platinum wire by means of a scrap of thin elastic. When I turn on that brass knob, just below the window, it connects a six-volt accumulator with the wires, the platinum becomes white-hot and

melts instantly" (252). The other device is a double-bullet cartridge for the officer's Mauser, which completes the illusion.

115. Maxwell Pyx, "The Adventure of the Knight's Nose," *Civil Service Observer* 18, no. 2 (February 1912): 29–31, at 30.

116. Pyx, "Knight's Nose," 29. Holmes, too, exhibits a showman's instincts, especially in his habit of revealing his reasoning all at once at the resolution of the case.

117. Pyx, "The Adventure of the Stepney Doctor," *Civil Service Observer* 17, no. 4 (April 1911): 76–78; concluded in 17, no. 5 (May 1911): 93–94; at 77. A development of this conceit is Raymond Chandler's chivalric conception of the urban detective as latter-day knight.

118. Pyx, "The Adventure of the Mysterious Incendiary," *Civil Service Observer* 16, no. 3 (March 1910): 47–48; continued in 16, no. 4 (April 1910): 67–68; concluded in 16, no. 5 (May 1910): 87–88; at 48.

119. Pyx, "Namarobi Extension," 8.

120. This note is sounded in the reception of Smith's RPS lecture, where one author noted how Smith caught his specimens in his rooms and his back garden and praised the lecture, writing that it "formed a most telling object-lesson of how to make an intensely interesting lecture out of the most ordinary and easily accessible of objects." This author also went on to praise Smith's "several humorous and sarcastic sallies," one of which came when he "apologized for talking English instead of Latin or Greek, languages of which too much is often heard at the RPS lectures" (The Magpie, "The 'A.P.' Causerie: Alas for Gamma Infinity!" *The Amateur Photographer and Photographic News* 48, no. 1260 [24 November 1908]: 488).

121. Pyx, "The Adventure of the Invisible Burglars," *Civil Service Observer* 18, no. 6 (June 1912): 108–110, at 110. For more on scientific detective literature, popular-science filmmaking, and trick films, see Chapter Five.

122. Frank P. Smith, "The True Story of the Juggling Fly," *Civil Service Observer* 15, no. 1 (January 1909): 13.

123. Pyx, "Missing Shadow," 93.

124. Melanie Keene, "'Every Boy and Girl a Scientist': Instruments for Children in Interwar Britain," *Isis* 98 (2007): 266–89, at 278. For experimental science sets for children in the German context, see Viola van Beek, "'Man lasse doch diese Dinge selber einmal sprechen': Experimentierkästen, Experimentalanleitungen und Erzählungen zwischen 1870 und 1930," *NTM: Zeitschrift für Geschichte der Wissenschaften, Technik und Medizin* 17, no. 4 (2009): 387–414.

125. McKernan, *Charles Urban*, 62.

126. "Percy Smith*," *Nature* 155 (5 May 1945): 538.

127. Victoria Carroll, *Science and Eccentricity: Collecting, Writing, and Performing Science for Early Nineteenth-Century Audiences* (London: Pickering & Chatto, 2008), 2, 164.

128. Carroll, *Science and Eccentricity*, 44.

129. "Mr. Percy Smith and his assistant, Miss Phyllis Bolté, produced twenty-four educational films last year" (Leslie A. Paul, "A Genius with Gadgets Gives Passports for Pests," *Tit-Bits*, 26 September 1931 [URB 8-2, 73]).

130. Both anecdotes are cited in Luke McKernan, "Smith, (Frank) Percy (1880–1945)," *Oxford Dictionary of National Biography* (New York: Oxford University Press, 2004); http://www.oxforddnb.com.libproxy.temple.edu/view/article/66096, accessed Oct. 4,

2009. Smith's singlemindedness also was registered in the obituaries: "he had no thought other than his work" ("Percy Smith*," *Nature* 155 [5 May 1945]: 538).

131. Lorraine Daston, "Attention and the Values of Nature in the Enlightenment," in *The Moral Authority of Nature*, ed. Lorraine Daston and Fernando Vidal (Chicago: University of Chicago Press, 2004), 100–126, at 118.

132. Percy Smith, "Spiders," *The Saturday Review*, 12 March 1910: n.p.; clipping in URB 8–1, 38–39.

133. Duncan, too, had a fascination for creatures generally deemed repulsive: "[worms] are shunned and avoided, and generally voted to be 'nasty, slimy things.' And yet, when you get to know them, and understand their ways, the worms, like so many humble and despised creatures, are not only interesting and entertaining, but are beautiful withal" (F. Martin Duncan, "Worms, and How to Photograph Them," *The Amateur Photographer* 38 [1903]: 48–49; cited in Boon, *Films of Fact*, 19).

134. Quoted in Oswell Blakeston, "Personally about Percy Smith," *Close-Up* 8, no. 2 (June 1931): 144.

135. The BFI website calls this a "short film," but since it begins with an intertitle, which is the source for the title, it is more likely that the film is a fragment. It can be viewed on the BFI's YouTube channel: https://www.youtube.com/watch?v=vKPbxcK58aI.

136. Some of the animated war maps are available to view at the BFI; Smith also used stop-motion animation to create films with the recurring characters "Bertie the bee" and "Archie the ant."

137. See Mary Field and Percy Smith, *The Secrets of Nature* (London: The Scientific Book Club, 1939); and my entry on "The Secrets of Nature" in *Encyclopedia of the Documentary Film*, ed. Ian Aitken (New York: Routledge, 2006), 3:1195–1197. See also Laura Frost, "Huxley's Feelies: The Cinema of Sensation in *Brave New World*," *Twentieth Century Literature* 52, no. 4 (winter 2006): 459–460, for Aldous Huxley's praise for Smith and documentary films more generally.

138. "Percy Smith*," *Nature* 155 (5 May 1945): 538; reprinted as "Percy Smith*," *Sight & Sound* 14, no. 53 (1945): 7.

Chapter 3

1. Emmanuelle Toulet, "Cinema at the Universal Exposition, Paris, 1900," *Persistence of Vision* 9 (1991): 31.

2. Richard Abel, *The Ciné Goes to Town: French Cinema 1896–1914* (Los Angeles: University of California Press, 1994), 7.

3. See François Jost, "Die Programmierung des Zuschauers," *KINtop* 11 (2002): 34–47, for a discussion of the program at the Gaumont-Palace. See also Jean-Jacques Meusey, *Paris-Palaces ou le temps des cinemas (1894–1918)* (Paris: CNRS Éditions, 1995), 285–291.

4. Frédéric Delmeulle, "Contribution à l'histoire du cinema documentaire en France: Le cas de L'Encyclopédie Gaumont (1909–1929)," Ph.D. thesis, Université de Paris III, 1999, 14.

5. Thierry Lefebvre, private communication. Lefebvre's information is contained in a filmography of popular-science films compiled from trade press information. These numbers are approximate due to the difficulties of precision when classifying certain films, an issue to which we will return, as well as the lack of definitive records.

6. Information about Comandon's career is drawn from Thierry Lefebvre, "Contribution à l'histoire de la microcinématographie: de François-Franck à Comandon," *1895* 14 (June 1993): 35–46; idem, "Jean Comandon et les débuts de la microcinématographie," *La Revue du practicien* 53 (2003): 2–5; Isabelle do O'Gomes, "Un laboratoire de prises de vues scientifiques à l'usine Pathé de Vincennes 1910–1926," in *Pathé, premier empire du cinema*, ed. Jacques Kermabon (Paris: Editions du Centre Pompidou, 1994), 140–141; and idem, "L'Oeuvre de Jean Comandon," in *Le Cinéma et la science*, ed. Alexis Martinet (Paris: CNRS Editions, 1994), 78–85. The Centre National de la Cinématographie (CNC) undertook an extensive restoration of Comandon's extant films; this archival effort led to a major publication, *Filmer la science, comprendre la vie: Le cinéma de Jean Comandon*, ed. Béatrice de Pastre and Thierry Lefebvre (Paris: CNC, 2012). This chapter was written before the restorations had been undertaken and the accompanying book had been published, and while I have inserted references to some of the most relevant new information, I urge the interested reader to consult this book, which provides the most complete, and nuanced extant account of Comandon's work and life.

7. See H. Siedentopf, "On the Rendering Visible of Ultra-Microscopic Particles and of Ultra-Microscopic Bacteria," *Journal of the Royal Microscopical Society* (October 1903): 573–578. It is certainly possible that F. Martin Duncan attended this lecture, although he does not seem to have used the ultramicroscope in his films. For an account of the development of the ultramicroscope, see David Cahan, "The Zeiss Werke and the Ultramicroscope: The Creation of a Scientific Instrument in Context," in *Scientific Credibility and Technical Standards in Nineteenth and Early-Twentieth Century Germany and Britain*, ed. J. Buchwald (Dordrecht: Kluwer Academic, 1996), 67–117. Cahan describes the ultramicroscope as an innovation as opposed to a discovery since its creation linked several previous technological refinements. See also Charlotte Bigg, "Evident Atoms: Visuality in Jean Perrin's Brownian Motion Research," *Studies in History and Philosophy of Science* 39 (2008): 312–322.

8. Augustus Paul von Wasserman discovered a complement fixation test for syphilis in 1906. The method of identification that Comandon was researching required more labor and expertise but was more accurate.

9. See Thierry Lefebvre, "Le cinéma scientifique contre vents et marées," in *Filmer la science, comprendre la vie*, 17–40; and Stéphanie Salmon, "Le docteur Comandon chez Pathé," in *Filmer la science, comprendre la vie*, 401–412.

10. "Perfectionnements aux dispositifs de prises de vues microcinématographiques" (No. 419. 305); cited in Lefebvre, "Contribution," 39, n. 15.

11. Jean Comandon, "Cinématographie, à l'ultra-microscope, de microbes vivantes et des particules mobiles," *Les Comptes Rendus de l'Académie des Sciences*, November 22, 1909, 939.

12. Ibid., 940.

13. Jean Comandon, "L'ultramicroscope et la cinématographie," *La Presse Médicale* 94 (November 1909): 843. The immediate technical precursor, however, was Victor Henri, whose microcinematographic study of Brownian motion was presented to the Académie in May 1908. Henri realized his experiments in the physiopathology laboratory of François-Franck and Lucienne Chevroton at the Collège de France. François-Franck was Marey's *préperateur*. Comandon studied with Henri, whom he calls "my mentor and friend," at the Sorbonne prior to his work with Gastou (841). See

also Laurent Mannoni, "Jean Comandon technicien," in *Filmer la science, comprendre la vie*, 47–60.

14. *Le Matin*, October 27, 1909. Lefebvre, "Jean Comandon," 4, cites the press articles. The presentation also led to a number of lectures for other learned societies—the Société des ingénieurs de France, the Société française de photographie, and the Société d'encouragement pour l'industrie nationale; see O'Gomes, "L'Oeuvre," 274, n. 1. See also Thierry Lefebvre, "Jean Comandon conférencier, 1909: les débuts," in *Filmer la science, comprendre la vie*, 413–422.

15. See Yuri Tsivian, "Media Fantasies and Penetrating Vision: Some Links between X-Rays, the Microscope, and Film," in *Laboratory of Dreams: The Russian Avant-Garde and Cultural Experiment*, ed. John E. Bowlt and Olga Matich (Stanford, CA: Stanford University Press, 1996), 81–99, esp. 82–86.

16. "Microbes Caught in Action," *New York Times*, October 31, 1909.

17. See Laurent Mannoni, *Étienne-Jules Marey: La Mémoire de l'oeil* (Paris: Le Cinémathèque Française, 1999), 256–258; cited in Lefebvre, "Comandon," 2.

18. See Victor Henri, "Étude cinématographique des mouvements browniens," note présentée par A. Dastre, séance de l'Académie des sciences 18 May 1908, 1024. See also [E. Benoit-Levy], "Cinéma: mouvement Brownien: la théorie et la pratique," *Phono-Ciné-Gazette* 84 (September 15, 1908), 725; and L. Chevroton and F. Vlès, "La cinématique de la segmentation de l'oeuf et la chronophotographie du développement de l'oursin," *Comptes Rendus de l'Académie des Sciences*, November 8, 1909, 806–809.

19. The *Berliner Klinische Wochenschrift*, no. 34, August 24, 1903, gives an account of the screening in its report of the July 29, 1903, meeting of the Berlin Society of Medicine; cited in Lefebvre, "Contribution," 42, n. 26.

20. Comandon, "L'ultramicroscopie et la cinématographie," 841.

21. For this comparison, see Marina Dahlquist, *The Invisible Seen in French Cinema before 1917* (Stockholm: Aura, 2001), 99. Lefebvre, "Contribution," 42, n. 22, suggests that Émile Cohl's earlier *fantoche* films like *Fantasmagorie* (August 1908), with their white lines on black background, an effect achieved by printing the negative of retraced drawings, approximate the ultramicroscopic aesthetic. Of course, not all of Comandon's microcinematographic films were made using the ultramicroscope, and other scientists were making microcinematographic films as well. For an argument that places Cohl into the context of Vlès and Chevroton's time-lapse microcinematography, among other things, see Thierry Lefebvre, "*Les Joyeux Microbes*: un film sous influence?" *1895* 53 (December 2007): 168–179.

22. See Lefebvre, "Jean Comandon," 4; O'Gomes, "L'oeuvre," 79; Lefebvre, "Jean Comandon conférencier"; and Salmon, "Le docteur Comandon chez Pathé."

23. On these changes, see Abel, *Ciné*, 32–34; and Salmon, "Le docteur Comandon chez Pathé."

24. Comandon, "L'ultramicroscope," 843.

25. P. Desfosses, "L'ultra-microscope et la cinématographie," *La Presse Médicale*, November 10, 1909, 914.

26. For detailed accounts of the various initiatives to institute visual education in France, see Bruno Beguet, "La vulgarisation scientifique au XIXe siècle," in *La Science pour tous*, ed. Bruno Beguet (Paris: Editions de la Réunion des musées nationaux, 1994), 4–48; Ségolène Le Men, "La science enfantine et l'apprentissage du regard," in *La Science*

pour tous; and Annie Renonciat, *Images lumineuses: Tableaux sur verre pour lanterns magiques et vues sur papier pour appareils de projection* (Paris: Institut National de Recherche Pédagogique, 1995), 149–182. For an excellent reading of the discourse of education in relation to cinema and science, see James Leo Cahill, "Forgetting Lessons: Jean Painlevé's Cinematic Gay Science," *Journal of Visual Culture* 11, no. 3 (December 2012): 258–287.

27. See François de la Bretèque and Pierre Guibbert, "Mission moralisatrice et romantisme social du cinéma du premières temps," in *Les Vingts premières années du cinéma français*, ed. Michèle Lagny et al. (Paris: Presses de la Sorbonne nouvelle, Editions de l'AFRHC, 1995); cited in Delmeulle, "Contribution," 39.

28. Boleslaw Matuszewski, "A New Source of History: The Creation of a Depository for Historical Cinematography," citation from http://tlweb.latrobe.edu.au/humanities/ screeningthepast/classics/clasjul/mat.html, trans. Julia Bloch Frey. The text is also available as "A New Source of History," trans. Laura U. Marks and Diane Koszarski, *Film History* 7 (1995): 322–324.

29. Quoted in Georges Sadoul, *Histoire du cinéma mondial des origins à nos jours*, 6th ed. (Paris: Flammarion, 1949), 49. Other figures in France who would gain prominence in their championing of the cinema's role in education were Edmond and Jean Benoît-Levy and G. Michel Coissac. See Jean-Jacques Meusy, "Qui était Edmond Benoît-Levy?" in *Les Vingt premières années du cinéma français*, ed. Michèle Lagny et al. (Paris: Presses de la Sorbonne nouvelle, Editions de l'AFRHC, 1995); and Valérie Vignaux, *Jean-Benoît Lévy ou le corps comme utopie. Une histoire du cinéma éducateur dans l'entre-deux-guerres en France* (Paris: AFRHC, 2007).

30. See Delmeulle, "Contribution," 45.

31. Henri Bousquet, *Catalogue Pathé des années 1896–1914, 1912–1913–1914* (Bures-sur-Vyette: Edition Henri Bousquet, 1995), 288. Pathé's arrogation of credit for the images became a target for criticism. Comandon's former advisor, Paul Gastou, complained, "It was in my laboratory at the St. Louis hospital that ultramicroscopic cinematography was born, which M. Pathé grabbed, mentioning neither the idea nor the origin" (Paul Gastou, *Le Laboratoire du praticien* [Paris: Poinat, 1912], cited in Lefebvre, "Jean Comandon," 3). Thierry Lefebvre renders a more gracious judgment, stopping short of calling Pathé a thief, writing instead about Comandon's "opportunism" and the "commercial phagocytosis" that took place with Pathé's employment of Comandon (Lefebvre, "Jean Comandon," 3; and idem, "Contribution," 43).

32. Program for the Cirque d'Hiver, February 28, 1910, quoted in Jean-Jacques Meusy, "La Diffusion des films de 'non-fiction' dans les établissements Parisiens," *1895* 18 (summer 1995): 188.

33. This print is in the collection of the BFI. This film is the first time the phrase "*vulgarisation scientifique*" appears as a classifying rubric in the catalogues. Do O'Gomes notes that a Spanish Pathé catalogue from 1904 contains two films that were classified under the rubric "*vulgarisation scientifique*" (Do O'Gomes, "Jean Comandon," 82). These one-minute films were apparently shot in an aquarium (Thierry Lefebvre, personal communication, July 5, 2004).

34. Cited in Bousquet, *Catalogue*, 317–318. The films were *Sang d'ovipares; Mouvement amiboide d'un leucocyte; Spirochetes de Vincent; Spirocheota gallinarum; Trypanosoma brucei; Trypanosoma lewisi; Microbes contenus dans l'intestin d'une souris; Fievre recurrente; Agglutination de spirocheota gallinarum; Spirochoeta pallida (de la syphilis); Sang*

humain; *Circulation du sang*; *Hemokonies*; *Action de l'eau sur le sang*, and *Faites bouillir votre eau*.

35. One category of Delmeulle's taxonomy of nonfiction production at Gaumont is the "commissioned film," which "seems more comprised as a vector for relatively complex business communication" (Delmeulle, "Contribution," 24).

36. It is unclear what the difference between this film and earlier films, such as *Peche aux homards* (Bousquet, *Catalogue*, 276) or *Peche aux harengs à Boulogne* (Bousquet, *Catalogue*, 267) might be.

37. Popularly, and misleadingly, known as the "walking fish," the axolotl is neotenic, which means that it can reach maturity without undergoing metamorphosis from the larval stage, when it has gills, to the terrestrial stage, when it develops lungs. Live specimens arrived in France in the 1860s, and it has since become a model organism. For an extensive account of its use as a laboratory animal, see Christian Reiß, "Der mexikanische Axolotl (*Ambystoma mexicanum*) als Labortier, 1864–1914: Verbreitungswege, Infrastrukturen, Forschungsschwerpunkte," Ph.D. dissertation, Friedrich-Schiller-Universität, Jena, 2014. See also the story by Julio Cortazar, "L'Axolotl," in *End of the Game and Other Stories*, trans. Paul Blackburn (New York: Pantheon Books, 1967).

38. As Thierry Lefebvre has noted, there was a fair amount of duplication in terms of subjects. See his comparative chart in "The Scientia Production (1911–1914): Scientific Popularization through Pictures," *Griffithiana* 47 (May 1993): 149.

39. Although Comandon is said to have overseen the production of the science films at Pathé, it is unclear to what extent he was involved in films that dealt with topics that were outside his interests and expertise; see Salmon, "Le docteur Comandon chez Pathé." He also acted as a supervisor for a series of surgery films. He remained an employee at Pathé until 1926, when he was let go amidst changes necessitated by the financial downturn. For his work for Albert Kahn, see Paula Amad, *Counter-Archive: Film, the Everyday, and Albert Kahn's Archives de la Planète* (New York: Columbia University Press, 2010); and *Jean Comandon* (Brussels: Hayez, 1967). After the crash of 1929, which decimated Kahn's fortune, Comandon relocated again, this time setting up his laboratory at the Institut Pasteur, where he would work until his retirement in 1967.

40. 80m in length, the catalogue description notes that 55m of this film were in color, which could mean either tinting or Pathé's stencil-coloring process.

41. See Salmon, "Le docteur Comandon chez Pathé," for details about the development and differentiation of popular-science films at Pathé.

42. Primary school, the *primaire*, which was compulsory as of 1882, encompassed grades one through five. The French *collège* is equivalent to the American middle school (grades six through nine).

43. The information in this and the following paragraphs about Léon Gaumont's education comes from Corinne Faugeron and Jean-Jacques Meusy, "Léon Ernest Gaumont, une exceptionnelle promotion sociale," in *Les Prémières années de la Société L. Gaumont et Cie, correspondance commerciale de Léon Gaumont, 1895–1899*, ed. Marie-Sophie Corcy, Jacques Malthête, Laurent Mannoni, and Jean-Jacques Meusy (Paris: Association française de recherche sur l'histoire du cinéma, 1998), 7–18.

44. Georges Orléans, manuscript memoir addressed to Léon Gaumont in December 1934, Gaumont papers, Bibliothèque du film; quoted in Faugeron and Meusy, "Léon Ernest Gaumont," 11.

45. Meusy and Faugeron, "Léon Ernest Gaumont," 10.

46. For an examination of how knowledge functioned as a social equalizer in England, see Allan Rauch, *Useful Knowledge: The Victorians, Morality, and the March of the Intellect* (Durham, NC: Duke University Press, 2002).

47. Jean-Marie Mayeur and Madeleine Rebérioux, *The Third Republic from Its Origins to the Great War, 1871–1914*, trans. J. R. Foster (Cambridge: Cambridge University Press, 1984); cited in Abel, *The Ciné Goes to Town*, 4. Gaumont frequently relied on the network of friends from his time at the *collège*, the so-called Barbistes, and he went on to serve on the school's board of trustees.

48. It was reincorporated as the Société des Etablissements Gaumont—S.E.G.—in December 1906.

49. For details of Gaumont's work with Demenÿ, see Mannoni, *The Great Art of Light and Shadow*, 439–450. At the same time as he was developing the Demenÿ device, Gaumont provided support for Gustav Eiffel's interest in X-ray research. See Corey et al., *Les Premières années de la société L. Gaumont et Cie*, 96–99, 100–107, 111–113, and 427–428. Demenÿ was of course already interested in the popular and commercial exploitation of his work with Marey; see Laurent Mannoni, "Glissements progressifs vers le plaisir: remarques sur l'oeuvre chronophotographique de Marey et Demenÿ," *1895* 18 (summer 1995): 10–51.

50. Leon Gaumont, handwritten addendum to a report addressed to him in 1945; Bibliothèque du film, Léon Gaumont Papers, cited in Delmeulle, "Contribution," 30, n. 34.

51. François-Franck and Chevroton, cited in Delmeulle, "Contribution," 29.

52. Delmeulle, "Contribution," 31.

53. See Delmeulle, "Contribution," 54. Gaumont had several *documentaire* rubrics: the "série Rouge," which contained the *documentaries* from the first ten years of the company (up until 1906–1907); the "séries D and E," which were mostly *actualités*; the "série Portraits," which consisted of very brief shots of luminaries; and the "série Enseignement," from which the *Encyclopédie* was drawn. The série Enseignement contained 1,500 films; the *Encyclopédie* contained 1,200. (See Delmeulle, "Contribution," 5.)

54. Gaumont *Encyclopédie* catalogue, 1929.

55. Delmeulle, "Contribution," 138. George Kleine's attempts to collect nonfiction films raised similar concerns; see Chapter Four.

56. Ibid., 130.

57. In another instance of parallelism, Urban attempted to recirculate a number of his documentaries in the 1920s under the title of "The Living Book of Knowledge." See McKernan, *Charles Urban*, Chapter Four.

58. The films preserved at the Cinémathèque Gaumont, which also are consultable at the Bibliothèque Nationale in Paris, are often missing considerable amounts of footage, as well as most or all of their intertitles. As a result, it is difficult to draw conclusions about the general character of the films or even to make confident pronouncements about specific films.

59. Quoted in Delmeulle, "Contribution," 32.

60. See Delmeulle, "Contribution," 62–63; Lefebvre, "The Scientia Production," 147; and Béatrice de Pastre and Emmanuelle Devos, "La Cinémathèque de la Ville de Paris," *1895* 18 (summer 1995): 107–121.

61. In accordance with archival practice, brackets indicate that this film's title is conjectural.

62. For a more detailed account of the Cinémathèque's history and its method of compiling films, see de Pastre and Devos, "La Cinémathèque de la Ville de Paris."

63. *Air liquide ou 140 degrés de froid* (Gaumont, July 1909), 139m, is a comedy where a scientist figure discovers a material that can instantly freeze people.

64. A comparison of the frames of the film preserved in the scenario collection at the Bibliothèque de l'Arsenal allows for definite identification. The second half of the film is taken from the second Pathé film, as is confirmed by a viewing of that film at the National Film and Television Archive in London. The total length of the Cinémathèque print is 346m.

65. See Christine Blondel, "Industrial Science as a 'Show': A Case-Study of Georges Claude," in *Expository Science: Forms and Functions of Popularisation*, ed. Terry Shin and Richard Whitley (Boston: D. Reidel Publishing Company, 1985), 249–258. See also, for more information on Claude, *La Science pour tous* (1990), 42. Claude's name for this popular-science show was Scientia.

66. For an excellent reading of French popular-science films in the collection of the Cinémathèque de la Ville de Paris that anticipates a number of my own observations, see Béatrice de Pastre, "La sangue ou la mise en scène du spectacle du vivant," in *Images, science, movement. Autour de Marey* (Paris: L'Harmattan, 2004), 95–102.

67. In "Les Glandines: Mollusques carnassiers de Mexique," *La Nature*, no. 2064 (December 14, 1912): 20, there is mention of a recent public lecture by Professor Bouvier at la Société nationale d'agriculture in Paris, who had received the animals from a certain Antoine Gineste, a monk living in Mexico, which suggests an intriguing possible link between academic research and the popular-science filmmaking unit at Éclair.

68. Announced in *Cinéma Journal* no. 200, June 22, 1912; subject in *Bulletin Pathé* n. 20, 1912; cited in Henri Bousquet, *Catalogue Pathé des années 1896 à 1914, 1912–1913–1914* (Bures-sur-Vyette: Edition Henri Bousquet, 1995), 557.

69. Paolo Cherchi Usai's blurb for the film when it was screened at the Giornate del Cinema Muto in 1995 picks up on this aspect of the film, calling it "A case study for vegetal rights."

70. Bibliothèque du Film, Paris, Léon Gaumont papers, letter from Georges Orléans to Charles Gaumont, May 29, 1912, quoted in Delmeulle, "Contribution," 34.

71. For a reevaluation of anthropomorphism and science, see *Thinking with Animals: New Perspectives on Anthropomorphism*, ed. Lorraine Daston and Gregg Mitman (New York: Columbia University Press, 2005).

72. Jean Henri Fabre, *Souvenirs entomologiques: Études sur l'instinct et les mœurs des insects* (1879–1907: Paris: Robert Laffont, 1989), vol. 1, 320; cited from *The Passionate Observer: Writings from the World of Nature by Jean Henri Fabre*, ed. Linda Davis, trans. Teixiera de Mattos (San Francisco: Chronicle Books, 1998), 5.

73. Lefebvre, "The Scientia Production," 141.

74. As Thierry Lefebvre has noted, early nonfiction films "are only truly understandable in the context of a detailed intertextuality" (Lefebvre, "Introduction," *1895* 18 [summer 1995]: 8).

75. Lefebvre notes that Fabre was "the inspiring force and the methodological model of the 'Scientia' production" ("The Scientia Production," 139).

76. Ibid., 88.

77. Lefebvre, "Popularization and Anthropomorphism," in *Uncharted Territory*, 95.

78. Mark-Paul Meyer, "Moments of Poignancy: The Aesthetics of the Accidental and the Casual in Early Nonfiction Film," in *Uncharted Territory*, 57.

79. Fabre, *Souvenirs entomologiques*, vol. 2, 793.

80. The most influential formulation of this view is the remark made at the Amsterdam workshop that nonfiction films "don't seem to exist in the regime of stylistic pressure that was clearly there for fiction filmmakers" (Ben Brewster, quoted in Hertogs and De Klerk, *Nonfiction from the Teens*, 32).

81. "Au milieu de cette bizarre pièce qui est la tête et la poitrine brillent deux yeux très convexes." Fabre's text reads, "Au milieu de cette bizarre pièce qui est à la fois la tête et la poitrine, brillent côte à côte deux gros yeux très convexes rappelant les superbes lentilles oculaires de la Lycose; apparemment yeux de myope de part et d'autre, à cause de leur forte convexité" (Fabre, *Souvenirs entomologiques*, vol. 2, 795).

82. Fabre, *Souvenirs entomologiques*, vol. 2, 792.

83. Note here that this type of editing underscores the commercial alliances of these types of films, especially when compared with scientific films. Thierry Lefebvre gives the example of a film by Lucienne Chevroton entitled *Développement de l'œuf d'oursin* (1909) that consists of a single shot that is roughly ten minutes long. Less extreme but in a similar vein, Paula Amad observes that, compared to commercial films, the Albert Kahn films tend to hold individual shots "too long" (Paula Amad, "Cinema's 'Sanctuary': From Pre-Documentary to Documentary Film in Albert Kahn's *Archives de la Planète* (1908–1931)," *Film History* 13, no. 2 [2001]: 148).

84. Stephen Bottomore mentions that the staff at Samuel "Roxy" Rothapfel's theaters "seems to have custom-assembled its own 'educationals,' out of bits of existing films, especially coloured or tinted scenes, and incorporating elements of the dramatic or comic (in pictures of animal life, for example). They assembled the elements so that the strongest scene was usually the last" (Bottomore, "Rediscovering Early Non-Fiction Film," 172).

85. George Maurice, "La Science au Cinéma," *Film-Revue*, 4 (17 January 1913): 13. For more on the relationship between epilepsy and comedy in the French context, see Rae Beth Gordon, *Why the French Love Jerry Lewis: From Cabaret to Early Cinema* (Stanford, CA: Stanford University Press, 2001).

86. Fabre, *Souvenirs entomologiques*, vol. 2, 820.

87. "Mais le Scorpion est maintenant sur ses gardes, l'arc de la queue tendu et les pinces ouvertes" (Fabre, *Souvenirs entomologiques*, vol. 2: 820).

88. This is the point in *L'Âge d'Or* (1930) when Luis Buñuel cuts from the footage of the Éclair film to footage that his crew shot itself. For a reading of this film that takes the scientific origin of the introductory footage into account, see Paul Hammond, *L'Âge d'or* (London: British Film Institute, 1997), especially 7–15. Buñuel's longstanding fascination with insects introduces another possibility for understanding these films, in which the subjects would be understood as figures of identification. How might fantasies about an electric body, as manifested, for instance, in the comedy *Zoe, femme torpille* (Pathé, November 1913), be related to the numerous popular-science films about the same animal (Cinès, Éclair, Pathé, all 1913)? For an account of the electric fish in the history of nineteenth-century biology, see Sven Dierig, "Urbanization, Place of Experiment, and How the Electric Fish Was Caught by Emil Du Bois-Reymond," *Journal of the History of the Neurosciences* 9, no. 1 (2000): 5–13.

89. See Frank Kessler, "Introduction: Visible Evidence—But of What? Reassessing Early Non-fiction Film," *Historical Journal of Film, Radio, and Television* 22, no. 3 (2002): 221–223, where he writes, "Not only are there different 'genres' and discursive forms, but furthermore there are different exhibition formats which influence or even determine the ways films could be read" (222).

90. Thierry Lefebvre, "De la science à l'avant-garde. Petit panorama," in *Images, science, mouvement. Autour de Marey* (Paris, L'Harmattan, Sémia, 2003), 103–109.

91. This type of programming often saw nonfiction as a moment of respite, a quiet interlude between the relative intensity of the comedies or the dramas. Roxy Rothapfel, for instance, discussed the educational as "something which delights the eye and soothes the mind without touching any emotional chords" (Rothapfel, quoted in Bottomore, "Rediscovering Early Non-Fiction Film," 172).

92. Yuri Tsivian, *Early Cinema in Russia and Its Cultural Reception*, trans. Alan Boder (Chicago: University of Chicago Press, 1998), 127, 129.

93. The magic-lantern lecture offered a model for extended nonfictional programs, as in Burton Holmes's travel lectures, Jacob Riis's exposés of urban poverty, passion plays, and boxing matches. See Charles Musser, *The Emergence of Cinema: The American Screen to 1907* (Berkeley: University of California Press, 1990), 38–42 and 193–223.

94. Ian Christie, "Sources of Visible Delight: Towards a Typology of Early Film Adaptation," in *Scene-Stealing: Sources for British Cinema before 1930*, ed. Alan Burton and Laraine Porter (Trowbridge: Flicks Books, 2003), 24. Both Stephen Bottomore, "Rediscovering Early Non-Fiction Film," and Jean-Jaques Meusey, "La Diffusion des films de 'non-fiction' dans les établissements Parisiens," indicate the presence of the science film in the program format before World War I.

95. Delmeulle, "Contribution," 119.

96. See Camille Flammarion, "Les Incendies du ciel," *Je Sais Tout* (March 15, 1910): 309–316; and Dr. Doyen, "Dans les abîmes de l'invisible," *Je Sais Tout* (January 15, 1911): 69–78.

97. Georges Dureau, *Ciné-Journal*, May 6, 1911; cited in Meusy, *Paris-Palaces*, 255.

98. Charles Le Fraper, *Le Courrier cinématographique*, July 29, 1911; cited in ibid.

99. *Ciné-Journal*, 166, October 28, 1911, 3.

100. Ben Singer, *Melodrama and Modernity: Early Sensational Cinema and Its Contexts* (New York: Columbia University Press, 2001), 129. Tom Gunning's formulation that the attraction goes underground, while not incompatible with this view, deemphasizes the role of attractions after the rise of the narrative feature, referring to special effects, for instance, as "tamed" attractions (Gunning, "Cinema of Attractions," 61).

Chapter 4

1. Louella Parsons, *New York Morning Telegraph*, August 12, 1923, sec. 5, 4; cited in Rita Horwitz, "George Kleine and the Early Motion Picture Industry," in *The George Kleine Collection of Motion Pictures in the Library of Congress: A Catalogue* (Washington, DC: Library of Congress, 1980), xiii.

2. See Horwitz, "George Kleine and the Early Motion Picture Industry," xiii–xv.

3. Christian Metz, *Film Language: A Semiotics of Cinema*, trans. Michael Taylor (Oxford: Oxford University Press, 1974), 94. For an account of how cinema came to be

defined as "harmless entertainment," see Lee Grieveson, "Not Harmless Entertainment: State Censorship and Cinema in the Transitional Era," in *American Cinema's Transitional Era: Audiences, Institutions, Practices*, ed. Charlie Keil and Shelley Stamp (Berkeley: University of California Press, 2004), 265–284. There he writes, "the effort to shift cinema from *harmful* to *harmless* became concentrated in pushing cinema away from an engagement with the public sphere of political debate or cultural negotiation, rendering cinema ostensibly apolitical, as a provider of 'harmless entertainment'" (274). See also Grieveson, *Policing Cinema: Movies and Censorship in Early-Twentieth-Century America* (Berkeley: University of California Press, 2004); and Richard Maltby, *Harmless Entertainment: Hollywood and the Ideology of Consensus* (Metuchen, NJ: The Scarecrow Press, Inc., 1983).

4. For a similar argument with regard to German cinema reformers' progressivism, see Scott Curtis, "The Taste of a Nation: Training the Senses and Sensibility of Cinema Audiences in Imperial Germany," *Film History* 6, no. 4 (winter 1994): 445–469, esp. 449.

5. Robert S. Birchard's entry on Kleine in the *Encyclopedia of Early Cinema* (New York: Routledge, 2005), 360–361, allows only that he "dabbled" in nontheatrical distribution in the 1920s, and makes no mention of his extensive and long-term involvement with nontheatrical cinema.

6. On the history of the modern museum, see Sharon Macdonald, "Collecting Practices," and Jeffrey Abt, "The Origins of the Public Museum," in *A Companion to Museum Studies*, ed. Sharon Macdonald (Malden, MA: Blackwell Publishing, 2006), 81–97 and 115–134. See also Tony Bennett, *The Birth of the Museum: History, Theory, Politics* (New York: Routledge, 1995); Steven Conn, *Museums and American Intellectual Life, 1876–1926* (Chicago: University of Chicago Press, 1998); Les Harrison, *The Temple and the Forum: The American Museum and Cultural Authority in Hawthorne, Melville, Stowe, and Whitman* (Tuscaloosa, AL: University of Alabama Press, 2007); and Karen Rader and Victoria Cain, *Life on Display: Revolutionizing U.S. Museums of Science and Natural History in the Twentieth Century* (Chicago: University of Chicago Press, 2014), esp. Ch. One, "'A Vision of the Future': The New Museum Idea and Display Reform, 1890–1915."

7. On Barnum, see Neil Harris, *Humbug: The Art of P. T. Barnum* (Chicago: University of Chicago Press, 1981); Andrea Stulman Dennett, *Weird and Wonderful: The Dime Museum in America* (New York: New York University Press, 1997); and James W. Cook, *The Arts of Deception: Playing with Fraud in the Age of Barnum* (Cambridge, MA: Harvard University Press, 2001).

8. See Daston and Park, *Wonders and the Order of Nature*, 329–364.

9. For an argument that also places an emphasis on the contemporary relevance of the cabinet tradition, see Horst Bredekamp, *The Lure of Antiquity and the Cult of the Machine: The Kunstkammer and the Evolution of Nature, Art and Technology*, trans. Allison Brown (Princeton, NJ: Princeton University Press, 1995). Beyond the scholarly engagement with this persistence, there has also been a significant extent to which the cabinet has become a part of the contemporary art world. For more on the cabinet's contemporary resonance, see the Conclusion.

10. Charles Musser, *A Guide to Motion Picture Catalogs by American Producers and Distributors, 1894–1908: A Microfilm Edition* (Frederick, MD: University Publications of America, 1985); consulted at http://edison.rutgers.edu/mopix/resource.htm (accessed August 9, 2009).

11. The Urban titles, which constitute the majority of the catalogue, are copied verbatim; a dispute that arose from this practice will be discussed in more detail later in the chapter. Further comparative work would be required to determine whether the other descriptions are copied or were created by Kleine, but it is likely that his method of composition would have been consistent for all catalogue entries.

12. In this sense, the front cover is similar to the title sequence of a film. For an extended consideration of how title sequences relate to the films they introduce, see Nicole de Mourgues, *Le Générique de film*, préface de Christian Metz, éd. (Paris: Méridiens Klincksieck, 1994).

13. See Sally Kohlstedt, "'Nature, Not Books': Scientists and the Origins of the Nature-Study Movement in the 1890s," *Isis* 96 (2005): 324–352.

14. For an account of the American Renaissance with an emphasis on architectural style, see the exhibition catalogue *The American Renaissance, 1876–1917* (Brooklyn: The Brooklyn Museum/Pantheon, 1979); on the architecture of expositions, see Robert W. Rydell, *All the World's a Fair: Visions of Empire at American International Exhibitions, 1876–1916* (Chicago, IL: University of Chicago Press, 1984); and Paul Greenhalgh, *Ephemeral Vistas: The* Expositions Universelles, *Great Exhibitions, and World's Fairs, 1851–1939* (Manchester: Manchester University Press, 1988); for the context of museum history, see Michaela Giebelhausen, "Museum Architecture: A Brief History," in *A Companion to Museum Studies*, ed. Sharon Macdonald (Malden, MA: Blackwell Publishing, 2006), 223–244.

There is a certain irony in the catalogue's invocation of the "classical" since what would come to be called "classical Hollywood cinema" was gaining steam and soon would relegate Kleine's vision for an educational cinema to the byways of cinema history. On this better-known cinematic classicism, see David Bordwell, Janet Staiger, and Kristin Thompson, *Classical Hollywood Cinema: Film Style & Mode of Production to 1960* (New York: Columbia University Press, 1985).

15. See Charles Musser and Carol Nelson, *High-Class Moving Pictures: Lyman H. Howe and the Forgotten Era of Traveling Exhibition, 1880–1920* (Princeton, NJ: Princeton University Press, 1991). For more on the iconography of the raised curtain, see the Conclusion.

16. [George Kleine], *Catalogue of Educational Motion Picture Films* (Chicago, IL: Bentley, Murray & Co., 1910), 1; hereafter abbreviated *Catalogue* (1910). For a helpful discussion of Kleine's rhetoric in the context of visual education, see Bill Marsh, "Visual Education in the United States and the 'Fly Pest' Campaign of 1910," *Historical Journal of Film, Radio, and Television* 30, no. 1 (March 2010): 21–36. Marsh's otherwise excellent article is hampered by the assumption that no prints of *The Fly Pest* exist; this chapter concludes with an analysis of this film.

17. For quotations by W. K. L. Dickson, Boleslaw Matuszewski, and others that provide examples of the idea that all film can be educational, see my "The Cinema of the Future: Visions of the Medium as Modern Educator, 1895–1910," in *Learning with the Lights Off: A Reader in Educational Film*, ed. Dan Streible, Dan Orgeron, and Marsha Orgeron (New York: Oxford University Press, 2011), 67–89.

18. The surgical films in the catalogue, by Dr. Doyen, are taken from the Eclipse catalogue; see *Catalogue* (1910), 36–39.

19. [George Kleine], "An Educational System by Visualization," *Catalogue* (1910), 5. "Motography" is one of many terms in use at the time to refer to motion pictures. See the

entry in Luke McKernan's blog: http://bioscopic.wordpress.com/2010/02/09/motography/ [accessed November 1, 2013].

20. [George Kleine?], "Education by Moving Pictures," *Catalogue* (1910), 2.

21. Ben Singer, "Early Home Cinema and the Edison Home Projecting Kinetoscope," *Film History* 2 (1988): 54.

22. *Anschauung,* a kind of immediate perceptual truth/insight, was the goal of Pestalozzi's method. For a more detailed account of how *Anschauung* functioned in Pestalozzi's writings, see Henning Schmidgen, "Pictures, Preparations, and Living Processes: The Production of Immediate Visual Perception (*Anschauung*) in Late-Nineteenth-Century Physiology," *Journal for the History of Biology* 37 (2004): 477–513, esp. 484 and 487.

23. My account of Pestalozzi's educational philosophy and its dissemination in the United States is indebted to Paul Saettler, *The Evolution of American Instructional Technology* (Englewood, CO: Libraries Unlimited, 1990), 36–41; "mud-pie factories" on 40.

24. "Education by Motion Pictures," *Catalogue* (1910), 3.

25. Herbert Spencer, *Education: Intellectual, Moral and Physical* (New York: D. Appleton, 1896), 155; cited in Anthony M. Platt, *The Child Savers: The Invention of Delinquency,* 2nd ed. (1969: Chicago, IL: University of Chicago Press, 1977), 58.

26. [George Kleine], "An Educational System by Visualization," *Catalogue* (1910), 5.

27. The Urbanora catalogue is identical save for the first few words, which read, "Our endeavour has been to produce" ([Charles Urban], "Introduction to Catalogue," *Catalogue: Scientific and Educational Subjects: Urbanora: The World's Educator* [London: n.p., 1908], 5).

28. [Kleine], "An Educational System by Visualization," *Catalogue* (1910), 6.

29. One note, on the catalogue's inside cover, reads, "Note from Mr. C. Urban, 'mostly taken from "Urbanora" cat.' AB, Oct. '37," while another, in Urban's handwriting, reads, "*263 pages* CUrban films copied from CU catalogues." (Charles Urban Papers, National Media Museum, Bradford, UK, URB 10/27; emphasis in original).

30. Clegg's letter appeared in the U.S. trade publications *Moving Picture News* and *Show World* and the British trade journal *Kinematograph Weekly* in the last week of April 1910.

31. George Kleine to C. M. Rogers, 27 April 1910; George Kleine papers, "Nontheatrical, General, 1909–1910" file, box 39. Eclipse, founded as a continental branch of the Charles Urban Trading Company, had recently had become independent.

32. C. M. Rogers to George Kleine, 17 May 1910; George Kleine papers, "Nontheatrical, General, 1909–1910" file, box 39.

33. George Kleine to Charles Urban, 27 April 1910; George Kleine papers, Historical file, box 26.

34. "I take it, however, that personalities are unimportant in this matter, the objects being to some extent philanthropic, and incidentally to place the maximum number of prints" (George Kleine to Charles Urban, 27 April 1910; George Kleine papers, Historical file, box 26).

35. Kleine uses the word "compilation" in both in the catalogue's dedication to Edison and in "An Educational System by Visualization."

36. Charles Urban, *Catalogue: Scientific and Educational Subjects: Urbanora: The World's Educator* (London: 1908), 7–8. Charles Urban papers, National Media Museum, Bradford, UK; URB 10–5.

37. While the wording and choice of font sizes on the catalogue's cover leave some room for uncertainty about Kleine's exact role (and indeed, some of his correspondents were under the impression that he had produced the films in the catalogue), Kleine was at this point in his career a distributor only, drawing from the output of, primarily, the Charles Urban Trading Company, Gaumont, Eclipse, Pathé, Essanay, Biograph, Edison, Lubin, Kalem, and Vitagraph. Later he would venture into production, with indifferent results. For more on his role with the Motion Picture Patents Company, see Robert Anderson, "The Motion Picture Patents Company: A Reevaluation," in *The American Film Industry*, ed. Tino Balio (Madison: University of Wisconsin Press, 1985), 133–152; and Scott Curtis, "A House Divided: The MPPC in Transition," in *American Cinema's Transitional Era: Audiences, Institutions, Practices*, ed. Charlie Keil and Shelley Stamp (Los Angeles: University of California Press, 2004), 239–264.

38. This copy of the catalogue is in the Billy Rose Theatre Collection at the New York Public Library.

39. For accounts of the cinema's emergence from other screen traditions, see Charles Musser, "Toward a History of Screen Practice," Chapter 1 of *The Emergence of Cinema: The American Screen to 1907* (Berkeley: University of California Press, 1994), 14–54; Laurent Mannoni, *The Great Art of Light and Shadow: Archaeology of the Cinema*, trans. and ed. Richard Crangle (1995; University of Exeter Press, 2000); and Iwan Rhys Morus, "Seeing and Believing Science," *Isis* 97, no. 1 (2006): 101–110.

40. For more on the history of cabinets of curiosity, see Paula Findlen, *Possessing Nature: Museums, Collecting, and Scientific Culture in Early Modern Italy* (Los Angeles: University of California Press, 1994); Krzysztof Pomian, *Collectors and Curiosity: Paris and Venice, 1500–1800*, trans. Elizabeth Wiles-Portier (Cambridge, MA: Polity Press, 1990); *Merchants and Marvels: Commerce, Science, and Art in Early Modern Europe*, ed. Pamela Smith and Paula Findlen (New York: Routledge, 2001); and *The Age of the Marvelous*, ed. Joy Kenseth (Hanover, NH: Hood Museum of Art/Dartmouth College, 1991).

41. [George Kleine], "Introduction," *Catalogue of Educational Moving Pictures* [Chicago: IL: G. Kleine, 1915], 3.

42. See Tom Gunning, "Early Cinema as Global Cinema: The Encyclopedic Ambition," in *Early Cinema and the "National,"* ed. Richard Abel, Giorgio Bertellini, and Rob King (Sydney: John Libbey & Company, 2008), 11–16. See also the discussion of Léon Gaumont in Chapter Three.

43. See Ben Brewster's comment in *Nonfiction from the Teens*, ed. Daan Hertogs and Nico De Klerk (Amsterdam: Stichting Nederlands Filmmuseum, 1994), 32. An example of this attitude underlies Charles Musser and Carol Nelson, *High-Class Moving Pictures*.

44. The limited success of these recirculation projects suggests that perhaps the material was not so ageless after all. With the beginnings of a cinephilic consciousness in the 1920s, film libraries for fiction films were formed, but the archival impulse during the 1910s was centered on nonfiction genres. Analogous uses for fiction footage are comparatively rare and idiosyncratic, as in Kuhleshov's experiments.

45. On the Gaumont encyclopedia, see Frédéric Delmeulle, "Contribution à l'histoire du cinema documentaire en France: Le cas de L'Encyclopédie Gaumont (1909–1929)," Ph.D. thesis, Université de Paris III, 1999; on the practices of the Cinémathèque de la Ville de Paris, see Béatrice De Pastre and Emmanuelle Devos, "La Cinémathèque de la Ville de

Paris," *1895* 18 (summer 1995): 107–121. See also Alexandra Schneider, "Time Travel with Pathé Baby: The Small-Gauge Film Collection as Historical Archive," *Film History* 19 (2007): 353–360.

46. See Lorraine Daston, "Warum Sind Tatsachen kurz?" in cut and paste *um 1900: Der Zeitungsausschnitt in den Wissenschaften*, ed. Anke te Heesen (Berlin: Kaleidoskopien, 2002), 132–144. Daston points out that the fact was coeval with modern scientific observational techniques, which she aligns with Francis Bacon. See also Mary Poovey, *A History of the Modern Fact: Problems of Knowledge in the Sciences of Wealth and Society* (Chicago, IL: University of Chicago Press, 1998); Ann Blair, *The Theater of Nature: Jean Bodin and Renaissance Science* (Princeton, NJ: Princeton University Press, 1997); and Ann Blair, "Humanist Methods in Natural Philosophy: The Commonplace Book," *Journal of the History of Ideas* 53 (1992): 541–551. Kleine's habits of borrowing without attribution have a certain resonance with the practices that were behind both the commonplace book and the cabinet of curiosity.

47. See *The Age of the Marvelous,* ed. Kenseth, for more on these items. A prominent argument for wonder as the predominant reaction to contact with the New World is Stephen Greenblatt, *Marvelous Possessions: The Wonder of the New World* (Chicago, IL: University of Chicago Press, 1992).

48. Frederick Starr, "The World before Your Eyes," *Chicago Tribune*, February 7, 1909; reprinted in *Catalogue: Scientific and Educational Subjects* (London: Charles Urban, 1909), 111.

49. For a thorough engagement with the alliance between early cinema and travel, see Jennifer Lynn Peterson, *Education in the School of Dreams: Travelogues and Early Nonfiction Film* (Durham, NC: Duke University Press, 2013).

50. Another well-known image of an early cabinet is the frontispiece to Ferrante Imperato's *Dell'historia naturale*, published in Naples in 1599; it is reproduced in Kenseth, ed., op. cit., 235.

51. Daston and Park, *Wonders and the Order of Nature*, 267, 266. See also Anke Te Heesen, *The World in a Box: The Story of an Eighteenth-Century Picture Encyclopedia*, trans. Ann M. Hentschel (Chicago, IL: University of Chicago Press, 2002), where she describes the encyclopedia as providing "a bewildering array of images and themes" (4).

52. Kleine, *Catalogue* (1910), 287–288.

53. Similar approaches to visual education became widespread in the course of the 1920s. The Keystone 600 set is another early example of visual educational materials where gestures at systematicity were overlaid on a more chaotic collection.

54. *Catalogue* (1910), 289; the description of the film does not clarify matters: "Upon the arrival of the Nile excursion steamers, the tourists after disembarking generally proceed by donkey to the scene of their contemplated visit. Much humor is added to the picture by some of the attitudes of the riders who probably had never mounted an animal before" (129).

55. Ibid., 288.

56. Ibid., 6, 5.

57. See the reproduction of the book of cabinet images produced for the Amsterdam apothecary Albertus Seba, *Cabinet of Natural Curiosities* (1731; New York: Taschen, 2005), which contained a hydra and other monsters (monstrous births, etc.).

58. For images of a cabinet chameleon, see the woodcut from Pierre Belon, *Les Observations de plusieurs singularitez et choses memorables*, Paris, 1553; compare this with the chameleon from F. Martin Duncan's films for Charles Urban between 1903 and 1906, probably included in *The Unseen World* series; see Chapter One.

59. Béatrice de Pastre, "La sangue ou la mise en scène du spectacle du vivant," in *Images, science, movement. Autour de Marey* (Paris: L'Harmattan, 2004), 95–102, makes a similar point.

60. For an account of science's turn away from monsters, see Daston and Park, *Wonders*, Chapters 4 and 5.

61. See Laurent Mannoni, *Great Art*, 94–98. The images in Robert Hooke's *Micrographia* (London, 1665) are a particularly well-known example of this type of observation. See Daston and Park, *Wonders*, on *Micrographia*; as well as Catherine Wilson, *The Invisible World: Early Modern Philosophy and the Invention of the Microscope* (Princeton, NJ: Princeton University Press, 1995); and Jutta Schickore, *The Microscope and the Eye: A History of Reflections, 1740–1870* (Chicago: University of Chicago Press, 2007), for more on the history of microscopic observation.

62. For an account of the first three fly films, see Chapter Two.

63. Frank P. Smith, "Flies and Their Foes, Through Microscope and Camera," *The Photographic Journal* (December 1908): n.p.; Charles Urban Papers, National Media Museum, Bradford, UK (URB 8/1) 49.

64. The statistics and the quotation come from George Kleine, "Memorandum: Supplementary to a brief submitted February 15, 1913, by George Kleine, to the Committee on Ways and Means, House of Representatives, Washington, D. C., recommending certain changes in the Tariff on moving picture films, positives and negatives," 7; George Kleine Papers, Manuscripts Division, Library of Congress, "Educational Institutions, 1913–1930" folder, box 18.

65. George Kleine to Charles Urban, 27 April 1910; George Kleine Papers, Manuscripts Division, Library of Congress, Historical file, box 26.

66. "Exchanges offered exhibitors at least a weekly change of films (most film theaters in rural areas changed at least once a week; many urban theaters changed twice a week, and at the height of the nickelodeon craze they offered a daily change of films in order to compete with neighboring theaters)" (André Gaudreault and Tom Gunning, "Introduction," *American Cinema: 1890–1909: Themes and Variations* [New Brunswick, NJ: Rutgers University Press, 2009], 15).

67. See Julie Lindstrom, "'Almost Worse than the Restrictive Measures': Chicago Reformers and the Nickelodeons," *Cinema Journal* 39, no. 1 (autumn 1999): 90–112.

68. I am indebted here to Scott Curtis's response to Marina Dahlquist's Chicago Film Seminar talk for the idea of *The Fly Pest* as an inoculation. For an earlier articulation of this notion, see Harry E. Kleinschmidt, "Educational Prophylaxis to Venereal Disease," *Social Hygiene* 5, no. 1 (January 1919): 27; cited in Anja Laukoetter and Christian Bonah, "Moving Pictures and Medicine in the First Half of the 20th Century: Some Notes on International Historical Developments and the Potential of Medical Film Research," *Gesnerus* 66 (2009): 121–146.

69. For accounts of American popular education campaigns aimed at raising awareness of flies as sources of disease, see Nancy Tomes, *The Gospel of Germs: Men, Women, and the Microbe in American Life* (Cambridge, MA: Harvard University Press, 1998); and

Martin Pernick, "The Ethics of Preventive Medicine: Thomas Edison's Tuberculosis Films; Mass Media and Health Propaganda," *Hastings Center Report* 8 (June 1978): 21–27.

70. "New War Is Begun to Kill Off Flies," *New York Times* (May 17, 1908): 5. See also "The New Moving Pictures—Their Recent Developments and Services to Commerce," *The New York Times* (December 12, 1909), SM4.

71. "Films in Anti-Fly Campaign," *New York Post*, December 13, 1909; reproduced in Kleine's broadsheet of fly-film publicity, Kleine papers, Historical file, box 26, "Fly Pest" folder.

72. Edward Hatch Jr., "The House Fly as a Carrier of Disease," *Annals of the American Academy of Political and Social Science* 37, no. 2 (March 1911): 169–179, at 174.

73. I take the head count from "Moving Picture Fight on Flies," *New York Press* (December 18, 1909); and the audience breakdown in "Fly Actors Big as Dogs in Moving Pictures," *New York Herald* (December 18, 1909); reprinted in Kleine publicity broadsheet; Kleine Papers, Historical file, box 26, "Fly Pest" folder.

74. Hatch, quoted in "Films in Anti-Fly Campaign," *New York Post* (December 13, 1909); reprinted in Kleine broadsheet.

75. "The House Fly Breeds Disease," *Poughkeepsie Eagle* (January 13, 1910); reprinted in Kleine broadsheet.

76. "Fly Costs 4,000,000 Lives," *New York City Press* (January 12, 1910); reprinted in Kleine broadsheet.

77. Watrous made the introductory remarks at five of those screenings. Richard Watrous to George Kleine, 6 February 1914; Kleine to Watrous, 16 February 1914; and Watrous to Kleine, 18 February 1914 (George Kleine Papers, Library of Congress, Manuscripts Division, Historical file, box 26). Kleine donated a print of the film to the ACA in 1914 at Watrous's request.

78. See Naomi Rogers, "Dirt, Flies, and Immigrants: Explaining the Epidemiology of Poliomyelitis, 1900–1916," *Journal of the History of Medicine and Allied Sciences* 44 (1989): 486–505. Somewhat later examples of this emphasis on the visual were L. O. Howard's photographs of the germs that grew in a Petri dish where a fly had walked; see Rogers, "Germs with Legs: Flies, Disease, and the New Public Health," *Bulletin of the History of Medicine* 63, no. 4 (winter 1989): 607. In this article, Rogers argues that anti-fly crusaders were misguided, especially in the way they mixed filth and germ theories of disease, but it is worth pointing out that although flies may not be as serious a vector for certain diseases as the rhetoric of the time suggested, they nevertheless did pose health risks that included miasis (infestation of maggots in living creatures), salmonella, and dysentery. Furthermore, the widespread adoption of screens against flies also protected households from the more significant threat of mosquitoes. See also Kirsten Ostherr, *Cinematic Prophylaxis: Globalization and Contagion in the Discourse of World Health* (Durham, NC: Duke University Press, 2005).

79. "Mr. H. Fly in Limelight Oval Makes Tabloid Drama Debut," *The Evening Telegram—New York* (February 25, 1910): 4; reprinted in Kleine broadsheet. Tomes notes that anti-tuberculosis campaigns used large models immediately prior to the introduction of *The Fly Pest*, "First used in Baltimore in 1904, an expanded and revised tuberculosis exhibit toured the United States between 1906 and 1912. When the exhibit opened in 1908 at the American Museum of Natural History in New York City, complete with a giant replica of the fly, tens of thousands flocked to see it" (Tomes, *The Gospel of Germs*, 121).

80. As a further example of the film's circulation in networks that were new for cinema at the time, it became part of the Louisiana Board of Health's traveling informational shows about tuberculosis. See Imported Film & Supply Co. to George Kleine, October, 19, 1910; Kleine Papers, Nontheatrical General File, 1909–1910.

81. J. N. Hurty, Secretary, Indiana State Board of Health, to the H. Lieber Co., April 25, 1910; Kleine papers, "Fly Pest" folder, box 26; "Gentlemen:- Your letter was promptly received, in regard to the matter of the Indianapolis police stopping the moving pictures which illustrate the fly pest. We regret exceedingly, that the police took this step. We think it a decided step backward. The pictures illustrated a condition that exists in almost every alley in Indianapolis. If people from day to day, can stand the original and exact conditions and can't stand pictures, that makes a condition which is strange to see. It is high time the pictures were being shown everywhere at all times, to arouse people to a sense of decency and cleanliness. We think those who object to seeing these pictures, are the ones that need to see them the most."

82. *Bulletin of the Municipal Commission on Tuberculosis of Saint Louis* 1, no. 10 (April 1910): 149; Kleine Papers, Historical file, box 26, "Fly Pest" folder.

83. 30 May 1910; Historical file, box 26; someone, probably Kleine, underlined the phrase "as we expected."

84. [Anonymous], "Menace of Flies Is Told by Film," clipping in Kleine papers, Historical file, box 26, "Fly Pest" folder. This screening was organized for local doctors at the Arcade theater. A flyer from the Bijou theater quoted *Moving Picture World*, which described the film as "revolting" but effective.

85. The issue of censorship links this film to an earlier moment in the reception of microcinematographic images, namely the reception of *Cheese Mites*. See also Emily Godbey, "The Cinema of (Un)Attractions: Microscopic Objects on Screen," in *Allegories of Communication: Intermedial Concerns from Cinema to the Digital* (Rome: John Libbey Publishing, 2004), 277–298, on the dread and disgust occasioned by microcinematography. For the proximity of the educational film to exploitation cinema, see Eric Schaefer, *Bold! Daring! Shocking! True!: A History of Exploitation Films, 1919–1959* (Durham, NC: Duke University Press, 1999).

86. George P. Chaney, "Campaigning against the Fly," *Technical World Magazine* (August 1910): 645.

87. See, for instance, Frank Parker Stockbridge, "How to Get Rid of Flies: The Way They 'Swat' Them in Topeka and Order Out the Boy Scouts to Slaughter Them—How They Trap Them in Wilmington," *The World's Work: A History of Our Time* vol. 23, November, 1911—April, 1912 (New York: Doubleday, Page & Company, 1912): 692–703. "This remarkable film . . . shows the development of the fly from the egg to maturity and conveys the lesson of its danger and general nastiness in a manner so graphic that it reaches the understanding even of the smallest children" (702–703) This article contains stills from *The Fly Pest*.

88. *Charles Urban Trading Co. Ltd. Catalogue, 1905–06* (London: Charles Urban, 1905–1906), 40; reproduced on reel 6 of *Early Rare British Filmmakers' Catalogues* (London: BFI/World Microfilms Publications, Ltd., 1982). An entry in Smith's notebook dated 9 August 1908 reads, "Took ground beetle head, head of blow fly, tree frog toilet, aphides on orchid and bee in holly hock," so it is possible that this shot was taken by Smith, in which case the similarity to Duncan's film would nevertheless be striking.

89. 75ft projected at 16fps would run 75 seconds, so allowing for an opening title constituting part of the length as well as allowing for the likelihood that some footage from the original film has been lost, the length is quite close.

90. See [Percy Smith,] "Cinematograph Work 1908 May 22 to 1910 Jun and 1930 Sep." Charles Urban Papers, National Media Museum, Bradford, UK, URB 8/3. "Foot of fly (photo) Flies tongue (photo)" entry for August 1909. The images are already present in Urban's collections, however; F. Martin Duncan made lantern slides that appeared in the Urban catalogue supplement of January 1904; series 1 (insects), no. 17 "foot of house-fly P.M. [photomicrograph]"; and 18. "tongue of blow-fly, P.M." (Urban catalogue, January 1904, 42; reel 6 of *Early Rare British Filmmakers' Catalogues*). Given that the catalogue description mentions the image of the fly's tongue, it is also possible that the microcinematographic shot of the tongue was also part of *Head of House Fly*.

91. See, for instance, the blurb in *Moving Picture World*, which writes about how the film "shows how it [the fly] carries contagion by illustrating the steps across the screen where every touch of the foot results in leaving the thousands of microbes which develops all sorts of contagious diseases" (Bijou publicity flyer in Kleine papers, Historical file, box 26, "Fly Pest" folder).

92. This moment evokes a more classical example of "curiosity" in its comparison of the fly's tongue to the trunk of an elephant, thereby creating a (monstrous) clash in scale. The catalogue description for *Blue-Bottle Flies Feeding* (Smith/Urban 1908), which also contained a shot (perhaps the same one) of a fly taking honey from the point of a needle, describes this moment as "a wonderful picture, showing the action of the trunk-like tongue" (Urban supplement 249, on reel 7 of *Early Rare British Film Catalogues*).

93. Barry Salt, *Film Style and Technology: History and Analysis*, 2nd ed. (1983: London: Starword, 1992), 91–92. An exception that Salt notes are insert shots, which does not apply to these shots.

94. See Thierry Lefebvre, "Popularization and Anthropomorphism: On Some Prewar 'Animal Films' (the Scientia Series)," in *Uncharted Territory: Essays on Early Nonfiction Film*, ed. Daan Hertogs and Nico de Klerk (Amsterdam: Stichting Nederlands Filmmuseum, 1997), 91–96, where he writes about how the popular-science film draws "repeatedly on certain standard forms, one of the most prominent being what I will call the 'identificatory zoom.' This actually corresponds to the classical rhetorical move of taking the reader or listener from the general to the particular. . . . So we may legitimately talk of a rhetorical and conceptual zoom" (91–92).

95. In the early 1910s, one in ten white infants died and one in seven black infants died; in 2000, one in 175 white infants died and one in seventy-five black infants died. Information taken from Michael Haines, "Fertility and Mortality in the United States," EH.Net Encyclopedia, edited by Robert Whaples. March 19, 2008. URL http://eh.net/encyclopedia/article/haines.demography

96. Rogers, "Germs with Legs," 610.

97. The BFI print is 378ft. The same film is preserved at the Nederlands Filmmuseum as *De Vliegen*. Other fly films are *Le plus dangereux des insects, la mouche* (Pathé, February 1913) 155m; *The House Fly* (Edison, 1912); and *La mouche (ou Le danger des mouches)* (Jean Comandon et Marius O'Galop, 1919), 8 minutes. A Pathé fly film from this era owned by a private collector contains an oscillation between these modes that is even more pronounced; there a juggling fly sequence forms part of a hygiene film.

98. See Jennifer Bean, "Movies and Progress," in *American Cinema, 1890–1910*, ed. André Gaudreault (New Brunswick, NJ: Rutgers University Press, 2008), 225–246.

Chapter 5

1. Gladys and Henry Bollman, *Motion Pictures for Community Needs: A Practical Manual of Information and Suggestion for Educational, Religious and Social Work* (New York: Henry Holt and Company, 1922), 19–20. My thanks to Charles Tepperman for sharing this quotation with me.

2. This characterization was especially prevalent in debates around censorship. "[The nickel theaters] minister to the lowest passions of childhood. They make schools of crime where murders, robberies and holdups are illustrated. The outlaw life they portray in their cheap plays leads to the encouragement of wickedness. They manufacture criminals to the city streets" (*The Chicago Tribune*, April 10, 1907, 10, cited in Lee Grieveson, "Why the Audience Mattered in Chicago in 1907," in *American Movie Audiences: From the Turn of the Century to the Early Sound Era*, ed. Melvyn Stokes and Richard Maltby [London: British Film Institute, 1999], 83). Feuillade's serials also were subject to censorship pressures.

3. This comment points to the serial's involvement in the development of special effects, an important area of overlap with popular-science cinema. For an account of the importance of popular science for the history of special effects, see Michelle Pierson, *Special Effects: Still in Search of Wonder* (New York: Columbia University Press, 2002), esp. Chapter One, "Magic, Science, Art: Before Cinema."

4. The quotation emphasizes the importance of the serial's advertising, which is related to how the serial was one of the first branches of the film industry to rely heavily on publicity. In addition, the serial is a heavily intertextual genre, relying a great deal on print media and the theater. See Ben Singer, "Serials," in *The Oxford History of World Cinema* (New York: Oxford University Press, 1996), 105–111.

5. Bill Nichols, *Representing Reality: Issues and Concepts in Documentary* (Bloomington: Indiana University Press, 1991), 3.

6. See Richard Abel, "The Éclair Trademark from Nick Carter to Zigomar," *Griffithiana* 47 (May 1993): 95. Francis Lacassin, "The Éclair Company and European Popular Literature from 1908 to 1919," *Griffithiana* 47 (May 1993): 77, gives May 22, 1910, as the date of the last novel.

7. See Richard Abel, "Exploring the Discursive Field of the Surrealist Film Scenario Text," in *Dada and Surrealist Film*, ed. Rudolf E. Kuenzli (Cambridge, MA: MIT University Press, 1996), 60–65.

8. See Abel, *Ciné*, 354–360.

9. For instance, Holmes first appears in *A Study in Scarlet* (1887) when Watson visits him in the chemical laboratory, and he excitedly tells Watson about how he has invented a test to detect hemoglobin. Doyle's medicolegal prophesy would become actual in 1901 when a test for hemoglobin was invented. See Jürgen Thorwald, *The Century of the Detective*, trans. Richard and Clara Winston (New York: Harcourt, Brace & World, 1964), 148–151.

10. Doyle, *A Study in Scarlet*, 12. See also the discussion of Holmes and scientific detection in Chapter Two.

11. Tom Gunning, "Lynx-Eyed Detectives and Shadow Bandits: Visuality and Its Eclipse in French Detective Stories and Films before World War I," *Yale French Studies*

107 (August 2005): 74–88. Gunning cites Roger Callois's remarks on how the detective genre alternates between "the ambitions of intelligence" and the "appetite for sensation" (Roger Callois, *Le Roman policier* [Buenos Aires: Editions des Lettres Français/Sur, 1941], 68; Gunning, "Lynx-Eyed Detectives," 79).

12. See Peter Brooks, *The Melodramatic Imagination: Balzac, Henry James, Melodrama, and the Mode of Excess* (New York: Columbia University Press, 1985).

13. Martha Vicinus, "Helpless and Unfriended: Nineteenth-Century Domestic Melodrama," *New Literary History* 13.1 (autumn 1981): 127–143, cited in Singer, *Melodrama and Modernity: Early Sensational Cinema and Its Contexts* (New York: Columbia University Press, 2001), 143.

14. Singer, *Melodrama and Modernity*, 12, 70, 78, 149.

15. Ben Singer, "Serial Melodrama and Narrative *Gesellschaft*," *The Velvet Light Trap* 37 (spring 1996): 76.

16. Georges Sadoul, *Le Cinéma français* (Paris: Flammarion, 1962), 17.

17. Abel, *Ciné*, 371.

18. Ibid., 387. Singer defines sensationalism as "a peculiar mode of scenic spectacle that tried to combine amazing sights with credible diegetic realism" (*Melodrama and Modernity*, 49). This understanding of sensationalism as a combination of astonishment and realism bears a strong resemblance to "fantastic realism." Singer also uses the phrase "spectacular realism," an even closer analogue (*Melodrama and Modernity*, 175).

19. See Vicki Callahan, *Zones of Anxiety: Movement, Musidora, and the Crime Serials of Louis Feuillade* (Detroit, MI: Wayne State University Press, 2005).

20. Robert Desnos, "Imagerie moderne," in *Nouvelle Hébrides et autres texts (1922–1930)* (Paris: Gallimard, 1978), 457. My translation of "merveilleux" as "fantastic" follows Robert Vilain, "An Urban Myth: *Fantômas* and the Surrealists," in *The Art of Detective Fiction*, ed. Warren Chernaik, Martin Swales, and Robert Vilain (New York: St. Martin's Press, 2000), 185, n. 10. Ado Kyrou opposes the fantastic to the marvelous, valorizing the latter as the properly Surrealist aesthetic category. Interestingly, though, the marvelous for Kyrou distinguishes itself from the fantastic by "having its feet on the ground," which is to say that the marvelous consists of a mixture of the fantastic and the realistic. Spiritualism, for instance, with its belief in the metaphysical, is not of interest to the surrealist aesthetic (Ado Kyrou, *Le Surréalisme au cinema* [1963; Évreux: Éditions Ramsay, 1985], 63–66, citation at 64).

21. See Fabrice Zagury, "'The Public Is My Master': Louis Feuillade and *Les Vampires*," supplement to *Les Vampires*, dir. Louis Feuillade, 399 min., Water Bearer Films, 1998, DVD.

22. Although this chapter restricts itself to French cinema, the American serial tradition is equally important and perhaps even more involved with a popular-scientific context. Indeed, it was the appearance of the "oxy-acetylene blow-pipe" in episode 3 of *The Exploits of Elaine* (1914) that first piqued my curiosity about the relations between the serial and popular science. My thanks to Madeleine Matz for steering me in this direction. Singer adduces a number of similarly socioeconomic contexts in which to read the American serial film, such as reading the antipathy among characters in serials as a function of the American immigrant experience.

23. R. A. Reiss, *Manuel de police scientifique (technique), vol. 1 (vols et homicides)* (Paris: Félix Alcan, 1911), 75.

24. Pierre Souvestre and Marcel Allain, *The Silent Executioner* (1911: New York, Ballantine, 1987), 57.

25. As Paolo-Cherchi Usai, "Les vies parallèles de Fantômas," *Les Cahiers de la Cinémathèque* 48 (1987): 71–76, points out, giant snakes were a trope in the Danish adventure film that predated *Fantômas*, so even the boa constrictor is not as fantastic as it may seem. Usai comments on the awkwardness of Feuillade's editing in this scene, speculating that it results from his lack of comfort with the conventions of action filmmaking. The roughness of the cuts and framings in the boa constrictor sequence, however, may well have as much to do with the recalcitrance of animals on film as they do with Feuillade-the-pictorialist being out of his element.

26. Tzevtan Todorov, *The Fantastic: A Structural Approach to a Literary Genre* (Ithaca, NY: Cornell University Press, 1975), 25.

27. For an overview of the crime film in the French cinema of this period, see Abel, *Ciné*, 354–388.

28. Abel, *Ciné*, 355.

29. *Ciné-Journal*, 9 March 1912, 57; quoted in Tom Gunning, "Attractions, Detection, Disguise: Zigomar, Jasset, and the History of Film Genres," *Griffithiana* 47 (May 1993): 125.

30. Gunning, "Attractions, Detection, Disguise," 113, 119.

31. Abel, *Ciné*, 361.

32. Gunning, "Attractions, Detection, Disguise," 121.

33. Ibid., 125. A further link between the traditions of the trick film and the crime melodrama appears in the affinity between Zigomar and Méliès. Gunning writes, "Zigomar is a modern narratized version of Méliès' Alcofrisbas" ("Attractions, Detection, Disguise," 125); and Abel writes, "In a sense, Georges Méliès's earlier satanic hero had returned . . . in a continually renewed, but always coolly restrained guise (except for his distinctive red hood)—a capitalist entrepreneur pushed to the point of excess, and completely at ease anywhere he happened to appear in contemporary society" (Abel, *Ciné*, 358).

34. Abel, *Ciné*, 360–361.

35. See Laurent LeForestier, "Une disparition in*struc*tive. Quelques hypotheses sur l'évolution des scenes à trucs chez Pathé," *1895* 27 (1999): 61–73.

36. In a particularly felicitous coincidence, the phrase "le bandit des grands chemins" also appears as an intertitle in the third Zigomar film, *Zigomar, peau d'anguille* (1913).

37. For an elaboration of the notion of the view, see Gunning, "Before Documentary," in *Uncharted Territory*, 9–24. Benjamin's evocation of the hands of the surgeon and the magician occurs in his essay "The Work of Art in the Age of Its Technological Reproducibility."

38. Abel, *Ciné*, 361; the first part of the quotation comes from *Ciné-Journal*'s review of *Le Cercueil de verre*, (10 February 1912): 56.

39. Marcel Allain and Pierre Souvestre, *Fantômas* (New York: Ballantine, 1987), 11.

40. Aside from the extraordinary number of copies printed during the series' initial publication (600,000 copies per volume and up), various translations, and numerous reprints (often abridged), the novels also gave rise to a small industry of Fantômas spinoffs: in print, comic books, in film, and on stage. After Souvestre's death of Spanish influenza in February 1914, Allain revived the series several times and went on to publish a vast amount of pulp fiction by himself. Beginning in 1925, Allain went on to write three new

series of Fantômas adventures on his own. For a bibliography of Allain's and Souvestre's extensive writings, see Francis Lacassin, "Bibliographie," in *Fantômas* (Paris: Robert Laffont, 1987), 1025–1072.

A number of other filmic incarnations of the character appeared, beginning with a twenty-episode American version of the serial directed by Edward Sedgwick for Fox (1920–1921). Initially titled *Fantômas*, each episode consisted of two reels, and the cast included Edna Murphy, Edward Roseman, Eva Balfour, John Walker, Lionel Adams, John Willard, and Irving Brooks. See Walter Lee, *Reference Guide To Fantastic Films: Science Fiction, Fantasy, and Horror* (Los Angeles: Chelsea-Lee Books, 1973). The film was retitled *The Exploits of Diabolos* after Allain filed a suit (see Usai, "Les vies parallèles de Fantômas"). No print of this serial is known to survive.

Fantômas also figured in six French feature-length films: *Fantômas* (Paul Fejos, 1931); *Fantômas* (Jean Sasha, 1946); *Fantômas contre Fantômas* (Robert Vernay, 1949); and a three-film Fantômas revival in the 1960s starring Jean Marais: *Fantômas* (1964); *Fantômas se déchaine* (1965); and *Fantômas contre Scotland Yard* (1966), all directed by André Hunebelle. (These last three films resemble the Batman films of the same period in the United States in their emphasis on camp.) In 1979 Antenne 2 (France) and Hamster Films (Germany) produced a four-episode TV series based on the Souvestre and Allain Fantômas novels; the episodes were directed by either Claude Chabrol or Juan-Louis Buñuel.

Jacques Champreux, Feuillade's grandson, was involved in two Feuillade hommages, Georges Franju's *Judex* (for which he served as a screenwriter, along with Feuillade scholar Francis Lacassin), and Franju's 1974 television series *Les Nuits Rouge*, where Champreux starred in the role of "L'Homme sans visage."

Much of the information about Fantômas's many incarnations, which also include a Mexican comic book and Julio Cortázar, *Fantomas contra los vampiros multinacionales* (1977), comes from the website www.fantômas-lives.com, written in part by Robin Walz. See also *L'encyclopedie de Fantômas* (Paris: Alfu/Autoedition, 1981); and Robin Walz, *Pulp Surrealism: Insolent Popular Culture in Early Twentieth-Century Paris* (Berkeley, CA: University of California Press, 2000), especially Chapter Two, "The Lament of Fantômas."

41. For a sampling of these images, see Patrice Caillot and François Ducos, *Gino Starace, l'illustrateur de Fantômas* (Amiens: Encrage, 1987).

42. For an overview of Bertillon's career, see Jürgen Thorwald, *The Century of the Detective*, 1–90.

43. See Thomas Keenan, "The Point Is To (Ex)Change It: Reading Capital, Rhetorically," in *Fetishism as Cultural Discourse*, ed. Emily Apter and William Pietz (Ithaca, NY: Cornell University Press, 1993), 152–185.

44. Allain and Souvestre, *Fantômas*, 5.

45. Tom Gunning, "Tracing the Individual Body: Photography, Detectives, and Early Cinema," in *Cinema and the Invention of Modern Life*, ed. Leo Charney and Vanessa R. Schwartz (Berkeley: University of California Press, 1995), 20.

46. For a reading of Feuillade according to the trope of invisibility, see Marina Dahlquist, "The Invisible Seen in French Cinema before 1917," Ph.D. dissertation, Stockholm University, 1999. There are similarities here with a scene in *Tih-Minh* where the kidnappers send a photograph of Tih-Minh that contains a newspaper with the current date to prove that she is still alive. The photograph soon turns completely black because the image had been improperly fixed, an explanatory intertitle tells us. In both cases, the

logics of appearance and disappearance of narrative information are underwritten by scientific explanations.

47. Reiss, *Manuel de police scientifique (technique)*, I:95–98. Reiss notes that criminal use of invisible ink is relatively rare and that most invisible inks are not, in fact, the products of sophisticated chemistry (he cites saliva, urine, and milk as the most common invisible inks), although he does admit that other authors have written about the employment of "invisible inks or other more or less complicated chemical compositions" (I:95).

48. Tom Gunning, "From the Kaleidoscope to the X-Ray: Urban Spectatorship, Poe, Benjamin, and *Traffic in Souls* (1913)," *Wide Angle* 19, no. 4 (1997): 39.

49. John Ashbery, "Introduction," Marcel Allain and Pierre Souvestre, *Fantômas* (New York: William Morrow and Company, Inc., 1986), 8.

50. Francis Lacassin, quoted in John Ashbery, "Introduction," 9.

51. Abel, *Ciné*, 376.

52. David Bordwell, "*La Nouvelle Mission de Feuillade*; or, What Was Mise-en-Scène?" *The Velvet Light Trap* 37 (spring 1996): 22.

53. In a description of *Seifenblasen* (Heron Films, 1910?), Roland Cosandey puts the close shot and *Fantômas* into suggestive contiguity, "Die 'photogénie' des Objekts in Grossaufnahme war eine Erfahrung, welche die modernen Künstler als Kinozuschauer wohl ebenso prägte wie auf anderem Gebiet *Fantômas*." [The 'photogénie' of the object in a close-up was an experience that probably marked modern artists as cinema spectators as much as, in another area, *Fantômas*.]. Roland Cosandey, *Welcome Home, Joye! Film um 1910: Aus der Sammlung Joseph Joye (NFTAV, London)*, trans. Elisabeth Heller, Stefan Kaiser, Corinne Siegrist-Oboussier (Basel: Stroemfeld/Roter Stern, 1993), 122.

54. The novel relates the detail that Fantômas remembers this trick from "the Tonkingese who lie stretched at the bottom of a river for hours at a time, breathing through hollow reeds" (Marcel Allain and Pierre Souvestre, *The Silent Executioner* [New York: Ballantine Books, 1987], 236).

55. Another example of this type of close-up occurs in the second episode of *Les Vampires*, when the Grand Vampire displays the poison ring. Here Feuillade cuts closer twice, and the second close shot is jarring and not strictly necessary.

56. Given the extent to which Allain and Souvestre cobbled together various preexisting elements of crime and detective fiction for their voluminous output requirements—elements from Maurice Leblanc, Emile Gaboriau, and Gaston LeRoux to name only the most apparent borrowings—it is fitting that this touchstone image would be borrowed from a failed advertising campaign. (For the story of the pink pills, see Vilain, "Fantômas and the Surrealists," 172; and Lacassin, "Introduction," 21–22.)

57. Chemistry is one of the sciences that figures most prominently in these films. The final Grand Vampire, as described in an intertitle, is "A chemist of genius, known among the Vampires by the frightening name 'Venomous.' In his depravity, he had dedicated his science to crime." He provides the closest iconographic moment for an argument about how the scientific supercriminal fits into the tradition of the mad scientist.

58. *Alias Jimmy Valentine* (Maurice Tourneur, 1914) also contains a cryptogram. It was based on the play *Alias Jimmy Valentine* by Paul Armstrong (New York, January 21, 1910), which was, in turn, based on O. Henry's short story "A Retrieved Reformation," published in *Cosmopolitan Magazine*, April 1903. O. Henry took the plot from the life of his friend Jimmy Connors while both of them were serving time in the Ohio State Penitentiary. See

http://www.afi.com/members/catalog/DetailView.aspx?s=1&Movie=16407. See also Shawn James Rosenheim, *The Cryptographic Imagination: Secret Writing from Edgar Poe to the Internet* (Baltimore, MD: The Johns Hopkins University Press, 1997).

59. The intertitles for *How Jones Lost His Roll* (Edison, 1903) self-assemble via stop-motion animation, and Edison himself mused about using cinema to teach spelling (see "How Thos. A. Edison Plans to Cure 'Hookey,'" *Chicago Daily Tribune* [December 10, 1911]: G4; my thanks to Paul Moore for drawing this article to my attention). But in these cases, while the technique is similar to Feuillade's shot, the element of decryption is missing. For an account of Guido Seeber's rebus films that points to the transformation of the decryption tradition, see Michael Cowan, "Moving Picture Puzzles: Training Urban Perception in the Weimar 'Rebus Films,'" *Screen* 51, no. 3 (autumn 2010): 197–218.

60. Gunning, "A Tale of Two Prologues," 32. Gunning remarks about Feuillade's prologues that, as opposed to the novel's refusal to reveal Fantômas's identity until later in the story, the film provides viewers with this information immediately; it "places them into a secure and knowing reading position, like that of detective Juve, who sees the figure behind the disguises and is able to see through Fantômas's powerful visual illusions."

61. Louis Lépine, "Préface," to Reiss, *Manuel de police scientifique*, I:5.

62. Reiss, *Manuel*, I:9.

63. Lépine, "Préface," I:5.

64. Bertillon himself saw fingerprinting as a competing system and mounted polemics against it. For more on this story, see Simon A. Cole, *Suspect Identities: A History of Fingerprinting and Criminal Identification* (Cambridge, MA: Harvard University Press, 2001).

65. This is the name of the magazine as given in the DVD released in the United States.

66. See Alan Rauch, *Useful Knowledge: The Victorians, Morality, and the March of the Intellect* (Durham, NC: Duke University Press, 2001).

67. See Tom Gunning, "Heard over the Phone: *The Lonely Villa* and the Terrors of Technology," *Screen* 32 (summer 1991): 184–196. For a contemporary manifestation of the scientific supercriminal, see Philippe Azoury and Jean-Marc Lalanne, *Fantômas, style moderne* (Paris: Éditions Centre Pompidou/Yellow Now, 2002), 94–97, where they suggest that Osama bin Laden is a new Fantômas. Along with their own analysis and reproduction of a wanted poster from the CIA website, they adduce the following quotation: "If bin Laden escapes, he risks becoming the Fantômas of the Arab world, the world's leaders' elusive adversary, and it will be impossible for the Americans symbolically to close the tragedy of September 11th" (Pascal Riché, *Libération*, 18 December 2001).

Conclusion

1. Mary Field and Percy Smith, *The Secrets of Nature* (1934; London: The Scientific Book Club, 1939), 86.

2. Miriam Hansen, "Benjamin and Cinema: Not a One-Way Street," *Critical Inquiry* 25, no. 2 (1999): 318.

3. Hansen, "Benjamin and Cinema," 332. The phrase "image world" is from Benjamin's draft notes for the "Artwork" essay, *Gesammelte Schriften*, ed. Rolf Tiedemann and Hermann Schweppenhäuser (Frankfurt am Main: Suhrkamp, 1972–1989), I:3:1040 and 1047; cited in Hansen.

4. *Secrets of Nature*, cited in Bousé, *Wildlife Films*, 59.

5. Walter Benjamin, "Das Kunstwerk im Zeitalter seiner technischen Reproduzierbarkeit (Zweite Fassung)," *Gesammelte Schriften*, 7:1:384; cited in Hansen, "Benjamin and Cinema," 340.

6. Hansen, "Benjamin and Cinema," 340.

7. Field and Smith, *The Secrets of Nature*, 88.

8. Benjamin, "Das Kunstwerk," cited in Miriam Hansen, "Benjamin, Cinema and Experience: 'The Blue Flower in the Land of Technology,'" *New German Critique* 40 (winter 1987): 205.

9. Benjamin, "The Work of Art in the Age of Mechanical Reproduction," *Illuminations*, trans. Harry Zohn, ed. Hannah Arendt (New York: Schocken Books, 1969), 232f.; cited in Hansen, "Blue Flower," 203–204.

10. Benjamin, "Short History of Photography," *Gesammelte Schriften* II.1:371; *Screen* 13.1:8; cited in Hansen, "Blue Flower," 210.

11. Benjamin, "The Work of Art"; cited in Hansen, "Blue Flower," 205.

12. See the *Telegraph*'s interest at http://www.telegraph.co.uk/news/newstopics/howaboutthat/10784353/Bug-performs-the-ultimate-workout.html; and http://sploid.gizmodo.com/bug-trapped-upside-down-does-hypnotic-workout-forever-1566894383/all; Digg.com, http://digg.com/video/bug-is-caught-in-a-feedback-loop; and Viralviralvideos.com, http://www.viralviralvideos.com/2014/04/23/bug-stuck-in-infinite-loop-as-it-walks-on-small-speck/

13. Several of the comments mention coming to the page only to read the comments, which suggests that "Bug Workout" is also a form of "customer review comedy," whose best-known example is the amazon.com page for Tuscan Whole Milk. For a related investigation of the recurrence of animal films in the age of digital media, see James Leo Cahill, "A YouTube Bestiary: 26 Theses on a Post-Cinema of Animal Attractions," in *The New Silent Cinema: Digital Anachronisms, Celluloid Specters*, ed. Paul Flaig and Katherine Groo (New York: Routledge/AFI, 2015).

14. My next book project, *The Living Book of Knowledge: Visions of the Motion-Picture Encyclopedia from Chronophotography to the Internet*, will pursue this issue.

15. [Michel Foucault], "The Masked Philosopher: Interview with Christian Delacampagne for *La Monde*, April 1980," in *Foucault Live (Interviews, 1966–84)*, trans. John Johnston, ed. Sylère Lotringer (New York: Semiotext[e], 1989), 198–199.

16. For PBS, see http://www.pbs.org/aboutpbs/news/20000611_curious.html; for the Discovery Channel, see http://www.discovery.com/tv-shows/curiosity; and for the naming of the Mars rover, see http://www.space.com/6764-flagship-mars-rover-curiosity.html.

17. See also Pierre Hadot, *The Veil of Isis: An Essay about the Idea of Nature* (New York: Belknap Press, 2008). For other examples see *Nature Unveiling Herself before Science* (Louis-Ernest Barrias, 1899) (reproduced as figure 4.12 in *Objectivity*), and illustrations in Anke te Heesen, *The World in a Box: The Story of an Eighteenth-Century Picture Encyclopedia*, trans. Ann M. Hentschel (Chicago, IL: University of Chicago Press, 2002), 99 and 100.

{ INDEX }

Pickstone, J. V., 55
Picture Theater News, 74
Pike, Oliver, 26, 55, 56, 82
Pisciculture pratique: La Truite (1910), 101
plant-growth films, 56, 67–79, 217n75, 218n89
Plants of the Underworld (Smith), 88
Poe, Edgar Allen, 179
Polytechnic theater, 21, 206n29
popularization, 7, 8, 10, 204n36
popular-science films
  as amusement, 21–2, 24, 40, 44, 52–3, 56, 79, 127, 138
  animal fight scenes in, 122, 125, 228n84
  audience for, 40
  by Comandon and Pathé, 92–102
  crime melodrama, 13–14, 158–88
  curiosity and, 3–5, 195–7
  by Duncan and Urban, 15–53
  educational role of, 23, 39, 44–6, 56, 68–9, 98–9, 130, 138, 148
  emergence of, 10, 15–16
  flourishing of in France, 90–128
  Gaumont and, 102–7
  historical background of, 1–11
  intertextuality in, 55, 107, 110, 161, 168
  Klein's collection of, 129–57
  long after-life of, 2–3, 195
  obscurity of, 6, 7
  popular conceptions of, 5, 19, 22, 156–7
  program format in, 125–8
  Smith and, 54–89
  spectacular display in, 11, 19, 37, 78, 82, 94, 106, 141, 166, 168
  term, 8, 9, 10
  violence in, 110, 113, 168
Porter, Edwin S., 53
program format, 229n91
  popular-science films and, 125–8
  Unseen World and, 37–40, 209n75
public health movement, 145–6, 236–7nn78–79
Pugilistic Toads and the Tortoise Referee (1903), 20, 28, 38–9
Pumfrey, Stephen, 8
Pyx, Maxwell, *see* Smith, F. Percy

Quaint Denizens of the Insect World (1907), 43
Quekett Microscopical Club, 55, 67, 79

raised-curtain motif, 197
The Red Codebook (1915), 180
  video stills from, *181, 182–3*
Reicher, Karl, 94
Reiss, R. A., 184, 243n47
religion, 74, 217n78
repetition, 194, 195

Riis, Jacob, 229n93
Rockefeller, John D., 129
Rogers, Charles, 137
Rogers, Naomi, 236– 7n78
Rosenthal, Joseph, 41
Rothapfel, Samuel "Roxy," 228n84, 229n91
Rousseau, Jean-Jacques, 135
Royal Photographic Society, 61

Sadoul, Georges, 162
Salisbury, E. J., 88
Satanas (1916), 186–8
  video stills from, *187*
Sazie, Léon, 159
Schatzkammern, 138
Schaudinn, Fritz, 92
science, 169–71
  ambivalent reception of, 169–70
  art and, 196
  detective stories and, 80–2, 84–5, 161, 188
  Gaumont and, 104–5
  professional/popular distinction in, 55
  See also popular-science films
Le Scorpion Languedocien (1912), 1–2, 12
  Fabre book and, 115–17, 119–25
  video stills from, *117, 119, 121, 123*
Secord, James, 2
The Secrets of Nature (Field and Smith), 189–90
"Secrets of Nature" films, 51, 88, 189, 190
Sedgwick, Edward, 242n40
sensationalism, 158, 167, 240n18
La Sensitive (1914), 113, *114*
serials, cinematic, 159–61
  advertising for, 239n4
  American tradition of, 241n22
  Fantômas, 159, 160, 162–4, 169–79
  Les Vampires, 159–60, 163, 169–70, 173, 243n57
  nonfiction and, 158–9
  popular-science films and, 13, 167, 188
  serialized fiction and, 127, 159
  series-serial distinction, 160
  Zigomar, 159, 160, 166–8
In the Shadow of the Guillotine (1913), 171–4
Sheldon, Edward, 135
Shell, Hanna Rose, 7–8
Sherlock Holmes series (Doyle), 79–82, 160–1, 218n93, 239n9
Singer, Ben, 128, 161, 240n18
Smith, Albert, 145
Smith, G. A., 16, 40
Smith, F. Percy, 12, 54–89
  Duncan and, 46, 51, 53, 54–5, 195
  eccentricity of, 85, 87–8
  juggling fly films by, 56–67, 143, 189, 195
  lectures by, 61, 214n25, 220n120